THE HEALTH CARE HANDBOOK

THE HEALTH CARE HANDBOOK

A Clear and Concise Guide to the
United States
Health Care System

ELISABETH ASKIN AND NATHAN MOORE

Washington
University in St. Louis

Printed in the United States of America

First Printing 2012

ISBN 978-0-615-65093-7

Please send questions, comments, and suggestions to:
info@HealthCareHandbook.com

Editing by Joyce Romine (StreamlineWorks.com)

Design by John Bennett (JohnBennettGraphics.com)

Cover Design by David Glaubke

Table of Contents

Foreword ix
Acknowledgments xi
Introduction xiii

Chapter 1: Health Care Systems and Delivery   1

Inpatient Care 2
    Ownership 3
    Services 5
    Organization 7
Hospital Issues 13
    Medical Errors 13
    Hospital-Acquired Infections 15
    Inpatient to Outpatient to Inpatient 15
Outpatient Care 17
    Delivery Formats 18
    Changing Practice Patterns 22
    Physician Shortage 24
    Primary Care Physician Shortage 26
Networks 28
National Health Care Organizations 29
Glossary 31
Suggested Reading 32
References 32

Chapter 2: Health Care Providers   36

Graduate Medical Education 37
Professional Credentialing 39
Health Care Providers 40
Glossary 73
References 73

Chapter 3: Insurance and Economics   77

Health Insurance Basics 79
    Coverage and Organization Formats 81
    Ways to Get Insurance 86
    Reimbursement Types 91

Why Does U.S. Health Care Cost So Much? 95
    Universal Reasons. 96
    Unique Reasons. 104
    Societal Reasons 108
Issues 112
    Defraying Costs 112
    Consequences of High Costs 113
    Certificate of Need 117
    Underpayment 119
    Emergency Department 119
Medical Malpractice 121
Glossary 127
Suggested Reading. 128
References 128

Chapter 4: Research, Pharmaceuticals,
and Medical Devices   133

Research. 134
    Institutions and Funding 136
    The Research Process 139
    Peer Review System 139
Pharmaceuticals. 141
    Government Regulation 142
    Intellectual Property 144
    Generics and Biosimilars 145
    Payments and PBMs 146
Medical Devices. 147
    Government Regulation 148
    Health Information Technology. 149
Issues 150
    Utility of Research Findings 151
    Evidence-Based Medicine. 153
    Comparative Effectiveness Research 156
    Government Regulation 158
    Why Are Drug Prices So High? 161
    Quality 168
Glossary 170
Suggested Reading. 172
References 173

Chapter 5: Policy and Reform 178

Cost, Access, Quality 179
Government Insurance Programs 183
    Medicare 183
    Medicaid 185
    CHIP 187
Reform 188
    State-Based Reform: Massachusetts 188
    National Reform: The Patient Protection and
    Affordable Care Act 189
Understanding the Affordable Care Act: FAQs . . 195
    How Will Things Change for Individuals? . . . 195
    What Exactly Is an Exchange? 200
    What Will Happen to Insurance? 203
    What Will Happen with Medicare? 205
    What Will Happen with Medicaid and CHIP? . 210
    What Are the New Insurance Types? 213
Impact of Health Care Reform 217
    Criticisms of the Affordable Care Act 217
    Politics of Reform 220
Glossary 226
Suggested Reading 228
References 229

About the Authors 240

Foreword

Incoming medical and other health professions students would certainly benefit from acquiring a foundational understanding of the complex structure of the American health care industry and the provisions of the recently enacted Patient Protection and Affordable Care Act. Elisabeth Askin and Nathan Moore recognized this need and, failing to identify a relatively brief, easily read introductory resource, proceeded to write a book that serves this purpose extremely well—not only for students but for many who are not well-informed.

When these Washington University medical students first sought my advice and mentorship, we discussed the obvious difficulties they would encounter; their time commitment to fully research and write the book might interfere with their medical education; the intrinsic complexity of the subject and the need to engage others to read, criticize and edit the manuscripts; and their own inexperience as authors. Undaunted, they proceeded to deliver a complete first draft four months later! The finalized version has taken less than a year—and they have maintained their good standing in the School of Medicine.

The finished product is an excellent educational volume. It will be valuable for its intended readership—medical and health professions students as well as a much wider audience, both professional and lay. The comprehensive subject matter includes fundamental and practical aspects of health care organization, finance and delivery, the nature of America's medical science enterprise, and key aspects of the PPACA, and it does so efficiently—in 200 narrative pages. Of special note is that it is not a dry recitation of concepts, definitions, and facts. Subjects are brought to life with helpful examples and occasional humor. Its readability stems in part from interesting and well-balanced descriptions, including important areas of uncertainty and controversy, differing points of view, and the students' own thoughtful perspectives on some issues. There is an extensive glossary and bibliography. The authors plan to see that the book is updated frequently in order to keep up with the inevitable changes in health and health care in the future.

The Health Care Handbook could not have been more timely given the uncertain future of health care in America. Perhaps it is too optimistic to think that the more professionals and others are well-informed about the issues, the more likely we are to make the right decisions for the health of our population. This has been an amazing accomplishment undertaken by two amazing students. It was a great experience for them as it was for me. It will be a great learning experience for all its readers.

WILLIAM A. PECK, M.D.

DIRECTOR, CENTER FOR HEALTH POLICY

ALAN A. AND EDITH L. WOLFF DISTINGUISHED PROFESSOR OF MEDICINE

FORMER DEAN, SCHOOL OF MEDICINE, WASHINGTON UNIVERSITY IN ST. LOUIS

FORMER CHAIR, ASSOCIATION OF AMERICAN MEDICAL COLLEGES

Acknowledgments

We received incredible support, commentary, and constructive criticism from our colleagues, family, and friends. First, we'd like to thank William Peck for his mentorship and high expectations. Second, we'd like to thank David Askin, husband and friend, for his unflagging willingness to be a sounding board, editor, idea-man, and cheerleader.

We would also like to thank our fantastic graphic designer John Bennett. We had research and graphics help from undergraduate students at Washington University in St. Louis: David Glaubke, Amber Anders, and Adira Weixlmann. We also received technical help from fellow medical student Marshall Strother. Further, we have relied upon the business and marketing acumen of Richard Mahoney, former CEO of Monsanto and current Executive in Residence at the Weidenbaum Center. His support has been crucial to finishing the book.

The Washington University School of Medicine community has supported this project from day one. When we decided that this was a resource other students should have, we had the immediate agreement and help of David Windus, the associate dean of Medical Student Education; Ed Dodson, the associate vice chancellor and associate dean for Admissions and Continuing Medical Education; Gregory Polites, assistant professor and assistant residency director in Emergency Medicine; and Alison Whelan, senior associate dean for Education. Finally, we have been honored and grateful to receive such incredible backing and interest from the dean of the School of Medicine, Larry Shapiro.

We received invaluable comments and advice from Ed Weisbart, Karen Dodson, Jennifer Black, Cheryl Herling, James Moore, Sam Moore, Charlie Kircher, and Liz Davlantes. We would also like to thank Thomas Ahrens, Jay Albertina, Renee Butkus, Chris Carpenter, Ruth Castellano, Christopher

Chen, Ronald Chod, Koong-Nah Chung, Don Clayton, Meagan Colvin, Ryan Crowley, Lauren Curley, Mike Daly, Bethany Davis, Kasey Davis, Tom DeFer, Susan Deusinger, Wendy Duncan, Mark Dunlop, Geralyn Eichelberger, Andy Flemings, Colleen Fowler, Mark Frisse, Spencer Gohre, Lynn Herling, Barbara Hill, Sarah Hoper, Lisa Hueckel, David Jaques, Harry Jonas, Ken King, Michael Lachtrup, Ken Lawson, Gerald Levey, Alan Levi, Steve Lipstein, Ken Ludmerer, Joanna May, Rebecca McAlister, Amanda Moore McBride, Jamie Meltzner, Brian Meyers, Heidi Miller, Pat Miller, Marina Mityul, Connie Mushill, Phil Needleman, Osamuede Osemwota, Andrew Pierce, Patricia Potter, David Pryor, Lori Rakita, Gail Rea, Eugene Rubin, Carl Saubert, Steve Schoenbaum, Aliza Shturman, Philip Stahl, Richard Suszek, Steve Taff, David Tan, Elizabeth Toolan, Victor Trogdon, Sandeep Vaheesan, Michael Valente, Judy VandeWater, Bob Wachter, Michael Weiss, Diane Duke Williams, and Ryan P. Young.

We would further like to give thanks to all of the professors and staff at Washington University School of Medicine for creating an atmosphere of such encouragement, assistance, and belief in students' potential.

Introduction

Why We Wrote This Book

When we were first getting interested in health care, a few years before starting medical school, we tried to cobble together an understanding of what health care even was. We found ourselves lost in a sea of confusion faced with highly specialized publications that were often ideologically bent. Sure, generalized textbooks are out there, but even those seemed to focus on policy without explaining the huge world of research and drug companies that we kept reading about in the news. Besides, let's face it: textbooks are boring. Even a motivated student can only read so much from textbooks without being required to.

In writing this book, we've worked hard to rid our knowledge base of huge gaps, vague opinions, and biased perceptions of some issues. But it shouldn't be so hard, especially not for health professions students, and especially not in a nation where health care is such a huge, important, costly industry. We should make it as easy as possible to understand the U.S. health care system.

Of course, timing was a useful motivator. When we first decided to write this book, the Affordable Care Act had just passed, and, as we publish, the Supreme Court has just ruled on the law's constitutionality. We are experiencing what is perhaps the most exciting and significant time in the history of health care in America, and it's increasingly clear how important "solving" the health care problem has become. We think it's very important that more people understand the issues that lay before us, and we want our book to help further that understanding.

Our Goals

The goal of this book is to provide a broad base of facts, concepts, and analysis so the reader gets a thorough overview of the American health care system. The goal is to be exhaustive in breadth rather than in depth. The goal is to make sure the reader never gets into an argument about health care only to have his opponent bring up an issue he's never even heard of.

In short, our goal is to provide a baseline level of facts and analysis so that readers may go forth with the ability not only to understand and evaluate what they read but also to form their own opinions.

The other goal of this book is to impress a single theme upon the reader: **_everything is always more complicated than you think._** (If we could have underlined that phrase obsessively in each copy of this book, we would have.) It's frustrating to know so much yet know so little; to think there's a solution if only it weren't thwarted by reality. But understanding these complications is necessary not only for understanding health care but also for developing informed, nuanced, realistic opinions. It would have been obnoxious to put this disclaimer on every page of the book, so we'll just ask you to keep it in mind as you read: _it's more complicated than this!_

Intended Audience

We're students ourselves, so we have firsthand insight about what students don't know, what they want to know, and what they need to know. As such, students are our primary focus for this book. On the other hand, we wanted to learn these things before we were students. Certainly these topics are relevant to all who have an interest in health care, public policy, or how our government spends money. And aren't we all students of what we want to learn? Thus, our focus is on "students" in the broad sense of the word.

A lot of people from different walks of life have read this book—from the CEO of a major hospital to experts whose research we cited to journalists to fellow students to our moms—and we have used their feedback to make the book as useful as possible to as many people as possible. That said, it's not quite feasible to set out to write a book for "everybody." We think the book will hold the most value for the following:

1. Students in undergraduate, graduate, and professional programs focused on medicine, nursing, dentistry, pharmacy, allied health, medical research, biotechnology, public health, public policy, economics, finance, health care administration, business, and law. Heck, throw in history and political science, too!

2. Health care professionals who want to expand their knowledge about what affects them in the workplace or who want a reference for continuing education.

3. Lay readers who are sufficiently interested in learning more about health care to have started reading a book about it. In short, if you ever find yourself confused by a news article about what an Accountable Care Organization is, or you don't have quite enough information to argue with your Uncle Dan about pharmaceutical companies, or you're annoyed that everything you read has an agenda—then this book is for you.

Limitations

This book can't cover everything, and it's not for everyone. There are certainly topics we decided not to include, and those we did include have depths we didn't plumb. If someone, for instance, has been working in health administration for the past 25 years, he'll think this book misses some important nuances.

Well, he would be right, and that's the point. Our book is a survey, not a deep dive. We've tried to address this limitation by pointing to suggested reading and reminding you of how complicated the issues are. However, if you're looking for an in-depth nuanced exploration of limited topics, this isn't the right book for you.

How to Read the Book

First, as we said previously, we don't want this to be a boring textbook. While the book is ordered as a progression of knowledge, it isn't necessary to read straight through, cover to cover. Rather, the book is separated into distinct sections, which you can flip around and/or read selectively to supplement knowledge you already have. (Though we should mention that Chapter 5 on Reform is harder to fully understand without the first four chapters if you don't already have background knowledge in health care.) See the extensive Table of Contents to get an idea of the sections and what you might want to peruse.

Second, we've done our best to streamline references to the glossaries and other parts of the book. Many words are defined within the text, but there are also glossaries at the end of each chapter. Further, you'll find cross-references in parentheses that point to other relevant sections.

Third, you should read with the golden triad of health care (Cost-Access-Quality) always at the back of your mind. Pretty much any information, problem, or solution falls into Cost, Access, and/or Quality, and the three are an interdependent cycle rather than separate pillars. We'll refer to the triad at various points in the book, and, even when we don't—even when you're just musing on the issues—you should wonder how not just one but all may be affected.

Finally, we want to hear from you! Please visit HealthCareHandbook.com to see the latest news on the book, and send all questions, comments, and suggestions to Info@HealthCareHandbook.com. We'll read each and every last email because we truly want your feedback.

ELISABETH ASKIN AND NATHAN MOORE, MAY 2012

Chapter 1
Health Care Systems and Delivery

Let's say your watch is running slow. You know the time is wrong, but, chances are, you don't know how to fix it. Instead, you take it to the watchmaker, who understands the inner workings of the gears and how their interaction produces that time, right or wrong. To truly understand the function, you must understand the mechanism. It's time to think like a watchmaker. Let's get started by examining the parts and how they work together to better understand the U.S. health care system. Then we'll discuss some of the issues facing that system today.

You may have noticed that health care has its own vocabulary. Most words and concepts will be explained as you read, but there's also a glossary at the end of the chapter.

Health Care Systems

Health care systems can be categorized in many different ways. We'll start with the two broadest categories—inpatient vs. outpatient care—and whittle down from there. First, let's define these terms:

Inpatient: Patient stays in a medical facility for at least one night; these are hospitals, mental institutions, and nursing homes.

Outpatient: Patient is examined, diagnosed, or treated at a medical facility but doesn't stay overnight. You're an outpatient when you're at a doctor's appointment, having a wart removed, or getting a colonoscopy.

The distinction can be tricky, though, because inpatient facilities—e.g., hospitals—usually have outpatient centers in them. So you don't have to be an inpatient to be treated at a hospital. This intersection reflects medical categories in general. They often blur, overlap, and mix and match.

Inpatient Care

Focusing on hospitals, let's examine the types of administration, types of services, organization, operations, and finally, some of the issues affecting hospitals.

Breakdown of 5643 U.S. Hospitals

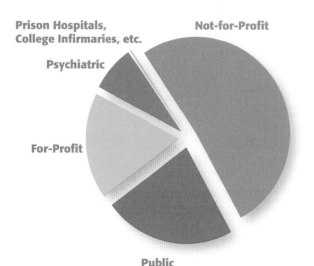

Prison Hospitals, College Infirmaries, etc.

Not-for-Profit

Psychiatric

For-Profit

Public

American Hospital Association, "Fast Facts," January 2012.

Note: This does not include long-term care hospitals.

HOSPITAL TYPES: OWNERSHIP

Public: Operated either by the federal, state, or local government.

- ▶ **Federal:** Three branches of the federal government operate hospitals—the Department of Defense for active military members, the Indian Health Service for Native Americans, and the Veterans Health Administration for military veterans.
  - ▶ **VA:** The Department of Veterans Affairs (VA) operates 152 hospitals and more than 1,300 outpatient facilities nationwide.[1] There are three interesting things to note about VA hospitals. First, their patients are more likely to be elderly and male than the general population. Second, they have high quality ratings; for example, one 2004 study compared the care received by VA patients to that of randomly selected community members and concluded that the VA care scored significantly higher in overall quality, chronic disease care, and preventive care.[2] Third, the VA was an early adopter of universal health care and electronic medical records.
- ▶ **State:** Typically long-term facilities for psychiatric patients. In 2010, there were 67 state government hospitals.[3]
- ▶ **Local:** Most local hospitals are safety-net, general hospitals that maintain a primary focus on free or reduced-cost care for underserved populations. In 2010, 1,001 hospitals were operated by local governments.[3]
- ▶ **Prisons:** Prison hospitals are administered by either federal, state, or local governments, or by private contractors.

Private: Hospitals not operated by the government. However, note that all hospitals that accept Medicare and Medicaid are, in some sense, *funded* by the government.

- ▶ **Not-for-Profit:** Not-for-profit, particularly religious, institutions are hospital mainstays, historically stemming from charity institutions for the poor. Any profit is reinvested in the hospital or community, rather than given to shareholders. These hospitals typically maintain a commitment to charity care, though this may not be their primary focus. Some not-for-profit hospitals function as safety net hospitals. Recognizing the value of the charity care that they provide, the government doesn't require these hospitals to pay taxes.[4]

> ‣ **Secular:** Most not-for-profit hospitals are owned and operated by non-religious civic organizations. They are governed by a board of directors that's comprised of locally prominent citizens.

> ‣ **Religious:** Many religious organizations have opened hospitals over the years, seeking to serve their own population, the underserved, or the community at large. Religious hospitals make up 9% of all hospitals in the U.S.,[3,5] and most of these are Catholic.[6] The direct impact of the religious organization on the day-to-day management of the hospital varies; in one arrangement, religious leaders comprise a portion of the board of directors but a lay CEO operates the hospital.

‣ **For-Profit:** For-profit hospitals are owned by private corporations and most of the hospital's profit is given to shareholders rather than reinvested into operations. Unlike not-for-profit hospitals, these organizations are required to pay government taxes. The largest operator of for-profit hospitals is the Hospital Corporation of America, which owns and operates 163 hospitals across the country.[7]

‣ **Physician-Owned Hospitals:** As of 2010, the U.S. had about 269 physician-owned hospitals.[8] The majority are for-profit institutions. These hospitals can be of any type but are more likely be single-specialty—especially orthopedics, oncology, or cardiology—than hospitals that don't have physician owners.[9] Expect to see a reduced number of these facilities in the coming years, as the Affordable Care Act (ACA) denies all Medicare reimbursements to new or expanding physician-owned hospitals.

PROS AND CONS

Like many things in health care, people have strong opinions about hospital ownership. Here's a quick guide to the common arguments you'll hear for and against the different types:

Government

‣ **For:** Government hospitals form a crucial part of the U.S. health care safety net for the most needy, and provide care, such as psychiatric services, that is unprofitable but necessary.

‣ **Against:** These hospitals are inefficient and mired in layers of bureaucracy, politics, and red tape.

Religious Not-for-Profit

▶ **For:** These hospitals provide the most—and most consistent—independent funding and commitment to charity care, and the underserved would be even less served without them.

▶ **Against:** The religious ideology of some hospitals restricts the care they offer to patients (e.g., Catholic hospitals don't offer in-vitro fertilization).[10]

Secular Not-for-Profit

▶ **For:** This model is best suited to serve the needs of the community without government administration.

▶ **Against:** These hospitals don't provide enough charity care to justify the billions in tax breaks they receive from the government.

For-Profit

▶ **For:** Financial incentives ensure that these hospitals provide the most efficient and cost-effective care for their patients, *and* they pay taxes.

▶ **Against:** These hospitals are more concerned with profits than patients and don't focus enough on quality of care or what services are best for the whole community.

Physician-Owned

▶ **For:** The medical staff is more committed because they also own the hospital, which leads to better care for patients.

▶ **Against:** Because the physicians benefit financially, they're more likely to utilize costly, high-reimbursement services for their patients.

HOSPITAL TYPES: SERVICES

Another way to classify hospitals is by services offered, which we detail here. Note that any of these types of hospitals may be associated with any sort of ownership.

General: Even aside from the soap opera, general hospitals are the most well-known types of hospitals. They supply a range of services, including emergency services, OB/GYN, internal medicine, surgery, and a variety of others.

▶ **Teaching:** The U.S. has nearly 400 teaching hospitals.[11] They're connected with medical schools, have residency programs, and are often referred to as "academic medical centers." Teaching hospitals explicitly include the training of medical students, new physicians, and other health care professionals as part of their mission. They're usually large hospitals located in major urban centers and provide a significant amount of charity care.

Specialty: Some hospitals—or sections of general hospitals—focus solely on a single specialty, such as cardiology, oncology, or women's medicine. Children's and psychiatric hospitals fall into this category as well.

▸ **Children's:** These are general hospitals for children. There are about 250 of these[12] in the U.S., many of which also serve as teaching and research institutions.

▸ **Psychiatric:** The U.S. has 444 of these institutions.[5] All focus solely on mental disorders, although they vary widely in breadth of services and in size. Psychiatric hospitals may treat mainly outpatients or short-term inpatients, or they may focus on long-term care. While voluntary entry is common, many include people who have been committed involuntarily, and some house the criminally insane.

NON-HOSPITAL INPATIENT FACILITIES

Thousands of non-hospital facilities also provide inpatient care. The most well known of these are **Skilled Nursing Facilities**, commonly called nursing homes, which provide 24-hour nursing care and assistance with daily living. In 2009, the 15,700 skilled nursing facilities in the U.S. had a total of more than 1.7 million patient beds.[13] Residents include the elderly as well as younger patients with severe disabilities. Though we may think of skilled nursing facilities as places where grandparents live out their days, they are not always permanent homes; stays can be as brief as three days, although patients typically have stays of 30 days or more. Most skilled nursing facilities are privately administered but often receive a large share of their funding through Medicare and Medicaid.

Two other types of inpatient facilities are:

▸ **Long-Term Acute Care Hospitals (LTACHs):** These serve patients who need intensive, hospital-level care for weeks or months. Patients in these hospitals typically have multiple, complex medical problems. In 2009, the 412 LTACHs in the U.S. had a total of around 27,250 beds.[14]

▸ **Inpatient Rehab Facilities (IRFs):** Also known as Acute Rehabilitation Hospitals, these facilities care for patients who require comprehensive rehabilitation along with considerable, but not hospital-level, medical management. Patients often enter these facilities after strokes, serious fractures, or joint replacement surgeries. In 2010, there were 1,180 IRFs in the U.S. for a total of 35,440 beds.[14]

HOSPITAL ORGANIZATION

In 2010, U.S. hospitals had a combined total of:[5]
▸ 941,995 staffed beds
▸ 37 million admissions
▸ $750 billion in expenses

A hospital is a pretty big business, and operating one is just as complex, if not more so, than operating any other large corporation. Far more services—and people—make the hospital run than any patient will ever encounter:

Board of Directors/Trustees: This small group sets the strategic vision for the hospital, provides oversight of the hospital's finances and quality, and hires and fires the senior administration, including the CEO. They are typically paid at for-profit institutions and serve without compensation at not-for-profit hospitals.

Administrative Services: These workers—the CEO, vice presidents, department heads, etc.—run the hospital on a day-to-day basis. They set hospital policy and oversee its execution, manage finances and budgetary planning, and handle marketing and public relations.[15]

Therapeutic Services: These workers provide the care normally associated with hospitals, such as physician visits, drugs, surgery, physical therapy, social work, psychiatry, etc. These are the services that directly make the patient feel better.

Diagnostic Services: These workers administer the laboratory, testing, and imaging facilities that help those in Therapeutic Services to figure out what care is needed.

Informational Services: These workers document and process information, such as medical records, billing, admissions, human resources, computer systems, and health education. Some of this may be performed by employees in dedicated roles (e.g., medical billers) and some by other staff (e.g., nurses performing registration).

Support Services: These workers maintain the hospital as a functioning facility. Areas of operation include food services, supply management, maintaining biotechnology equipment, and housekeeping.

STRUCTURE

The organizational structure of a hospital can vary significantly depending on size, ownership, service type, network facilitation, and history. Here's a visual depiction of the organization of one typical hospital:

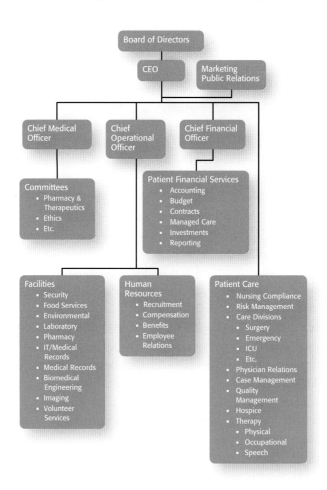

THE HOSPITAL-PHYSICIAN RELATIONSHIP

While physicians are included in the organizational chart, most of the physicians who provide inpatient care aren't actually hospital employees. In most businesses, workers are employees who receive their salary from the owner of the business, who in turn sets hours and working conditions for employees. However, hospital-physician relationships developed in a time when physicians were their own bosses. When a patient was too sick to be treated as an outpatient, the physician would admit the patient to a local hospital, where he or she would direct the patient's care. Upon discharge, the patient received separate bills—one from the physician for the care received and another from the hospital for use of a bed, supplies, and hospital staff.

Traditionally, physicians operated as independent contractors, and hospitals contracted with them in several ways, including:

▸ Independent physicians who worked primarily in outpatient settings could maintain privileges to admit their patients to one or more hospitals.

▸ Multiple physicians aligned to offer their services together as a "medical group"; one or more hospitals/health care networks then contracted with the group to provide patient care in their facilities.

▸ At some academic medical centers, physicians were employed by a medical school or academic physician organization and maintained an exclusive contract with an affiliated hospital.

For any of these relationships, all of which are still common today, physicians order and use hospital resources (i.e., spend hospital money) without being directly employed by the hospital (the usual way that employers exert control over their employees). The upshot is that hospitals may have to use different methods than a traditional employer to influence physician behavior—behavior that has far-reaching effects on many health care issues, such as cost control and quality improvement.

However, this traditional hospital-physician relationship is evolving. A small percentage of physicians has always been hospital employees—emergency physicians, ICU physicians, or pathologists, for example—but today, a growing number of physicians in all specialties are eschewing their traditional independence in favor of direct employment by a hospital, health care network, or insurance company. One large example is Kaiser Permanente, a California-based HMO (Chapter 2) that directly employs physicians. For other hospitals, many of the physicians they employ are hospitalists who only treat hospitalized patients and don't maintain an outpatient clinic. For more information, see "Changing Practice Patterns" later in this chapter.

Looking at the organizational chart, it's more obvious that there is a distinction between administrative services and medical services. Administrators are running a business, whereas the health care staff is practicing medicine. For the most part, these goals align, but at times they diverge, and power struggles may arise.[16]

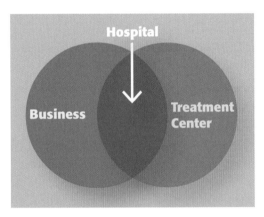

Most salient is when what health care staff considers good medicine is what administrators consider unnecessary expenditures (and, as administrators would point out, unnecessary expenditures for one patient may lead to fewer resources to properly care for other patients, which is bad medicine). Length of stay is one area of possible disagreement; longer hospital stays are expensive for hospitals[a] but they also may be necessary for optimal health. Another is equipment purchases and prioritizing what treatments are offered.

For instance, an increasing number of prostate surgeries are performed with high-tech robotic equipment; these systems cost upwards of a million dollars each. When considering whether to purchase one, the surgeon

---

a   Of course, this depends on the type of insurance that's paying for the patient stay. Longer hospital stays are more expensive for the hospital if the reimbursement is on a DRG basis (page 92) or if the patient is uninsured; however, per diem reimbursement systems often make longer hospital stays profitable for the hospital.

(who uses the equipment) and administrator (who pays for it) are likely to ask different questions:

Surgeon

▸ Will this improve my patients' outcomes?
▸ Will this make surgeries easier and/or quicker for me?
▸ What's the learning curve for the new instrument? Will the hospital staff be properly trained?
▸ Will I lose patients if I don't have this system?

Administrator

▸ Will this improve patients' outcomes?
▸ Is the system a good value? Could this same amount of money be spent elsewhere in the hospital and help more patients?
▸ Will insurance companies reimburse more now to compensate for our increased costs?
▸ Will I lose physicians if I don't have this system?

Though both medical and administration staff want what is best for patient care, they may emphasize different aspects of what that means. This can lead to a discrepancy in ethos between the administration, representing the business aspect of a hospital, and the medical staff, representing the treatment aspect. As you might imagine, given that physicians aren't employees, this discrepancy can be difficult to resolve.

Another fact to consider is that most, but not all, health care professionals besides physicians are directly employed by the hospital. Also, the organizational chart doesn't indicate whether the hospital is part of a network (page 28), but some are, and just like any business franchise, the central office will set some policies.

COMMITTEES

Each hospital has a number of committees, usually headed by the medical staff, that make decisions regarding hospital management, regulation, and the care delivered in that institution. A few of these committees include Pharmacy and Therapeutics (which determines which drugs may be prescribed), Credentialing (which approves new health care providers), Infection Control, and Quality Improvement.

Committees are an essential part of running a hospital, and they may include members from all sectors of the organization. One of the most important committees found at any hospital is the Credentialing Committee; this is the group that determines whether a physician will be granted "privileges" to admit patients to the hospital. (No patient can be admitted to a hospital unless an approved physician agrees to direct his or her care; hence, the term "admitting" or "attending" physician for that provider who directs a patient's care.) If a physician in the community would like to be able to admit patients, he or she is subjected to a thorough background check, including previous malpractice claims, by the Credentialing Committee. Physicians may have admitting privileges at multiple hospitals, and it's often in hospitals' best interest to grant privileges, as this brings in more patients and more revenue.[b]

Another important committee is the Ethics Committee. Aside from certain laws that detail what health providers can and can't do, physicians and hospitals aren't obligated to follow a specific, universal ethical code.[17] While individual professions do have codes of conduct, these not only aren't binding but also are often quite loose to allow for specifics. The hospital's Ethics Committee reviews complex cases and scenarios to assist providers and patients with their decision-making. Examples may include:

▸ Should treatment be continued for a 25-week-old premature baby who isn't expected to survive on his or her own?

▸ Should a surgeon tell a patient about things that went wrong in surgery, even if he or she doesn't think they will affect the patient's outcome?

▸ Should nurses continue offering narcotics to a pediatric patient whose immune system is failing?

Ethics committees aren't elected; they're typically made up of volunteer health care staff, hospital administrators, and community members, often including local religious leaders.

---

b   This committee is usually a subcommittee of the board of directors, and is staffed by attending physicians and hospital administrators. This can create an odd incentive structure. While the administrators may wish to increase the number of admitting physicians to bring in more revenue, the current physicians are incentivized to limit the number of physicians with privileges in order to decrease competition.

PATIENT CARE TEAMS

The hospitalized patient is served by a number of physicians, nurses, and other allied health professionals, often referred to as a "care team," who work together to diagnose and treat the patient. The composition of the care team and members' responsibilities vary by patient and institution, but the team is usually headed by an attending physician who directs patients' care and delegates tasks to the other members of the team. A typical care team may include:

- An attending physician
- Physician interns and residents (in all teaching institutions)
- Physician consultants
- Nurses and other health care professionals
- Health professions students

HOSPITAL ISSUES

As you can see, hospitals are complicated organizations. They weren't *designed* but instead arose from existing institutions and grew organically— at times inefficiently—to meet society's needs. As with many large organizations, hospitals have some issues. Let's go through a few that aren't only important for society but also relevant to health reform.

Medical Errors

The report *To Err is Human: Building a Safer Health System* was published in 1999 by the Institute of Medicine (IOM, page 30). The report shed light on medical errors, suggesting that 48,000-96,000 people died every year from these errors, more than from Alzheimer's disease or drug overdose.[18] This publication had a huge impact,[19] initiating research about communication, guidelines, and information technology to prevent errors.

Before we discuss this sensitive topic, let's define some important terms. An "adverse event" is any harm that occurs to a patient because of his or her medical care or stay in a health care institution. An adverse event may occur when a mistake has been made as well as when best practices have been followed, but a bad outcome still resulted. "Medical errors" refer more specifically to *preventable* adverse events that occur due to errors during the delivery of care. Examples include a physician making an incorrect diagnosis, a nurse giving medicines to the wrong patient, an IV pump failing during surgery, and a blood test not being ordered due to miscommunication between hospital staff.

Types of Errors

Diagnostic
- Error or delay in diagnosis
- Failure to employ indicated tests
- Use of outmoded tests or therapy
- Failure to act on results of monitoring or testing

Treatment
- Error in the performance of an operation, procedure, or test
- Error in administering the treatment
- Error in the dose or method of using a drug
- Avoidable delay in treatment or in responding to an abnormal test
- Inappropriate (not indicated) care

Preventive
- Failure to provide prophylactic treatment
- Inadequate monitoring or follow-up of treatment

Other
- Failure of communication
- Equipment failure
- Other system failure

Leape et al, "Preventing Medical Injury," May 1993.

The medical errors that loom largest in popular consciousness may be cases in which physicians have operated on the wrong limb. However, these cases are exceedingly rare. The most common medical errors aren't even due to mistakes or negligence. Rather, most errors occur because of deficiencies within the incredibly complex health care delivery system. Think of a large hospital—a fast-paced, stressful environment with thousands of employees and a dizzying array of computer systems and medical devices. A momentary lapse of attention or miscommunication by any employee or device at any time of day can lead to a bad outcome for a patient. Thus, efforts to stem medical errors don't simply target negligent action by providers but instead often focus on improving health care system design and on enhancing the transfer of information between providers.

To Err is Human suggests that "mistakes can best be prevented by design-ing the health system at all levels to make it safer—to make it harder for people to do something wrong and easier for them to do it right."[19] The Affordable Care Act of 2010 addressed some of the IOM's suggestions about coordination for patient safety by mandating the creation of a National Quality Strategy.

Hospital-Acquired Infections

Hospital-acquired infections (HAIs), also called nosocomial infections, are diseases that result from hospital treatment; they're infections or condi-tions that arise *due to* the care patients receive. Obviously, this is the reverse of how things are supposed to be, yet HAIs are all too common. Common HAIs include urinary tract infections from catheters, blood stream infections from IV lines, and surgical site infections. The most recent analy-sis, from the Centers for Disease Control and Prevention (CDC), estimated that the total number of HAIs for the year 2002 was 1.7 *million* and that more than 98,000 patients died from these infections.[20] As if that weren't bad enough, HAIs are also expensive—another CDC report calculated that HAIs cost hospitals between $35–$45 billion per year.[21]

Although it may not be possible to completely eliminate HAIs, many pre-ventive measures have been shown to help. For instance, proper hand hygiene has been shown to significantly reduce infection rates.[22] But it's worth noting that the CDC guidelines for properly washing hands are two-and-a-half pages long—which may be why researchers estimate that only about 40% of health care workers actually adhere to these guidelines.[23] As with so many issues in health care, behavior change is both absolutely nec-essary and incredibly difficult.

Trending from Outpatient to Inpatient to Outpatient

In the olden days, physicians usually made home visits, or house calls, so the majority of patients were by definition outpatients. With the advent of antiseptic facilities and surgery, hospitals ceased to be places where sick people went to die and started to be places where sick people went to get well. So the 20th century saw the rise of the inpatient.

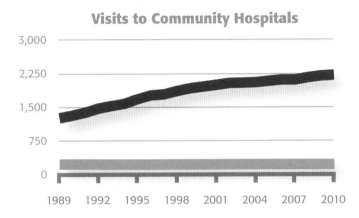

Visits to Community Hospitals

American Hospital Association Chartbook, "Inpatient Admissions per 1,000 Persons, 1990–2010" and "Total Hospital Outpatient Visits per 1,000 Persons, 1990-2010," March 2011.

However, over the past 20 years, the balance has again shifted and out-patient care represents an increasing share of dollars and attention. Today, outpatient care accounts for about 40% of health care spending,[25] but, as you can see from the figure above, outpatient care accounts for a much greater proportion of hospital visits. This trend in hospitals toward outpatient care is primarily due to three outside forces:

▸ Technological advances and improvements in clinical care have reduced the hospital time needed to recover from many medical conditions and surgical procedures.

▸ A growing number of outpatient physicians are directly employed by hospitals and health care networks (page 28).

▸ In the 1980s, Medicare switched its payment structures to reimburse hospitals by lump sums based on Diagnosis Related Groups (see Chapter 3) rather than by the length of the patient stay. Since hospital stays are expensive, this was a strong financial motivator for hospitals to shift health care delivery practices to favor shorter inpatient stays.

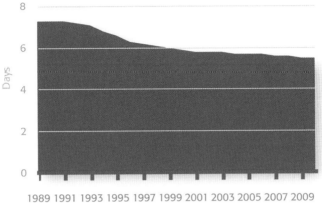

Average Length of Stay in Community Hospitals

American Hospital Association Chartbook, "Average Length of Stay in Community Hospitals, 1990-2010," March 2011.

This shift to shorter hospital stays has pros and cons. Though many patients may be glad not to spend the night in a hospital, discharging patients before they're ready has negative consequences both for health (due to incomplete care) as well as for costs (through readmissions and avoidable health outcomes). On the other hand, keeping patients in the hospital for too long puts them at increased risk for hospital-acquired infections and medical errors, and each extra day in the hospital can cost $10,000 or more. For now, though, the drive to reduce length of stay shows no signs of stopping. This trend is instructive in two ways:

▸ As an example of the way that changes in payment structure lead to changes in care delivery, which is also an example of how the components of our triad—Cost-Access-Quality—are intertwined.
▸ As an example of the conflict, as discussed in the "Hospital Organization" section, between the hospital as a business and as place of care, and the difficulty in synchronizing quality and efficiency.

Outpatient Care

Outpatient care is often referred to as "ambulatory" care, the idea being that you can walk on your own. However, the strict definition of an outpatient is a person receiving medical care without staying overnight at a health care facility, though that doesn't necessarily mean that the person is not ill or receiving significant care. Outpatient visits may include minor surgery, check-ups, physical therapy, mammograms, and lab testing, to name a few examples. Clearly, these are pretty varied treatments, and the ways outpatient care is delivered are quite variable as well.

That variation in care is reflected in this section, as we look at some of the types of facilities, services, and organizations common in outpatient care, keeping in mind that these may mix and match. We'll also look at some issues affecting outpatient medicine.

Outpatient Visits to Physicians in 2008[13]
80% to Physicians' Offices 60% Primary Care / 40% Specialist
9% to Hospital-Based Outpatient Services
10% to the Emergency Department

DELIVERY FORMATS FOR OUTPATIENT MEDICINE

Private Practice: An outpatient clinic owned and operated by the health care professionals who practice there. Private practice has traditionally been the dominant form of outpatient care in the U.S. Private physician practices are often classified by the number of physicians employed:

▸ **Solo Practice:** As simple as it gets—a single physician of any specialty who owns the office in which he or she sees patients.
▸ **Group Practice:** Any private medical practice that includes more than one physician. This ranges from dual practices to groups of more than 1,000 physicians. Group practices can be further classified by the type of care they offer: primary care, single specialty, multi-specialty, or comprehensive (primary care + specialty).

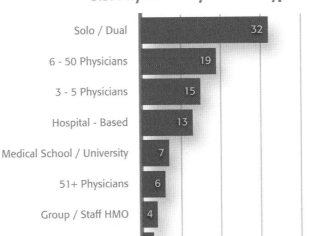

U.S. Physicians by Practice Types

The Physicians Foundation, "Health Reform and the Decline of Physician Private Practice," October 2010. *Used by permission.*

Hospital/Health Care Network: As discussed in the "Inpatient Care" section, an increasing number of physicians are employed directly by hospitals or health care networks. In many cases, a private group practice will be purchased by a hospital or health care network, and the physicians in that practice become network employees. These physicians may be integrated into normal hospital operations, be housed in a separate section of the building, or practice in traditional community-based locations.

Community Health Center (CHC): These are government-supported institutions that provide low-cost care to underserved and low-income populations. CHCs often focus on primary care but may offer a range of services in a "one-stop shop" format. For instance, some CHCs offer laboratory testing, OB/GYN, and dental services in addition to primary care. In 2011, more than 1,200 CHCs were providing care to 20 million patients annually.[26,27] Many CHCs are also designated as Federally Qualified Health Centers, which enables them to receive extra funding from Medicare, Medicaid, and CHIP. FQHCs are slated to receive expanded funding under the ACA (page 216).

Free/Charitable Clinic: These clinics also offer care for underserved and low-income populations. Their main difference from CHCs is that free and charitable clinics are not government-supported; instead, they're operated by private not-for-profit organizations. Another difference is that free clinics, as you might suspect, may offer care without any charge to the patient.

Local Government: Apart from funding other institutions, many city and county health departments directly offer a limited range of outpatient services, including immunizations and screening for diseases such as tuberculosis and HIV.[28]

Health Maintenance Organization (HMO): These tend to be networks rather than physical facilities, but rules were made to be broken. A good example is Kaiser Permanente, which is an insurer that owns its own facilities and employs its own physicians. (See page 81 for more information about HMOs.)

Emergency Department (ED): Care received in the ED is considered outpatient care because those patients have not yet been admitted to the inpatient section of the hospital. Emergency Medicine is a separate medical specialty that requires three to four years of residency training. However, the current demand for emergency physicians is greater than the supply. Many EDs, especially those in rural areas, are staffed by physicians who have completed residencies in fields other than emergency medicine. (For more on ED-specific issues, see page 119.)

Urgent Care Center (UCC): UCCs bridge the gap between primary care and the ED. They're open on evenings and weekends, appealing to patients who can't get same-day appointments with their primary care physicians, need medical care outside of normal office hours, or don't have regular primary care physicians. However, UCCs aren't equipped to deal with trauma or true medical emergencies. UCCs are primarily staffed by physicians trained in family medicine, and about half of all centers are physician-owned. The most common services offered by UCCs are cut and fracture care, X-rays, school and employment physicals, and immunizations. Approximately 8,700 UCCs were operating in 2011, with each center seeing an average of 342 patients per week.[29]

Retail Clinic: These small medical clinics in convenient locations (e.g., Walgreens) offer quick, inexpensive, protocol-based care for limited medical conditions, such as strep throat, minor burns, and vaccinations. Patients who present with urgent or more complicated conditions are referred to EDs, UCCs, or other local physicians. Most retail clinics are staffed by nurse practitioners, although some employ physician assistants and physicians. The number of retail clinics nationwide has grown from 60 in 2006 to more than 1,000 in 2011.[30]

Ambulatory Surgery Center (ASC): Although surgical services are often closely linked with hospitals, more than 40% of surgeries in the U.S. are actually performed in outpatient settings. ASCs are like surgical clinics, where patients can undergo minor surgical procedures that don't require hospital stays. The most common procedures performed at the 5,349 ASCs in the U.S. are colonoscopies, endoscopies, and cataract removals.[31] More than 80% of ASCs are owned at least in part by physicians; similar to physician-owned hospitals, conflict of interest is an issue. For instance, studies indicate that physician-owners of ASCs are more likely to recommend surgery for their patients than are other physicians.[32]

Home Care: About 12 million Americans receive health care in their homes[33] rather than traveling to health care institutions. Many patients are discharged from hospitals while needing long-term treatment and oversight, which can be accomplished for less cost in the home than in an inpatient facility. The primary professionals who provide home care are home health aides and nurses.

Hospice: Also called palliative care, these programs aim to provide maximal quality of life for patients with terminal illnesses. Patients select hospice care when they decide to shift the focus of their care from trying to cure their conditions to providing comfort from their symptoms, including pain control. Specialized multidisciplinary teams of health care professionals provide hospice care, usually in the home, but also in hospitals, long-term care facilities, and hospice inpatient institutions. More than 40% of the people who died in 2009 were under the care of a hospice program at the time of death.[34] Hospice care is less expensive than inpatient care, and, interestingly, patients in hospice care may live longer than those who continue medical treatment.[35]

Non-Physician Services: Many other health care professionals provide outpatient care as well. Dentists, chiropractors, podiatrists, physical therapists, and optometrists are just a few of the providers who practice primarily in outpatient settings.

Complementary and Alternative Medicine (CAM): More than one-third of Americans regularly use complementary (used with conventional medicine) or alternative (used in place of conventional medicine) therapies, which include herbal or natural products, acupuncture, and homeopathic care. Most CAM is provided in the outpatient setting. Although some insurance plans provide reimbursement for CAM services, the majority of spending is out of pocket and totals more than $30 billion annually.[36] Upon hearing the rate of use and spending on CAM, it's not surprising that the federal government has established a National Center for CAM to study the field.

Patient-Centered Medical Home: This model for is comprehensive and coordinated outpatient care. For more information, see page 213.

Boutique/Concierge Practice: These clinics focus on patients who would like a high level of service (e.g., short wait times, long appointments and physicians who are available 24/7) and are willing to pay for it. Boutique or concierge practices typically charge an annual membership fee along with separate appointment fees and can therefore afford to keep the total patient load pretty low and have more time for each patient.

ISSUES IN OUTPATIENT MEDICINE

Outpatient medicine is just as susceptible to issues as inpatient medicine. Let's go through a few issues, as we did with hospitals, which are both important to society and relevant to health care reform.

Changing Practice Patterns

For physicians who work primarily in outpatient settings, the dominant trend over the last 30 years has been a shift from working in solo private practices to group practices owned by a hospital or health care network. In fact, the proportion of physicians in solo practice has declined by more than 40% during this time period,[37,38] and a growing number of physician practices are now owned by hospitals or health care networks.[c] This represents a funda-

---

c   Some physicians are directly employed by insurance companies rather than hospitals or health care networks. This arrangement is discussed in Chapter 3.

mental change for physicians, who traditionally have been their own bosses, and for hospitals, where new administrative systems have to be designed to incorporate physicians as employees rather than as independent workers.

Why is this change occurring? For hospitals and health care networks, physician employees represent access to patients. Remember, physicians can send their patients to a number of hospitals; hospitals must then constantly compete for physician preference. Although the outpatient practices of physician employees, especially in primary care, may be unprofitable for the network,[39] money is made when patients are referred to specialists, sent for lab testing, or admitted to the hospital. Also, new payment systems that reward comprehensive services, coordination of care, and risk reduction favor large networks that can provide primary, inpatient, and specialist care.

For the physician, a contract with a hospital or health care network offers several advantages over private practice: a guaranteed salary, steady access to patients, more integrated care for their patients, and a better work-life balance. Keep in mind that a physician in solo practice is running a small business in addition to practicing clinical medicine; having access to health care network staff who take care of administrative demands such as billing, scheduling, negotiating with insurance companies, and record keeping is no small thing. Ironically, many physicians also find it easier to get personal health insurance at affordable prices after becoming employed by a network.

So, how will this dramatic change in the hospital-physician relationship affect patients? A variety of outcomes are possible. In the best case scenario, the integration of primary care and specialist physicians with hospital administration will foster greater coordination between providers, fewer duplicated labs and procedures, and more efficient delivery of care, leading to better outcomes and lower costs for patients. In the worst case scenario, the loss of physician autonomy will allow hospital administrators to dictate clinical practice to favor profit over quality care and cause physician morale to drop. This, along with decreased market competition due to dominance of a few large, integrated hospital-physician networks, then leads to poorer outcomes and higher costs for patients. The true result will likely fall somewhere in between, but expect the changing nature of the hospital-physician relationship to remain an important and controversial issue for the foreseeable future.

Physician Shortage

A major expansion of health insurance coverage due to the ACA and a rapidly aging population will significantly increase demand for medical services in the coming years, and a number of national organizations have recently sounded alarms that the supply of physicians won't be able to keep pace. One of these organizations, the Association of American Medical Colleges, forecasts a shortfall of 130,000 physicians by the year 2025.[40] In addition, the unequal distribution of physicians throughout the country means that some areas are already experiencing a shortage; the federal government already designates more than 20% of the U.S. population as living in a "health professional shortage area."[41] A national consensus is growing that the supply of physicians needs to be expanded, but to do so will require changes to an already controversial system.

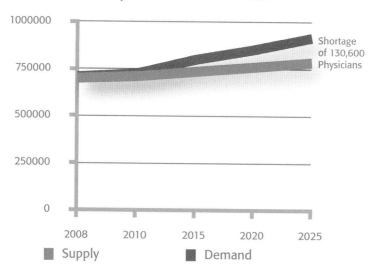

Difference Between Physician Supply and Demand Projected from 2008–2025

Shortage of 130,600 Physicians

■ Supply   ■ Demand

Association of American Medical Colleges, "Physician Shortages to Worsen Without Increases in Residency Training," September 2010. Used by permission.

In 2010, there were 79,020 medical students in the U.S., of whom 18,665 were newly enrolled.[42] That same year, there were 113,142 medical residents in the U.S.[43] (There are more residents than students because many residencies are longer than the four years of medical school and also because many residencies are filled by international medical graduates.) Many more people would like to become physicians, but the bottleneck (and barrier) to actually becoming one is the limited number of medical school and residency slots, which in turn limits physician supply and contributes to the shortage.

The number of residents is limited by two main entities:[44] first, by the Department of Health & Human Services, which, largely through Medicare, funds most residency programs; second, by the Accreditation Council for Graduate Medical Education (ACGME), which approves any new residencies in each specialty through Residency Review Committees.

There are arguments both for and against limiting the number of medical students and residents (which is, ultimately, a limit on physicians). Here's a point-counterpoint summary of the arguments.

Point: Limiting Physician Number is Good	Counterpoint: Limiting Physician Number is Bad
▸ Entering medical students can be assured that, though they're taking on massive debt (an average of $117K per student),[45] they will definitely get jobs when it's all over.	▸ Competition is limited, keeping salaries artificially high.
▸ These limits reflect maintenance of high standards by accreditation organizations and medical licensing boards.	▸ Standards are too high, blocking students who would make good physicians.
▸ The U.S. already has more physicians per capita than it has ever had,[46] and areas of the U.S. with more physicians per capita don't have better health outcomes but do have higher costs and poorer coordination of care.[47]	▸ These limits lead to a patient-to-physician ratio that's too high, especially in primary care and in rural areas.
▸ It would be expensive—and drive up costs further—to fund many new residency programs.	▸ Physicians must put in long hours to compensate for the small workforce, leading to sleep-deprived and overworked physicians.
	▸ The U.S. population is aging, and older people require more medical care.

Primary Care Physician Shortage

The percentage of U.S. physicians choosing to work in primary care has been on the decline for some time, and today less than 40% of practicing physicians are in primary care.[48] The reasons for this trend are many: higher pay for specialists than for primary care physicians (PCPs), the low status of primary care in most academic medical centers, and unpleasant workloads (too much paperwork, too many patients per day). Compounding the problem, hundreds of primary care residency slots have been cut or converted to specialty training positions,[49] ensuring that the number of new PCPs will fall.

General Practitioners, Specialists, and Other Doctors as a Share of Total Doctors

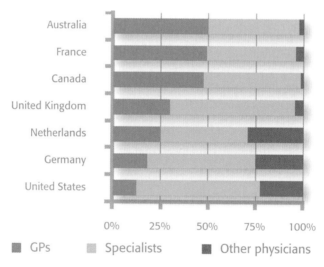

Organisation for Economic Co-operation and Development "Health Data 2011," June 2011.

Note: Specialists include pediatricians, ob/gyn, psychiatrists, medical specialists and surgical specialists. Other doctors include interns/residents if not reported in the field in which they are training, and doctors not elsewhere classified.

So, why should we care? What's so bad about fewer primary care physicians and more specialists? To answer, let's use the triad of Cost-Access-Quality.

Cost: In 2005, a systematic review of research about primary care usage and health outcomes found that "areas with higher ratios of primary care physicians to population had much lower total health care costs than did other areas, possibly partly because of better preventive care and lower hospitalization rates. [...]In contrast, the supply of specialists was associated with more spending and poorer care."[50]

Access: Primary care is the easiest way for most people to access health services, both for ongoing wellness or disease management and for appropriate referrals to specialists. In rural areas, if there's a shortage of primary care physicians, then there's almost certainly a shortage of specialists as well.

Quality: Use of primary care leads to better health outcomes. The same systematic review as above found that primary care was associated with better outcomes in all-cause mortality, heart disease mortality, stroke mortality, infant mortality, low birth weight, life expectancy, and self-rated health.[50] Primary care creates this benefit through six mechanisms:

- Greater access to needed services
- Better quality of care
- A greater focus on prevention
- Early management of health problems
- The cumulative effect of the main primary care delivery characteristics
- The role of primary care in reducing unnecessary and potentially harmful specialist care[50]

From this list, one can conclude that a shortage of primary care providers may lead to poor quality, high costs, and restricted access. Health care reform may only exacerbate this problem—over the next decade, millions of newly insured Americans will be looking for primary care providers. They may be in for a rude surprise when they find that many primary care providers won't take new patients with Medicare and Medicaid (see Underpayment on page 118), and of those that do, the wait for an appointment may be one month or more.[51]

So how can we fix the problem of a primary care provider shortage in the U.S.? Here are some potential solutions, although each has pros and cons:

- Make medical education free.
- Encourage and incentivize medical students to enter primary care.
- Tweak current payment systems (like Relative Value Units, page 93) to increase reimbursement for primary care services.

- Use alternate payment systems (like capitation, page 92) that reward health promotion and coordination of care rather than costly procedures.
- Reduce the hassles of primary care practice (e.g., less paperwork, longer patient visits, etc.).
- Increase the number of residency positions in primary care training programs.
- Shift more of the primary care workload to nurse practitioners (page 57) and physician assistants (page 66).
- Expand the Patient-Centered Medical Home and other delivery structures that put the PCP in charge of coordinating patient care across medical specialties.
- Establish more three-year medical schools—cheaper and faster—aimed at producing family physicians.

Networks

As of 2009, 88% of community hospitals were part of a system or network.[5] A health care delivery system or network is an organization that owns and operates multiple hospitals and/or outpatient facilities.

A **Horizontal Network** is a conglomeration of multiple institutions of the same type. An example is Shriners Hospitals, which owns and operates 22 pediatric hospitals across the country.

A **Vertical Network** contains different types of services. An example is Kaiser Permanente, which is an insurer, an owner of hospitals and outpatient centers, and an employer of physicians.

A more common form of integration, though less robust than a network, is a **Group Purchasing Organization (GPO)**, where multiple institutions join to purchase products so they have greater negotiating power and receive better prices. More than 95% of hospitals belong to a GPO.[52] Unlike networks, however, the members of a single GPO are not necessarily owned or operated by the same organization.

Please note that many organizations of health care providers are also called networks. Those are detailed in Chapter 3.

National Health Care Organizations

A number of organizations, both within and outside of the government, play a role in making sure that health care in the U.S. is safe and effective. We detail the major groups here.

Governmental

Department of Health & Human Services (HHS)

This government agency deals with almost all aspects of health in the U.S. The HHS Secretary sits in the Cabinet. Divisions include Medicare, Medicaid, Centers for Disease Control and Prevention (CDC), National Institutes of Health (NIH), Agency for Healthcare Research and Quality (AHRQ), and the Food and Drug Administration (FDA), along with non-health programs, like Head Start and Faith-Based and Neighborhood Partnerships. The HHS budget accounts for nearly one-quarter of the total federal budget.[53]

Occupational Safety and Health Administration (OSHA)

This division of the Department of Labor regulates and inspects workplace conditions to ensure that the environment is safe for employees. For example, OSHA creates regulations on medical equipment to reduce accidental needlesticks in hospitals. OSHA covers most private and federal workplaces.

National Institutes of Health (NIH)

The NIH is the main governmental institution responsible for biomedical and health research; it's a major source of funding for medical research in the U.S. The NIH awards grants to medical researchers across the country as well as employs and funds its own research staff. It maintains a number of centers and institutes, including the National Institute for Medical Health and the National Cancer Institute.

Centers for Disease Control and Prevention (CDC)

The CDC is the primary governmental agency for public health and epidemiology. For example, the CDC is responsible for tracking and coordinating the national response to the spread of diseases such as swine flu.

Agency for Healthcare Research and Quality (AHRQ)

The AHRQ is the primary government agency for health systems and outcomes research. Studies focus on cost, access, and quality of U.S. health care; much of the data is used in the formation of new clinical practice guidelines (page 154).

Surgeon General

The Surgeon General is the federal government's spokesperson to the nation on matters of health. He or she often spearheads large public health campaigns, such as encouraging Americans to quit smoking. The Surgeon General represents the U.S. government in a number of committees and private organizations and is the head of the Public Health Service Commissioned Corps.

Non-Governmental

Institute of Medicine (IOM)

The IOM is a branch of the National Academy of Sciences. It's an independent, not-for-profit organization comprised of academics and other health care experts that produces reports on topics relevant to the nation's health, such as childhood obesity and medical errors. Reports are commissioned and funded by a variety of sources, including the federal government and private organizations.

The Joint Commission (TJC)

TJC is a non-governmental, not-for-profit organization that accredits hospitals and other health care facilities in the U.S. Accreditation is dependent on adherence to a broad set of standards that cover everything from physician credentialing to placement of bathrooms. Although hospitals aren't required to be accredited by TJC, many government and private insurance programs will not reimburse non-accredited hospitals. Hospitals are examined by TJC for reaccreditation every three years.

American Medical Association (AMA)

Established in 1847, the AMA is the largest and most powerful professional organization of U.S. physicians and medical students. While fewer than 30% of physicians today belong to the organization, it remains an influential force in both policy and politics.

Accreditation Council for Graduate Medical Education (ACGME)

The ACGME is responsible for the accreditation of post-MD medical train-ing programs within the United States. Accreditation is accomplished through a peer review process and is based upon established standards and guidelines.

Glossary

ACA: The Affordable Care Act—the new health care reform law. See Chap-ter 5, which is entirely about it.

Allied Health: Allied health refers to health care workers who are not phy-sicians, nurses, or dentists but are still vital to patient care. Many of these roles are detailed in the "Providers" section of Chapter 2.

Consult: When one physician formally asks another health care provider to contribute to a patient's care. Typically, a consult is called when the patient has a problem outside of the attending physician's expertise, and the con-sulting provider is asked to evaluate the patient and offer an opinion on the condition and possible treatments. Consulting providers are usually specialist physicians, but consults can also be asked of a broad range of other professionals, including mental health providers, occupational and physical therapists, and dietitians. A consult isn't the same as a referral.

Medicaid: A joint federal-state public health insurance program aimed at covering low-income adults and children. See the section on Medicaid in Chapter 5.

Medicare: A federal public health insurance program aimed at covering adults over the age of 65. See the section on Medicare in Chapter 5.

Patient Dumping: The hospital practice—through various means—of decreasing the likelihood that patient populations with low reimbursement rates will come to that particular hospital for their care. For instance, hospi-tals may restrict their services to the uninsured so that those patients flood hospitals with greater charity care provisions.

Suggested Reading

To Err is Human, by the Institute of Medicine. *This text on medical errors can be found for free online. Although it was written in 1999, it's still very relevant and referenced often.*

Delivering Health Care in America, by Leiyu Shi and Douglas Singh. *This tome is over 600 pages long, meaning it probably has just about everything you would want to look up. The newest edition will include a chapter on the Affordable Care Act.*

Essentials of the US Health Care System, by Leiyu Shi and Douglas Singh. *In case 600 pages is a little too daunting for you, this is the shortened (around 300 pages) version of the same book as above.*

Understanding Health Policy, by Thomas Bodenheimer and Kevin Grumbach. *This book is more accessible and less textbookish than the preceding two.*

Health Affairs (journal), http://www.healthaffairs.org. *This is the premier journal for health service research and policy commentary. It's printed monthly, so check back often for new information.*

The Health Care Blog, http://www.thehealthcareblog.com. *This blog includes submissions from physicians, economists, PhDs, and pundits on a huge range of topics across the political spectrum. As with Health Affairs, we recommend reading periodically to stay informed and up-to-date.*

References

1. Where do I get the care I need? http://www.va.gov/health/MedicalCenters.asp. Department of Veterans Affairs. Accessed Apr 12, 2012.
2. Asch SM, McGlynn EA, Hogan MM, et al. Comparison of Quality of Care for Patients in the Veterans Health Administration and Patients in a National Sample. *Annals of Internal Medicine*. 2004;141(12):938-945.
3. D. Culbertson. American Hospital Association. Personal Communication.
4. Anderson K, Gevas G. The Tax Status of Not-for-Profit Hospitals Under Siege & The Financial Implications of Recent Attacks. http://www.drinkerbiddle.com/files/Publication/3798d6f1-868f-4950-9b2e-0a98767c99cc/Presentation/PublicationAttachment/188499da-64f6-45dd-a800-1335d664ca97/HCNationalCityWhitePaper.pdf. National City. Accessed Aug 26, 2011.
5. Fast Facts on US Hospitals. http://www.aha.org/aha/resource-center/Statistics-and-Studies/fast-facts.html. American Hospital Association. Accessed Apr 12, 2012.
6. Health Care Reform - Facts & Statistics. http://www.usccb.org/healthcare/facts.shtml. United States Conference of Catholic Bishops. Accessed Aug 5, 2011.

7. About Our Company. http://hcahealthcare.com/about/. HCA Healthcare. Accessed Apr 20, 2012.

8. Weaver C. Physician-Owned Hospitals Racing To Meet Health Law Deadline. http://www.kaiserhealthnews.org/Stories/2010/October/28/physician-owned-hospitals.aspx. Kaiser Health News. Accessed Aug 5, 2011.

9. Iglehart JK. The Emergence of Physician-Owned Specialty Hospitals. *New England Journal of Medicine*. 2005;352(1):78-84. http://dx.doi.org/10.1056/NEJMhpr043631.

10. Uttley L, Pawelko R. No Strings Attached: Public Funding of Religiously-Sponsored Hospitals in the United States. http://www.mergerwatch.org/storage/pdf-files/bp_no_strings_hilights.pdf. MergerWatch.

11. Teaching Hospitals. https://www.aamc.org/about/teachinghospitals/. Assocation of American Medical Colleges. Accessed Aug 26, 2011.

12. History of Children's Hospitals. http://www.childrenshospitals.net/AM/Template.cfm?Section=Facts_and_Trends&CONTENTID=12693&TEMPLATE=/CM/ContentDisplay.cfm. . Accessed Aug 5, 2011.

13. Health, United States, 2010: With Special Feature on Death and Dying. http://www.cdc.gov/nchs/data/hus/hus10.pdf. National Center for Health Statistics. Accessed Aug 26, 2011.

14. Report to the Congress: Medicare Payment Policy. http://www.medpac.gov/documents/Mar12_EntireReport.pdf. Medicare Payment Advisory Commission. Accessed Apr 12, 2012.

15. Health Sciences Curriculum. http://www.cte.unt.edu/health/curriculum.html. University of North Texas. Accessed Aug 5, 2011.

16. Rundall TG, Davies HT, Hodges CL. Doctor-manager relationships in the United States and the United Kingdom. *Journal of healthcare management / American College of Healthcare Executive*s. 2004;49(4):251-68; discussion 268-70.

17. Frequently Asked Questions in Ethics. http://www.ama-assn.org/ama/pub/physician-resources/medical-ethics/code-medical-ethics/frequently-asked-questions.page?. American Medical Association. Accessed Aug 5, 2011.

18. WISQARS Leading Causes of Death Reports. http://webappa.cdc.gov/sasweb/ncipc/leadcaus10.html. National Center for Injury Prevention and Control, Centers for Disease Control and Prevention. Accessed Aug 26, 2011.

19. Kohn LT, Corrigan J, Donaldson MS. *To err is human: Building a safer health system.* Vol 6. Natl Academy Pr; 2000.

20. Klevens RM, Edwards JR, Richards CL, et al. Estimating health care-associated infections and deaths in US hospitals, 2002. *Public health report*s. 2007;122(2):160.

21. Scott R. The Direct Medical Costs of Healthcare-Associated Infections in US Hospitals and the Benefits of Prevention. Centers for Disease Control and Prevention, March 2009.

22. Allegranzi B, Pittet D. Role of hand hygiene in healthcare-associated infection prevention. *Journal of Hospital Infectio*n. 2009;73(4):305-315.

23. Erasmus V, MSc, Daha T, Brug H, PhD, et al. Systematic Review of Studies on Compliance with Hand Hygiene Guidelines in Hospital Care. *Infection Control and Hospital Epidemiolog*y. 2010;31(3):283-294.

24. TrendWatch Chartbook. http://www.aha.org/research/reports/tw/chartbook/index. shtml. American Hospital Association. Accessed May 4, 2012.

25. Jensen E, Mendonca L. Why America Spends More on Health Care. http://nihcm. org/pdf/EV_JensenMendonca_FINAL.pdf. National Institute for Health Care Management.

26. About our Health Centers. http://www.nachc.org/about-our-health-centers.cfm. National Association of Community Health Centers. Accessed Aug 26, 2011.

27. M. Jester. National Association of Community Health Centers. Personal Communication.

28. Beitsch LM, Brooks RG, Menachemi N, Libbey PM. Public health at center stage: new roles, old props. *Health Affair*s. 2006;25(4):911.

29. Weinick R, Bristol S, DesRoches C. Urgent care centers in the U.S.: Findings from a national survey. *BMC Health Services Researc*h. 2009;9(1):79. http://www. biomedcentral.com/1472-6963/9/79.

30. Retail Clinics in the United States. http://www.merchantmedicine.com/Home. cfm?view=Retail. Merchant Medicine. Accessed Apr 12, 2012.

31. Cullen KA, Hall MJ, Golosinskiy A. *Ambulatory surgery in the united states, 2006.* US Dept. of Health and Human Services, Centers for Disease Control and Prevention, National Center for Health Statistics; 2009.

32. Hollingsworth JM, Ye Z, Strope SA, Krein SL, Hollenbeck AT, Hollenbeck BK. Physician-Ownership Of Ambulatory Surgery Centers Linked To Higher Volume Of Surgeries. *Health Affair*s. 2010;29(4):683-689.

33. Basic Statistics about Home Care. http://www.nahc.org/facts/10HC_Stats.pdf. The National Association for Home Care & Hospice. Accessed Aug 5, 2011.

34. Hospice Care in America. http://www.nhpco.org/files/public/Statistics_Research/ Hospice_Facts_Figures_Oct-2010.pdf. National Hospice and Palliative Care Organization. Accessed Aug 5, 2011.

35. Connor SR, Pyenson B, Fitch K, Spence C, Iwasaki K. Comparing hospice and nonhospice patient survival among patients who die within a three-year window. *Journal of pain and symptom managemen*t. 2007;33(3):238-246.

36. Nahin R, Barnes P, Stussman B, Bloom B. Costs of complementary and alternative medicine (CAM) and frequency of visits to CAM practitioners: United States, 2007. *National health statistics report*s. 2009;18.

37. Kletke PR, Emmons DW, Gillis KD. Current trends in physicians' practice arrangements. From owners to employees. *JAMA: The Journal of the American Medical Associatio*n. 1996;276(7):555.

38. Kane C. Policy Research Perspectives: The Practice Arrangements of Patient Care Physicians, 2007-2008: An Analysis by Age Cohort and Gender. http://www. ama-assn.org/resources/doc/health-policy/prp-200906-phys-prac-arrange.pdf. American Medical Association. Accessed Sept 14, 2011.

39. Kocher R, Sahni NR. Hospitals' race to employ physicians—the logic behind a money-losing proposition. *New England Journal of Medicin*e. 2011.

40. Physician Shortages to Worsen Without Increases in Residency Training. https://www. aamc.org/download/150584/data/physician_shortages_factsheet.pdf. Association of American Medical Colleges. Accessed Feb 4, 2012.

41. Kirch DG, Vernon DJ. Confronting the complexity of the physician workforce equation. *JAMA: The Journal of the American Medical Association*. 2008;299(22):2680.

42. U.S. Medical School Applicants and Students 1982-1983 to 2010-2011. https://www. aamc.org/download/153708/data/charts1982to2011.pdf. Association of American Medical Colleges. Accessed Aug 26, 2011.

43. The ACGME at a Glance. http://www.acgme.org/acWebsite/newsRoom/newsRm_ acGlance.asp. Accreditation Council for Graduate Medical Education. Accessed Aug 5, 2011.

44. Nicholson S. Barriers to entering medical specialties. http://www.nber.org/papers/ w9649. National Bureau of Economic Research.

45. Medical School Graduation Questionnaire: 2011 All Schools Summary Report. https://www.aamc.org/download/263712/data/gq-2011.pdf. Association of American Medical Colleges. Accessed Apr 12, 2012.

46. Kliff S. We have more doctors per capita than ever before. http://www. washingtonpost.com/blogs/ezra-klein/post/we-have-more-doctors-per-capita-than-ever-before/2011/12/16/gIQAKIfByO_blog.html. . Accessed Dec 27, 2011.

47. Goodman DC, Fisher ES. Physician workforce crisis? Wrong diagnosis, wrong prescription. *New England Journal of Medicine*. 2008;358(16):1658-1661.

48. The Physician Workforce: Projections and Research into Current Issues Affecting Supply and Demand. http://bhpr.hrsa.gov/healthworkforce/reports/physwfissues. pdf. Health Resources and Services Administration. Accessed Apr 12, 2012.

49. Weida NA, Phillips Jr RL, Bazemore AW, et al. Graham Center Policy One-Pager: Loss of Primary Care Residency Positions Amidst Growth in Other Specialties. *Am Fam Physician*. 2010;82(2):121.

50. Starfield B, Shi L, Macinko J. Contribution of primary care to health systems and health. *Milbank Quarterly*. 2005;83(3):457-502.

51. Bodenheimer T, Pham HH. Primary care: current problems and proposed solutions. *Health Affairs*. 2010;29(5):799-805.

52. A Primer on Group Purchasing Organizations. http://www.higpa.org/resource/ resmgr/research/gpo_primer.pdf. Health Industry Group Purchasing Association. Accessed Aug 26, 2011.

53. HHS: What We Do. http://www.hhs.gov/about/whatwedo.html. Department of Health & Human Services. Accessed Dec 27, 2011.

Chapter 2
Health Care Providers

Health care is a huge industry in the U.S. It currently accounts for more than one-tenth of all American workers and is projected to add more jobs than any other sector of the economy over the next 10 years.[1] The health care workforce can be just as complicated as the rest of the health care system. If you walk into a hospital and start checking out work badges, you may end up more confused about who's who than you were before. What's a CNS? Is a DO the same as an MD? What does an LVN do? This chapter serves as a handy reference guide to the health care workforce—a quick snapshot of the many important professions who make health care happen.

Graduate Medical Education

Physicians' degrees are awarded after completion of four years of medical school, but graduates must complete postgraduate residency training before they're allowed to practice medicine. Residency programs are generally hospital-based and are governed by the Accreditation Council for Graduate Medical Education (ACGME). Those who seek to practice medicine must apply, interview, and rank the residency programs they're interested in. Programs, similarly, rank the students they would accept as residents. These rank lists are combined by the National Resident Matching Program using an algorithm to match students with residencies; those students who enter "the match" are obligated to accept their given positions.

In 2010, there were 8,887 residency programs in 26 specialties, with 113,142 active residents.[2] Specialties include well-known fields such as internal medicine, general surgery, pediatrics, and anesthesiology and also smaller disciplines like medical genetics and nuclear medicine.

Historically, first-year residents (i.e., PGY1—Post-Graduate Year 1) were considered interns. Internship was a year of rotating among many specialties. Some specialties still require a separate internship year of general training, usually in internal medicine, before commencing specialty training, while other disciplines have integrated the internship year into the normal residency program. Residency lasts from three years (family medicine, pediatrics, etc.) to six or more years (neurosurgery), and training can further be extended with sub-specialty fellowships.

Residents are considered trainees (like apprentices), not employees, and thus their work is not subject to federal wage and hour regulations. This means that, legally, they aren't required to receive overtime, breaks, and other worker benefits. Salaries reflect that residents are trainees: residents don't have to pay tuition, but their wages are more like educational stipends than physicians' incomes. Resident salaries begin at around $45,000 and increase each year by a few thousand dollars. These wages come mostly from Medicare funds, the limited nature of which also determines the number of residency slots. The Balanced Budget Act of 1997 placed a limit on the number of Medicare-supported resident slots, meaning that there has been a steady cap on the number of residents. This has obvious implications for the number of physicians, as discussed on page 25. The Affordable Care Act (ACA) doesn't change this cap, though it does redistribute some funds.

A number of other health care professions, including pharmacy, optometry, and dentistry, offer post-graduate residencies as well, but these residencies aren't required for practice.

Residency Work Hours

Work hours for residents have long been controversial. Historically, residents lived in the hospital and worked up to 120 hours per week. That leaves slightly less than seven hours per day to do anything else, like sleep and eat. Aside from the idea that these kinds of hours are difficult psychologically, research also shows that overworked, fatigued residents make more mistakes, driving up the medical error rate. Amid such criticism, in 2003, the ACGME limited residency work hours for all programs to 80 per week. In addition, as of July 2011, shifts for PGY1 are limited to 16 hours (PGY2 and beyond may be scheduled for 24-hour shifts).

However, few on either side of the issue consider this to be a satisfactory conclusion, so the debate continues.

Point: More Hours Are Better	Counterpoint: Fewer Hours Are Better
▸ The more hours you spend in the hospital, the more you learn; residency is an intense training period by necessity and shouldn't be diluted.	▸ Long work hours encourage more students to enter high-paying specialties so that the money will make up for their time.
▸ Patient mortality has not decreased after the institution of the 80-hour work week.[3]	▸ It's inhumane to physicians (psychologically, physiologically, and emotionally) and drives off potential physicians from entering the field.
▸ Old hours were so long that residents didn't have to rush; now they have to rush constantly and have less time to learn.	▸ Sleep-deprived residents make more errors and decrease patient safety.[5]
▸ Medicine is a career, and training physicians should be completely devoted to it at the expense of other parts of life.	▸ Oversight on residents is weak, meaning many errors will go unnoticed by supervising physicians.

- Shorter shifts mean more shift changes, and more shift changes mean more medical errors.[4]
- 80 hours isn't really a limit; residents may work more hours yet only report 80.
- You can't expect to reduce training by 20% without an accompanying reduction in quality.

- Physicians should value work-life balance.
- We should be seeking to reduce shift change errors in general, not ignoring the problem by increasing shift lengths.
- The U.S. government limits pilots' and truckers' work hours, why not physicians'?

Professional Credentialing

Licensing

Licensing is legal approval from a state government to practice a profession. Specific requirements differ from state to state and by profession but often include graduation from an accredited educational program, passing an examination, and supervised clinical experience. Licenses must be renewed every few years; usually, this requires a fee and completion of a certain number of hours of continuing education in the field. Only those who are licensed are allowed to use certain titles associated with each profession. For example, in a state that licenses dietitians, only those people who have completed the educational requirements and been licensed by the state government may call themselves "dietitians." On the other hand, any person, with or without qualification, may call himself or herself a "nutritionist" because that is not a licensed profession. In addition, separate licenses must be granted for practice in different states. For example, it's illegal for a chiropractor licensed in Virginia to practice in West Virginia without first completing the process for a new state license.

Certification

Board certification is a formal recognition of competence from a non-governmental, national professional organization. Two types of certification are common. For professions that are licensed, certification allows workers to demonstrate proficiency in specialty practice areas. For professions that aren't licensed, certification is a way of demonstrating quality to employers and the public. Some health care institutions require certification, even if the law doesn't, and even if not required, nationally certified professionals are more likely to be hired and to earn higher wages than uncertified workers.

Scope of Practice

In every state and for each licensed profession, laws regulate what members of that profession can and cannot do. This is termed the "scope of practice," and it determines what diagnoses, treatments, and procedures a health care professional may perform in each state. Scope of practice regulations may differ significantly from state to state for the same profession.

For example, nurse practitioners (NPs) have prescribing authority in all 50 states; however, each and every aspect of their authority varies across the country. Thirteen states allow NPs to prescribe with complete autonomy. The remaining states require some physician oversight, which differs by state from co-signing controlled substance prescriptions to engaging in "collaborative practice agreements" to creating written standard protocols. In some states, NPs are only allowed to prescribe medications from a limited formulary set by the state. In addition, 19 states require a separate application for licensed NPs who wish to prescribe, and nine states limit their prescriptive authority for controlled substances.[6]

Take 50 states and 32 professions, and things can get confusing very quickly. Let's try to simplify them here.

Note: Many of the practitioners discussed here hold doctorate degrees—DPT, MD, DO, DDS, etc.—that are specific for each profession. These are "clinical" degrees; that is, they provide education geared toward working with patients. A research doctorate (PhD), on the other hand, provides an education that focuses more on conducting and evaluating scientific experiments than on clinical practice. People in any of the professions listed here can complete PhDs. Anyone who has completed a doctorate degree—research, clinical, or both—may be referred to as a "doctor," but at many institutions, that title is reserved for physicians.

Health Care Providers

This is a quick guide to the health care professionals you're most likely to come across. Each table includes the total number of persons in that profession, gender (when available), what they do, how they're educated, how much they're paid, and where they work.

Assistant / Aide	NA / CNA / AA / CDA / PCT / many more
▸ Total Number	3.8 million[7]
▸ Education	▸ Education before working varies widely; many receive no formal training and learn on the job. Others attend one-year programs and receive certificates or diplomas or two year programs that result in associate's degrees. Programs are available in high schools, technical and vocational schools, and community and junior colleges.
▸ Licensing	▸ Licensing varies by state and by profession. Many states do not require licensing for assistants or aides, while others have specific laws regulating their scope of practice. Most professions have national organizations that offer voluntary certification through exams and continuing education.
▸ Job Description	▸ This category encompasses a wide variety of health care workers (excluding Physician Assistants and Medical Assistants) who are directed and supervised by licensed health care professionals. Aides are usually classified by the occupation of their supervisors: Occupational Therapy Aides, Anesthesia Aides, etc. Generally, they don't participate in diagnosing or selecting treatment for the patient. Aides and assistants perform a wide range of vital tasks in all health care settings. Contact with patients can be extensive or quite minimal, depending on specific job requirements.
	▸ The largest subtype, accounting for more than 40% of all aides and assistants, is Nursing Aides. Also known as orderlies or patient care technicians, nursing aides work under the supervision of Nurses and Practical Nurses. They can perform many basic patient care duties, including helping patients eat, dress, and bathe; serving meals, making beds, and tidying up rooms; taking vital signs; helping patients ambulate; and escorting them to surgery or imaging. Nursing aides are also the primary caregivers in most nursing homes.
▸ Average Salary	▸ Ranges from $12.09 hourly / $25,140 annually for nurse aides to $24.66 hourly / $51,300 annually for occupational therapy assistants.[8]
▸ Work Location	▸ Assistants and aides are found in every setting where health care is practiced.

Audiologist	AuD
▸ Total Number	12,800[7] Female 82%[9] Male 18%[9]
▸ Education	▸ Most programs are four years, although some are three years. These programs include a mix of classroom and laboratory learning and supervised clinical work. During the first two or three years, students study the development, anatomy, physiology, and pathology of the auditory and vestibular systems as well as the evaluation, rehabilitation, and psychological aspects of hearing and balance disorders. Generally, the last nine-12 months of training are spent in an externship in a supervised clinical setting.[10]
▸ Licensing	▸ Licensed in all 50 states. Some states regulate the practice of audiology and the dispensing of hearing aids separately, requiring an additional Hearing Aid Dispenser license.[7]
▸ Job Description	▸ Audiologists work with patients who have hearing, balance, or other ear problems like tinnitus. They use a variety of tests to determine the severity and cause of hearing and balance disorders and determine treatments on their own or in conjunction with the patient's medical team. Audiologists often fit and program hearing aids, bone-anchored hearing aids, middle ear implants, and cochlear implants; examine and clean ear canals; and provide rehabilitative strategies for patients with hearing loss. Many audiologists work for companies whose employees are at risk for noise-induced hearing loss, and others work in schools, where they administer hearing screening tests and other rehabilitative and diagnostic services.
▸ Average Salary	▸ Hourly: $33.58 Annually: $69,840[8]
▸ Work Location	▸ 50% General Outpatient, 27% Hospitals, 19% Schools and Colleges[8]

Health Care Chaplain / Hospital Chaplain	CC / BCC / CCC
▸ Total Number	14,290 employees, many more volunteers[7]
▸ Licensing	▸ Health care chaplains are not state-licensed. Voluntary board certification in clinical pastoral services is available from several organizations; requirements include a master's degree in theology, endorsement from a religious institution, 1,600 hours of clinical training, and one year of supervised experience in a health care institution. Many chaplains in health care institutions are community clergy who have not received board certification but have often received other types of training in health care chaplaincy.
▸ Job Description	▸ Health care chaplains are responsible for attending to the spiritual needs of patients, especially in hospitals, nursing homes, and hospice services. Approximately 55% of hospitals employ chaplains, and religiously affiliated hospitals are more likely than secular hospitals to employ chaplains.[11] Chaplains may be trained clergy of any religion. Chaplains often spend time one-on-one with patients but may also work with patients' families, consult with case managers in discharge planning, and lead regular services in hospital chapels. In some hospitals, chaplains are part of an interdisciplinary care team and are consulted to perform spiritual assessments and to determine a plan of care for the patient. Chaplains are often called to provide bereavement support for patients and their families in the last hours of life.
▸ Average Salary	▸ Hourly: $22.17 Annually: $46,110[8]
▸ Work Location	▸ 47% Hospitals, 29% Home Health, 12% Nursing Homes, 12% Other[8]

Chiropractor	DC

- ▶ Total Number — 49,100 Female 22%[12] Male 78%[12]

- ▶ Education
  - ▶ Programs grant doctoral degrees after four years; that time is split between science classwork and supervised clinical rotations. Special emphasis is placed on musculoskeletal anatomy, spinal adjustment, manipulation, and radiology. After graduation, a chiropractor may undergo additional training to receive a diploma in one of 10 specialties, including orthopedics and acupuncture; passage of an examination and completion of 300-400 hours of additional clinical experience is required. About 12% of chiropractors have a specialty.[12,13]

- ▶ Licensing
  - ▶ Licensed in all 50 states.

- ▶ Job Description
  - ▶ Chiropractors diagnose and treat patients with disorders of the musculoskeletal system, especially back and neck pain. Many chiropractic treatments deal specifically with manipulation of the spine. Chiropractic is based on the principle that spinal joint misalignments interfere with the nervous system and can result in lower resistance to disease and many different conditions of diminished health.
  - ▶ Chiropractors take patients' health histories; conduct physical, neurological, and orthopedic examinations; and may order laboratory tests. X-rays and other diagnostic images are important tools because of chiropractic emphasis on the spine and its proper function. Chiropractors also analyze patients' posture and spines using specialized techniques. For patients whose health problems can be traced to the musculoskeletal system, chiropractors manually adjust the spinal column.
  - ▶ Some chiropractors use additional treatments in their practices, including heat, water, light, massage, ultrasound, electric currents, and acupuncture. They may apply supports such as straps, tape, braces, or shoe inserts. Chiropractors cannot prescribe drugs[a] or perform major surgery.

- ▶ Average Salary
  - ▶ Hourly: $38.38   Annually: $79,820[8]

- ▶ Work Location
  - ▶ Most chiropractors work in outpatient facilities and many own their own practices.

a New Mexico has recently passed a law allowing chiropractors who have completed advanced training to prescribe a limited formulary.

Counselor

▸ Total Number	356,200[7]	
▸ Education	▸ All states require at least a master's degree.	
▸ Licensing	▸ Required to be certified by passing a state-recognized exam. May be voluntarily nationally certified through the National Board for Certified Counselors.	
▸ Job Description	▸ Rehabilitation counselors help people with both physical and emotional disabilities resulting from birth defects, illness or disease, accidents, or other causes. They provide personal and vocational counseling; offer case management support; and arrange for medical care, vocational training, and job placement.	
	▸ Mental health counselors work with individuals, families, and groups to address and treat mental and emotional disorders and to promote mental health. They are trained in a variety of therapeutic techniques to address issues such as depression, anxiety, substance addiction and abuse, suicidal impulses, stress, trauma, low self-esteem, and grief.	
	▸ Substance abuse and behavioral disorder counselors help people who have problems with alcohol, drugs, gambling, and eating disorders. Counseling can be done on an individual basis but is frequently conducted in a group setting and can include crisis counseling, daily or weekly counseling, or drop-in counseling supports.	
	▸ Marriage and family therapists apply family systems theory to enhance communication and understanding among family members and help to prevent family and individual crises. They may work with individuals, families, couples, or groups.[7]	
▸ Average Salary	▸ Median annual wages are as follows: substance abuse and behavioral disorder counselors, $37,030; mental health counselors, $36,810; rehabilitation counselors, $30,930; and marriage and family therapists, $44,590.[8]	
▸ Work Location	▸ Most counselors work in outpatient settings. A growing number of counselors are self-employed and work in group or private practices.	

Dentist	DDS / DMD
▸ Total Number	141,900[7] Female 20%[14] Male 80%[14]
▸ Education	▸ Dental education is similar to that of optometrists and podiatrists; these graduate-level programs last four years and are split between two years of science classwork and two years of supervised clinical rotations.
	▸ After graduation, dentists may complete optional postgraduate programs in order to specialize in one of nine areas, including oral and maxillofacial surgery (OMFS), orthodontics, and public health. About 18% of dentists have a specialty.[7] Some OMFS specialists complete a six-year, joint dentistry/general surgery residency and receive an MD degree upon completion, along with the DDS degree received at dental school graduation.
▸ Licensing	▸ Licensed in all 50 states.
▸ Job Description	▸ Dentists are the primary providers of tooth, gum, mouth, and masticatory system care in the U.S. They can perform many of the duties of physicians, including taking histories, ordering and interpreting imaging, making diagnoses, prescribing medication, and performing surgery, but their work is restricted to the oral cavity and masticatory system. Some dentists, especially dental surgeons, have full hospital privileges, while most others have courtesy privileges or no hospital relationships.
▸ Average Salary	▸ Hourly: $79.58 Annually: $165,530[8]
▸ Work Location	▸ Almost entirely outpatient, and many own their own practices.

Dietitian	RD / LD / LDN
▸ Total Number	60,300[7] Female 96%[15] Male 4%[15]
▸ Education	▸ Education may take place at either the undergraduate or graduate level. Two paths can be taken: a coordinated program that combines instruction and clinical rotations or a didactic classroom program followed by a separate clinical rotation internship. Undergraduate students in these programs take courses in foods, nutrition, institution management, chemistry, biochemistry, biology, microbiology, and physiology. In either case, the student must complete at least 900 hours of clinical rotations before being eligible to take a certification exam.
▸ Licensing	▸ Laws regulating dietitians and nutritionists vary by state, and in some states, the professions are not regulated at all. 47% of registered dietitians are state-licensed.[15] The title "Registered Dietitian" denotes that the person has graduated from an accredited dietetics program and passed the national certification exam from the Commission on Dietetic Registration.
▸ Job Description	▸ Dietitians make detailed nutritional histories and assessments of patients and work with other health professionals to develop appropriate diets for patients inside and outside the hospital. This often involves designing diets in response to medical conditions like diabetes or treatments like chemotherapy. Dietitians are also centrally involved in selecting the feeding method (e.g., parenteral) and composition of nutritional support for patients who cannot eat, often as part of a multidisciplinary nutrition support team. 20% of RDs specialize in areas such as pediatric or oncology nutrition.[15]
▸ Average Salary	▸ Hourly: $26.13 Annually: $54,340[8]
▸ Work Location	▸ 34% Hospitals, 9% Nursing Homes, 8% Outpatient, 7% Government[8]

Emergency Medical Technician / Paramedic	EMT

▸ **Total Number** — 210,700 (excluding volunteers)[7] Female 29%[16] Male 71%[16]

▸ **Education**
- ▸ There are five levels of EMT training, in order of increasing length: First Responder, EMT-Basic, EMT-Intermediate/85, EMT-Intermediate/99, and EMT-Paramedic. A high school diploma is usually required before enrolling in an EMT program. EMT-Basic programs require approximately 110 hours of training. EMT-Paramedic programs require around 1,000 hours of training, split between classroom learning and supervised clinical experience, over an average of 15 months.[16] Paramedic programs cover anatomy and physiology as well as clinical skills, including advanced airway support, IV fluid management, cardiovascular management, and the use of some medications.

▸ **Licensing**
- ▸ EMTs and paramedics are licensed in all 50 states. Most states require certification by the National Registry of EMTs (NREMT), while others require state-specific certification.

▸ **Job Description**
- ▸ EMTs and paramedics are responsible for quickly responding to emergency situations, assessing and stabilizing victims' medical conditions, and transporting victims to the nearest medical facility via ambulance or helicopter. EMTs and paramedics operate in emergency medical services systems where physicians provide medical direction and oversight. Scope of practice depends on the level of training and varies by state. Typical duties are the following:
- ▸ EMT-Basic: Non-invasive procedures such as bag-valve-mask ventilation, splinting, and automated external defibrillation.
- ▸ EMT-Intermediate: Starting IV lines, placing nasogastric tubes, and administering a limited number of medications, such as epinephrine and albuterol.
- ▸ EMT-Paramedic: Administering a greater number of medications orally or intravenously, including antipsychotics and narcotics; interpreting EKGs; endotracheal intubations; blood transfusions; and thoracic decompressions.[17]

▸ **Average Salary**
- ▸ Hourly: $16.01   Annually: $33,300[8]

▸ **Work Location**
- ▸ Most work on ambulances or medical evacuation (Medivac) helicopters or as part of emergency response teams with police and firefighters.

Health Care Administrator

▸	Total Number	283,500[7]
▸	Education	▸ Health care administrators come from a variety of educational backgrounds. Some attend two- or three-year master's programs in health administration (MHA), public health (MPH), business administration (MBA), or public administration (MPA); some schools offer public health, business administration, and public administration programs with a health care focus. Many other health care administrators don't have graduate training but learn while working at a health care institution. Others are health care professionals, like physicians and nurses, who have been promoted to administrative positions without any specific training beyond their medical education. Of Health Care Administrators working today, the highest education level completed is: 52% bachelor's degree, 41% master's degree, and 3% associate's degree.[18]
▸	Licensing	▸ All states require nursing home administrators to be licensed, and some states require licensing for administrators of assisted living facilities. A license is not required for other areas of health care administration.
▸	Job Description	▸ Health care administrators plan, direct, coordinate, and supervise the delivery of health care. These workers are either specialists in charge of specific clinical departments or generalists who manage entire facilities or systems. This broad category includes a wide range of workers, from CEOs of large health care networks to budgeting managers at small group practices. Some health care professionals, especially those in solo practice, also perform administrative duties, but most health care institutions are operated by full-time health care administrators.
		▸ Some administrators, known as information managers, are responsible for the maintenance and security of all patient records. As electronic health records become more prevalent throughout the field, information managers will be crucial in building and maintaining these systems.[7]
▸	Average Salary	▸ Salaries vary widely depending on the size of the institution and the specific administrative position, ranging from $40,000 per year for mid-level managers at many outpatient and group practices to $5 million or more annually for CEOs of private insurance companies.
▸	Work Location	▸ 38% Hospitals, 10% Physicians' Offices, 7% Nursing Homes, 6% Home Health[8]

Home Health Aide / Personal Health Aide   HHA / PHA

▸ Total Number	1.7 million[7] Female 90%[19] Male 10%[19]
▸ Education	▸ No specific education is required for home health aides; most employers and states do not require high school diplomas. Home health aides are usually trained on the job by nurses, other home health aides, or supervisors.
▸ Licensing	▸ Home health aides who work for agencies that receive reimbursement from Medicare or Medicaid must complete 75 hours of training, 16 hours of supervised practical experience, and an examination. Training includes courses on personal hygiene, safe transfer techniques, reading and recording vital signs, infection control, and basic nutrition. Some states require additional training. Voluntary certification is available from the National Association for Home Care and Hospice.
▸ Job Description	▸ Home health aides provide help to the disabled, chronically ill, elderly, cognitively impaired, and others who need assistance in their own homes or in residential facilities. They also assist people in hospices and in day programs and help individuals with disabilities go to work and remain engaged in their communities.
	▸ Aides provide light housekeeping and homemaking tasks such as laundry, changing bed linens, shopping for food, and planning and preparing meals. Aides also may help clients get out of bed, bathe, dress, and groom. Some accompany clients to doctors' appointments or on other errands.[7]
	▸ They may go to the same home every day or week for months or even years and often visit four or five clients on the same day. However, some aides may work solely with one client who is in need of more care and attention.
▸ Average Salary	▸ Hourly: $10.25 Annually: $21,320[8]

Medical Assistant	MA / CMA / RMA / CCMA / NCMA
▸ Total Number	483,600[7] Female 88%[20] Male 18%[20]
▸ Education	▸ Education before working varies widely; some receive no formal training and learn on the job. Others attend one-year programs and receive certificates or diplomas or two-year programs which result in associate's degrees. Programs are available in high schools, technical and vocational schools, community and junior colleges, and universities. Of Medical Assistants working today, the highest level of education completed is: 41% high school diploma, 37% medical assistant certificate or diploma, and 22% associate's degree.[18]
▸ Licensing	▸ No state requires licensing for medical assistants, although some require permits for certain procedures like injections and phlebotomy. ▸ Multiple organizations offer voluntary certification programs and examinations for medical assistants, including the American Association of Medical Assistants and American Medical Technologists. About 12% of the total medical assistant workforce is certified.[20]
▸ Job Description	▸ Medical assistants are jack-of-all-trades helpers for physicians and other health care professionals. They perform administrative and clinical duties to keep offices running smoothly and to ensure patients are cared for. Specific tasks vary widely by place of employment, but common responsibilities include taking vital signs, preparing and maintaining examination and treatment areas, preparing patients for examination, assisting with procedures and treatments, preparing and administering medications, screening patients and following up on test results, collecting and processing patient specimens for medical tests, scheduling appointments, submitting insurance claims, and monitoring third-party reimbursements.[20] ▸ Many medical assistants advance to other professions in the health care fields, like medical administration or nursing.
▸ Average Salary	▸ Hourly: $14.31 Annually: $29,760[8]
▸ Work Location	▸ 62% Physicians' Offices, 12% Hospitals, 10% Offices of other health care professionals[8]

Medical Coder	CPC / CCS / RHIT

▸ Total Number   172,500[7]

▸ Education
▸ Education before working varies widely; many receive no formal training and learn on the job. Others attend six-month or one-year training programs and receive certificates or diplomas or two-year programs which result in associate's degrees. Programs are available in high schools, technical and vocational schools, and community and junior colleges. Of Medical Coders working today, the highest level of education completed is 65% high school diploma, 21% program diploma/certificate, and 10% associate's degree.[18]

▸ Licensing
▸ Medical coders are not licensed by any state. Several organizations, including the American Health Information Management Association and the American Academy of Professional Coders, offer voluntary national certification.

▸ Job Description
▸ Medical coders specialize in codifying patients' medical information for reimbursement purposes. They assign a code to each diagnosis and procedure using classification systems software. The classification system determines the amount for which health care providers will be reimbursed if the patient is covered by Medicare, Medicaid, or other insurance programs using the system. Coders may use several coding systems, such as those required for ambulatory settings, physician offices, or long-term care.

▸ Average Salary
▸ Hourly: $16.83   Annually: $35,010[8]

▸ Work Location
▸ 37% Hospitals, 24% Physicians' Offices, 7% Nursing Homes[8]

Medical Scientist

▸ **Total Number** 109,400[7]

▸ Education	▸ There are no specific educational requirements to become a medical scientist, but most have a PhD in an area of the biological sciences. PhD programs are university-based, generally last between three and six years, and require a combination of science classwork and independent research, usually in the laboratory. Before graduation, students must compile and present dissertations of their original research. After graduation, most medical scientists spend one to three years in postdoctoral apprenticeships in laboratories with established scientists to gain more hands-on research experience.
	▸ Students wishing to perform clinical research often enter joint MD/PhD programs; these "medical science training programs," housed at medical schools, generally last eight to nine years. Upon graduation, students are granted both an MD and a PhD.
▸ Licensing	▸ No states license medical scientists; however, those who administer drug or gene therapy to human patients or who otherwise interact medically with patients—draw blood, excise tissue, or perform other invasive procedures—must be licensed physicians (MD or DO).
▸ Job Description	▸ The driving force behind clinical medicine is research, and the people who do the research are known as medical scientists. Medical scientists conduct biomedical research to advance knowledge of life processes and of other living organisms that affect human health, including viruses, bacteria, and other infectious agents. They also engage in laboratory research, clinical investigation, technical writing, drug development, regulatory review, and related activities. For example, medical scientists involved in cancer research may formulate a combination of drugs that will lessen the effects of the disease. They can then work with physicians to administer these drugs to patients in clinical trials, monitor their reactions, and observe the results. Medical scientists examine the results of clinical trials and adjust the dosage levels to reduce negative side effects or to induce better results. In addition to developing treatments for medical conditions, medical scientists attempt to discover ways to

prevent health problems. For example, they may study the link between smoking and lung cancer or between alcoholism and liver disease. Many health professionals divide their time between clinical practice and research activities.

▸ Average Salary	▸ Hourly: $41.69	Annually: $86,710[8]
▸ Work Location	▸ 37% Research and Development, 20% Academic, 13% Pharmaceutical Industry[8]	

Medical Transcriptionist   MT / CMT / RMT

▸ Total Number	105,200[7]
▸ Education	▸ Education before working varies widely; many receive no formal training and learn on the job. Others attend one-year programs and receive certificates or diplomas or two-year programs which result in associate's degrees. Programs are available in high schools, technical and vocational schools, and community and junior colleges. The curriculum includes coursework in anatomy, medical terminology, legal issues relating to health care documentation, and grammar and punctuation.
▸ Licensing	▸ No states require licensing for medical transcriptionists, but voluntary certification is available through the Association for Healthcare Documentation Integrity.
▸ Job Description	▸ Medical transcriptionists listen to dictated recordings made by physicians and other health care professionals and transcribe them into medical reports, correspondence, and other administrative material. To understand and accurately transcribe dictated reports, medical transcriptionists must understand medical terminology, anatomy and physiology, diagnostic procedures, pharmacology, and treatment assessments. They also must be able to translate medical jargon and abbreviations into their expanded forms.[7]
▸ Average Salary	▸ Hourly: $16.12 Annually: $33,530[8]
▸ Work Location	▸ Most transcriptionists work at hospitals and physicians' offices, but increasingly more work off-site or at home, where they receive dictations and submit documentation electronically.

Nurse	RN

▸ Total Number   2.6 million[7]   Female 93%[35]   Male 7%[35]

▸ Education   ▸ Several educational paths are available to become an RN.

    ▸ Bachelor's Degree (BSN): A three- to four-year program at a university. All four years may be completed at one institution, or the time may be split between a university and a nursing college.

    ▸ Accelerated BSN: A 12- to 18-month program for students with non-nursing bachelor's degrees, leading to a BSN at a university or a nursing college.

    ▸ Associate's Degree (ASN, AAS, ADN): A two-year program at a community or junior college.

    ▸ Diploma: A three-year program at a hospital-based school of nursing or a community college.

    ▸ Master's Entry Level (MN, MSN, CNL): A three- to four-year graduate program for students with non-nursing bachelor's degrees.

    ▸ Completion of one of these five educational routes allows a graduate nurse to take the national licensure exam to become a registered nurse. Successful completion of the exam indicates minimum competency, and results are accepted by every state; however each state has its own Nurse Practice Act which must be adhered to in order to maintain licensure to practice.

    ▸ Master's programs are available for RNs who wish to become nurse educators or nurse practitioners (see next page). There are also a number of programs for nurses with associate's degrees or diplomas to advance to a BSN. The highest level of education completed among nurses working today is: 48% bachelor's degree or higher, 39% associate's degree, and 13% diploma.[18]

    ▸ Some RNs go on to complete advanced education and training in certain specialties; about 16% of nurses are certified in one of these specialties. Certification is available in more than 70 areas, including psychiatry and oncology.

▸ Licensing   ▸ Licensed in all 50 states.

55

▸ Job Description	▸ Nurses are the largest group of employees in the health care field, and they often spend more time with the patient and family members than any other health care professional. Every new patient admitted to a hospital undergoes a nursing assessment by an RN to determine the patient's physical condition and functional status; during the course of the patient's stay, nurses maintain a plan of care and perform interventions within their scope of practice. Such interventions include symptom management, patient and family education, skin and wound care, and grief counseling. Other actions are specified by institutional protocol or in the "patient orders" that are submitted by physicians and other health care providers. Because nurses spend the most time with patients, they often confer with the other members of the care team regarding the management of patients.
	▸ RNs are responsible for a broad range of patient care activities, including vital sign monitoring; starting, regulating, and maintaining IVs and catheters; medication administration; evaluating responses to treatment; obtaining blood and tissue specimens for laboratory testing; identifying developing problems; ambulating patients; supervising and directing practical nurses and nurse's aides; discharge planning and instruction; and charting and maintaining the medical record. Nurses are employed in a variety of inpatient and outpatient institutions in a number of roles, and their work responsibilities vary accordingly.
	▸ In most hospitals, nurses are assigned to a care team in a single location or medical unit in the hospital. A "clinical nurse manager" is the RN responsible for administration and supervision of that unit; when the nurse manager is off duty, another RN acts as a "charge nurse," supervising the other RNs and patients and conferring with the medical staff. All hospitals employ a Chief Nursing Executive (title may differ by institution) to provide central nursing administration.
▸ Average Salary	▸ Hourly: $32.56 Annually: $67,720[8]
▸ Work Location	▸ 62% Hospitals, 11% General Outpatient, 8% Public Health, 6% Home Health[8]

Advanced Nursing Professions

Advanced Practice Nurses (APRN) are RNs who have completed specialized graduate training and have a broader scope of practice for diagnosis and treatment than do RNs. There are four types: Clinical Nurse Specialists, Nurse Anesthetists, Nurse Midwives, and Nurse Practitioners. The U.S. has more than 260,000 practicing APRNs.[37-40] All four types are licensed separately in all 50 states.

RNs who wish to become advanced practice nurses must complete master's programs (MSN). Most programs are two years in length and require a BSN for admission. Some programs require clinical work experience as an RN before applying.

After graduation from a master's program, an APRN may enter a two-and-a-half- to four-year program to obtain a doctoral degree (DNP, DNS, DNSc) in nursing. Some of these graduates use their doctoral education to become experts in specialized fields like diabetes or pediatrics, while others go on to health care administration.

- **Nurse Practitioners** (NP / CNP / CRNP) can perform most of the duties of physicians, such as taking histories, making diagnoses, prescribing medication, and performing limited procedures. In many states, they must be supervised or have a collaborative practice agreement with physicians; such supervision may range from consultations after each patient encounter to meetings every few months. About one-fifth of NPs have hospital admitting privileges.[41] NPs are allowed to prescribe medications in all 50 states, but some states also require the co-signature of a physician and/or restrict the prescription of controlled substances. Average yearly salary is around $97,000.[37]

- **Clinical Nurse Midwives** (CNM / CNMW / CM / NM / CPM) are mid-level providers of OB/GYN services with an emphasis on pregnancy and childbirth. Their scope of practice is similar to that of NPs and PAs; they can diagnose and treat most conditions in the field of OB/GYN, but in most states, they must have a professional relationship with a physician. CNMs can also treat male partners for STDs and provide medical care for the normal newborn for the first month of life. They are legally allowed to write prescriptions in some states but not in others. Their median average salary is around $85,000.[42]

- **Clinical Nurse Specialists** (CNS) have a similar education and scope of practice as NPs but with a somewhat different focus. Whereas NPs treat individual patients with a variety of conditions, CNSs usually focus on a single condition or specialty for which they provide advanced nursing care. For example, a CNS may specialize in neonatology; in the Neonatal ICU, that CNS would work with the most complex and difficult patients. CNSs are allowed to prescribe medications in some states. Also, many CNSs work with hospital administration in case management and in improving health care delivery and interdisciplinary teamwork.

- **Nurse Anesthetists** (NA / CRNA) specialize in administering sedation and anesthesia. Scope of practice varies by state; some require physician relationships, but more than a quarter of CRNAs work without physician supervision.[43] NAs are the primary providers of anesthesia in many rural locations. Unique in nursing, more than 40% of NAs are male.[41] Median salary is $160,000 per year.[44]

Practical Nurse / Vocational Nurse	LPN / LVN

▸ Total Number   753,600[7]   Female 95%[45]   Male 5%[45]

▸ Education	▸ Practical nursing education programs are usually 12-18 months of training with a focus on practical clinical education. Programs are offered in high schools, technical and vocational schools, community and junior colleges, hospitals, and colleges and universities. Most, but not all, programs require a high school diploma before entering. Of practical nurses working today, the highest level of education completed is: 72% high school diploma and 23% associate's degree.[18]
▸ Licensing	▸ Licensed in all 50 states.
▸ Job Description	▸ Practical Nurses provide patient care under the direction of an RN or a physician. They perform many of the same duties as RNs but are not allowed to perform certain procedures and functions (specifics vary from state to state). For example, they may be allowed to remove catheters and IV lines but not place them. Major functions of LPNs in the hospital include administering medications; taking and recording vital signs; dressing wounds; feeding patients; assisting patients with dressing, hygiene, bathroom care, and walking; monitoring inputs and outputs; and placing EKG leads. In the outpatient setting, LPNs may also be responsible for making appointments and other clerical duties in the physician's office or for assisting patients with activities of daily living, if employed in nursing homes or in home health care. Often, LPNs are charged with directing and supervising nursing aides and other support personnel. Many LPNs go on to become RNs at a later date.
▸ Average Salary	▸ Hourly: $19.88 Annually: $41,360[8]
▸ Work Location	▸ 30% Nursing Homes, 20% Hospitals, 12% Physicians' Offices, 9% Home Health Care[8]

Occupational Therapist	OT / OTR / MOT / MSOT / OTD
▸ Total Number	104,500[7] Female 95%[21] Male 5%[21]
▸ Education	▸ Master's degree (MOT) programs generally last two to two-and-a-half years and include classroom instruction in anatomy, biology, physiology, behavioral science, and occupational therapy theory and skills. Before graduation, 24 weeks of supervised clinical experience also are required. Doctoral programs (OTD) usually last two-and-a-half to three years and are similar to master's programs but require one additional year of classwork or research and one additional clinical or research experience.
▸ Licensing	▸ Licensed in all 50 states.
▸ Job Description	▸ Occupational therapists are trained to help people with medical conditions and disabilities achieve greater function and independence in their lives by promoting meaningful activities or "occupations." Occupations include activities of daily living (ADL) such as dressing, cooking, eating, working, and going to school; the goal of occupational therapy is to improve patients' performance and participation in individual and community activities and, therefore, increase well-being. Physical exercises may be used to increase strength and dexterity to restore function after illness or injury, while compensatory or alternative strategies may be taught for coping with permanent disabilities. For example, OTs select and teach the use of adaptive devices like wheelchairs, orthoses, eating aids, and dressing aids. They also design or build special equipment needed at home or at work, including computer-aided adaptive equipment. Therapists also may collaborate with patients and employers to modify the work environment so that patients can more easily function in the workplace.
	▸ Hospital-based OTs are often centrally involved in the discharge planning process, along with nurses, case managers, and physical therapists. The OT assesses the patient in order to recommend the appropriate level of care for the patient post-discharge—e.g., nursing home, rehab, home with assistance, etc.
▸ Average Salary	▸ Hourly: $35.28 Annually: $73,380[8]
▸ Work Location	▸ 24% Hospitals, 23% General Outpatient, 13% Schools, 10% Nursing Homes[8]

Optometrist		OD
▶ Total Number	34,800[7] Female 28%[22] Male 72%[22]	
▶ Education	▶ Optometry education is similar to that of dentists and podiatrists. Three to four years of undergraduate work are required before admission to a doctoral program of optometry, which lasts four years. The first two years consist of classroom and laboratory work, followed by two years of supervised clinical rotations. Although a residency is not required, about 10% of optometrists complete additional training in a specialty area, like pediatrics or contact lens fitting.[22]	
▶ Licensing	▶ Licensed in all 50 states.	
▶ Job Description	▶ Optometrists are the primary providers of eye care in the U.S. They perform many of the duties of physicians, including taking histories, ordering and interpreting imaging, and diagnosing conditions of the eye, but are prohibited from performing surgery in all but a handful of states. Optometrists can prescribe medication in most states but may be barred from prescribing controlled substances. Optometrists are commonly confused with other eye health professionals. To clarify, ophthalmologists are physicians who specialize in eye care, and opticians make, fit, and help patients select eye glasses and contacts.	
▶ Average Salary	▶ Hourly: $51.32	Annually: $106,750[8]
▶ Work Location	▶ Most optometrists work in outpatient settings, and many own their own practices.	

61

Pharmacist	PharmD / R.Ph / BS Pharmacy	
▸ Total Number	269,900[7] Female 46%[24] Male 54%[24]	
▸ Education	▸ Programs take four years to complete. Applicants to pharmacy programs don't need bachelor's degrees, but most complete at least two years of undergraduate work. Many programs combine undergraduate and graduate work into a six-year degree. Major areas of instruction include chemistry, pharmacology, business management, pharmacy practice, and clinical practice. Classroom learning is combined with laboratory instruction and supervised clinical rotations. One- to two-year postgraduate residencies are often required for pharmacists who wish to work in clinical settings; about 15% of pharmacists[25] complete one of these residencies in general, clinical, or specialty pharmacy practice.	
▸ Licensing	▸ Licensed in all 50 states.	
▸ Job Description	▸ Pharmacists are responsible for receiving prescriptions and preparing medicines for patients, along with educating patients about medications and working with physicians to reduce dangerous drug interactions and side effects. Pharmacists who work in hospitals or other institutions as a part of health care teams may also be consulted by physicians and asked to help select medications or design medication regimens for inpatient treatment. In some states, pharmacists who develop "collaborative practice agreements" with physicians are allowed to prescribe a limited number of drugs.	
▸ Average Salary	▸ Hourly: $52.29	Annually: $109,380[8]
▸ Work Location	▸ 54% Pharmacies, 27% Hospitals, 10% Other Outpatient, 3% Industry[8]	

Physical Therapist	PT / DPT / MPT / MSPT / BSPT
▶ Total Number	185,500[7] Female 68%[26] Male 32%[26]
▶ Education	▶ In the last 10 years, most PT programs have changed from granting master's degrees (two- to two-and-a-half-year programs) to doctoral degrees (three-year programs). The curriculum typically includes supervised clinical rotations and science classwork in subjects like anatomy, physiology, pathophysiology, exercise physiology, neuroscience, biomechanics, pharmacology, pathology, and radiology.
▶ Licensing	▶ Licensed in all 50 states.
▶ Job Description	▶ Physical therapists treat and occasionally diagnose individuals with conditions that limit movement, strength, balance, coordination, flexibility, and functional independence. Common conditions they treat include musculoskeletal injuries such as sprains, chronic pain, broken bones, arthritis, and amputations, along with neurological disorders such as stroke, multiple sclerosis, and cerebral palsy. Treatments may include therapeutic exercise, stretching and range-of-motion exercises, functional training, manual therapy, assistive and adaptive devices and equipment, temperature changes, therapeutic ultrasound, and electrical stimulation. PTs often prescribe long-term exercise plans for patients to complete following treatment to improve functional independence and to stop further symptoms from developing. About 6% of PTs are board-certified in one of eight specialties, including sports medicine and women's health.[27]
	▶ Physical therapists are often confused with physiatrists (also known as PM&Rs), who are physicians who specialize in physical rehabilitation. PTs and physiatrists often work together in caring for patients with musculoskeletal injury.
▶ Average Salary	▶ Hourly: $37.50 Annually: $77,990[8]
▶ Work Location	▶ 35% General Outpatient, 25% Hospital, 11% Home Health, 7% Nursing Homes[8]

Physician	MD (Allopathic) / DO (Osteopathic)
▸ Total Number	661,400 (93% MD / 7% DO)[7] Female 29%[31] Male 61%[31]
▸ Education	▸ Allopathic medical education requires an undergraduate degree, four years of medical school, and three to eight years of residency training. The first two years of medical school are pre-clinical and classroom-based. Students take anatomy, biochemistry, physiology, pharmacology, psychology, microbiology, and pathology, among others. The second two years are clinic- rather than classroom-based. Medical students work as part of the care team in hospitals and clinics. Schools mandate certain rotations (usually in internal medicine, family practice, obstetrics and gynecology, pediatrics, psychiatry, and surgery) and allow for elective rotations in the fourth year of schooling.
	▸ Osteopathic education is very similar to allopathic education in length, structure, and content, with a few key differences. Osteopathic education is more focused on treating the patient holistically, considering physical, mental, and environmental causes of disease. Also, students receive extensive training in manipulation of the musculoskeletal system as a means of treating disease. Most osteopathic schools emphasize primary care rather than specialty medicine. Finally, DOs have two choices for their residency training: they can join DO-only residency programs accredited by the American Osteopathic Association or joint MD/DO residency programs accredited by the ACGME.
▸ Licensing	▸ Licensed in all 50 states.
▸ Job Description	▸ Physicians diagnose and treat injury and disease. Physicians examine patients; obtain medical histories; and order, perform, and interpret diagnostic tests. They also educate and advise patients. Physician specialties include anesthesiology, family medicine, internal medicine, pediatrics, obstetrics and gynecology, neurology, radiology, psychiatry, and surgery.
	▸ Osteopathic physicians have the same scope of practice as allopathic physicians, and most of the distinctions between the two doctrines have disappeared in the last 50 years. Historically, osteopathic physicians focus more on preventive medicine and holistic treatment, including musculoskeletal manipulation, than do allopathic physicians. DOs are more likely to pursue careers in primary

▸ care or in rural or underserved communities than are allopathic physicians. Other than that, their practices are virtually indistinguishable, and DOs and MDs often work together.

▸ Although only 22% of health expenditures go directly to physician services, physicians' clinical decisions determine up to 90% of total health expenditures.[32]

▸ Average Salary[33, b]		HOURLY	ANNUALLY
	▸ Primary Care	$60.65	$149,053
	▸ Internal Medicine/Pediatric Subspecialties	$84.85	$235,815
	▸ Surgery	$92.10	$260,830
▸ Specialty	▸ 37% are in primary care, and 63% are in specialties.[34]		

b   These salaries are drawn from a different source than those on page 107 to provide a more accurate hourly salary.

Physician Assistant	PA / RPA / LPA

▸ Total Number   74,800[7]   Female 65%[23]   Male 35%[23]

▸ Education ▸ PA education is similar to that of physicians but can be completed in less time. Training programs take two to three years and include instruction in human anatomy, physiology, clinical pharmacology, clinical medicine, physical diagnosis, and medical ethics. Programs also include supervised clinical training in several areas. Most programs grant master's degrees upon graduation, but some grant bachelor's degrees, associate's degrees, or certificates. Postgraduate residency is not required but is available for PAs who want more training or who want to specialize in a specific field, like surgery or emergency medicine.

▸ Licensing ▸ Licensed in all 50 states.

▸ Job Description ▸ Physician Assistants can perform most of the duties of physicians, such as taking histories, making diagnoses, prescribing medication, and performing limited procedures, but they must do so under physician supervision. Supervision can vary from direct observation by a physician to daily meetings between the PA and physician. However, in some rural or inner-city clinics, physicians may only be present for one or two days per week, and PAs act as the principal care providers for most patients. Surgical PAs assist surgeons during procedures and suture wounds but do not perform surgery themselves. PAs are allowed to prescribe medications in all 50 states, but some states also require the co-signature of a physician or restrict the prescription of controlled substances.

▸ Average Salary ▸ Hourly: $41.89   Annually: $87,140[8]

▸ Work Location ▸ 55% Physicians' Offices, 23% Hospitals, 9% Other Outpatient[8]

Podiatrist		DPM
▸ Total Number	12,200[7] Female 26%[28] Male 74%[28]	
▸ Education	▸ Podiatry schools require completion of at least 90 hours of undergraduate study before admission. Podiatry programs are similar to those of dentists and optometrists; program length is four years, split between two years of basic science and two years of supervised clinical rotations. After graduating from podiatry school, 92% of DPMs complete two- to four-year residencies to receive advanced medical training.[28] After completing residency, a podiatrist can become board-certified in surgery or in primary podiatric medicine.	
▸ Licensing	▸ Licensed in all 50 states.	
▸ Job Description	▸ Podiatrists are the primary providers of foot and ankle care in the U.S.[29] They can perform many of the duties of physicians, including taking histories, ordering and interpreting imaging, making diagnoses, prescribing medication, and performing surgery, but their work is restricted to the foot and ankle. Hospital relationships vary by institution; some podiatrists are granted full hospital admitting privileges, and some must co-admit with physicians. Many podiatrists specialize in areas such as sports medicine or pediatrics.	
▸ Average Salary	▸ Hourly: $64.14 Annually: $133,410[8]	
▸ Work Location	▸ Almost entirely outpatient, and many own their own practices.[8]	

Clinical Psychologist	CP / LCP / LP / PsyD

▸ **Total Number** 152,000[7] Female 58%[30] Male 42%[30]

▸ **Education**
  - ▸ Clinical psychology education occurs in graduate-level programs that require a bachelor's degree before entering. Programs last between four and five years and include classroom education, original research, and writing and presenting a dissertation. Graduates wishing to pursue clinical careers then enter a "match," similar to that of physicians, which places them at health care institutions across the country for one-year clinical internships.

▸ **Licensing**
  - ▸ Licensed in all 50 states. In most states, licensure requires a doctoral degree in psychology, a one-year postdoctoral fellowship, a dissertation, supervised clinical experience, and completion of a national certification exam. Additional examinations are also required by many states.

▸ **Job Description**
  - ▸ Clinical psychologists are mental health providers who focus on the mind and behavior. They assess and diagnose mental disorders, such as mood, anxiety, behavior, and adjustment disorders, using the DSM-IV, and treat these conditions through talk therapy. The four main types of clinical psychology practice are psychodynamic, humanistic, cognitive-behavioral, and family therapy. Targets for these therapy approaches range from unconscious thoughts to family system interactions to actual behavioral changes. Some psychologists complete advanced training to become board-certified in a specialty. Health Psychologists are a specialty of clinical psychologists who often work in health care settings. Their activities include identifying strategies to promote adherence and increase coping, making behavioral changes to support physical and emotional health, and helping with pain management.
  - ▸ Clinical psychologists are often confused with psychiatrists, physicians who specialize in mental health disorders and have full prescribing privileges. Clinical psychologists without prescription authority often refer patients who need medication to psychiatrists. In New Mexico and Louisiana, clinical psychologists who complete additional training are allowed to prescribe psychotropic medication along with therapy.

▸ **Average Salary**
  - ▸ Hourly: $34.87   Annually: $72,540[8]

▸ **Work Location**
  - ▸ 56% General Outpatient, 26% Academic Institution, 7% Business and Government[8]

Social Worker	LSW / LICSW / LCSW / CSW / LCS / LMSW
▸ Total Number	276,000[7] Female 81%[47] Male 19%[47]
▸ Education	▸ Social work education is conducted both at the undergraduate and graduate levels. Bachelor's degree-granting programs last three to four years and are offered at universities or colleges. The curriculum includes classes on social work values and ethics, human behavior and the social environment, social welfare policy and services, and social research methods, and at least 400 hours of supervised field experience. Master's degree programs require students to have an undergraduate degree, which does not have to be in social work. Master's programs usually last two years and include a minimum of 900 hours of supervised field instruction or internship. Classes are tailored to fields of interest.
▸ Licensing	▸ Many states offer a tiered system of social work licenses depending on the individual's level of education and clinical experience, including Social Worker, Clinical Social Worker, and Independent Clinical Social Worker.
▸ Job Description	▸ Social workers in hospitals and other medical settings are often responsible for helping patients with non-medical issues that nevertheless affect their health. For example, a major responsibility of many hospital-based social workers is to make discharge plans for patients to ensure that they will leave the hospital to a safe place where they can recuperate and recover function. This may include finding shelter for homeless patients, arranging home health care services, finding funding for patients' prescriptions, transferring patients to rehabilitation centers, and planning for follow-up visits at the hospital or clinic. Social workers often help indigent patients apply for government support like Medicaid and also manage advanced directives, patient support groups, and patient transportation.
	▸ Social workers are also found in a number of other health care roles, including therapist; in fact, clinical social workers working as therapists are the nation's largest group of mental health service providers.[48] They are employed in a variety of settings, including outpatient clinics, substance abuse rehabilitation centers, employee assistance programs, and private practice. Social workers focus on mental health problems in the context of a

patient's overall lifestyle and will often work to change lifestyle or living conditions to alleviate mental problems. Services may include individual and group therapy, outreach, crisis intervention, social rehabilitation, and teaching skills needed for everyday living.

▸ Many social workers work outside the medical field. They are not discussed here.

▸ Average Salary	▸ Hourly: $22.04	Annually: $45,862[8]
▸ Work Location	▸ 21% Hospital, 15% Individual and Family Services, 9% Outpatient Clinics, 9% Government[8]	

Speech-Language Pathologist / Speech Therapist	SLP

- ▶ Total Number — 119,300[7]   Female 95%[46]   Male 5%[46]

- ▶ Education
  - ▶ Speech-language pathology training occurs in graduate programs, with undergraduate coursework in communication sciences as a prerequisite. The programs last two to three years and include classroom instruction in normal and abnormal functioning of the communication and swallowing organs and systems along with supervised clinical rotations.

- ▶ Licensing
  - ▶ Licensing and regulation for speech-language pathologists varies by state. The American Speech-Language-Hearing Association offers voluntary certification, including a national examination, which satisfies the licensing requirements for most states.

- ▶ Job Description
  - ▶ Speech-language pathologists work with people who cannot produce speech sounds or cannot produce them clearly; those with speech rhythm and fluency problems, such as stuttering; people with voice disorders, such as inappropriate pitch or harsh voice; those with problems understanding and producing language; those who wish to improve their communication skills by modifying an accent; and those with cognitive communication impairments, such as attention, memory, and problem-solving disorders. They also work with people who have swallowing difficulties.
  - ▶ For individuals with little or no speech capability, speech-language pathologists may select augmentative or alternative communication methods, including automated devices and sign language, and teach their use. They teach patients how to make sounds, improve their voices, or increase their oral or written language skills to communicate more effectively. They also teach individuals how to strengthen muscles or to use compensatory strategies to swallow without choking or inhaling food or liquid.

- ▶ Average Salary
  - ▶ Hourly: $33.60   Annually: $69,880[8]

- ▶ Work Location
  - ▶ 52% Schools, 16% General Outpatient, 11% Hospitals, 4% Nursing Homes[8]

Technician / Technologist   XT / RDMS / CPhT / NMT / CVT / many more

▸ Total Number	1.3 million[7]
▸ Education	▸ Education before working varies widely; some receive no formal training and learn on the job. Others attend six-month to one-year programs and receive certificates or diplomas, two-year programs resulting in associate's degrees, or four-year programs resulting in bachelor's degrees. Programs are available in technical and vocational schools, community and junior colleges, and universities.
▸ Licensing	▸ Many states do not require licensing for technicians or technologists. Most professions have national organizations that offer voluntary certification by passing standardized exams and completing continuing education.
▸ Job Description	▸ This category encompasses a wide variety of health care workers (excluding EMTs) who deal primarily with specialized medical equipment. Examples include sonographers, who operate ultrasounds; pharmacy technicians, who prepare medicines; and radiology technologists, who operate imaging equipment like CT or MRI scanners. Specific responsibilities vary by title and institution. Generally, a health care professional, such as a physician, will order a test or treatment for a patient; technicians and technologists are then responsible for using their equipment to complete the order in a timely and accurate manner. Some technicians and technologists, like cardiovascular technicians, have portable equipment and may perform tests in patients' hospital rooms; others, like MRI technologists, require patients to visit a central location. Technicians and technologists work under the broad supervision of physicians, but most of their day-to-day activities are performed independently.
▸ Average Salary	▸ Salaries range from $14.24 hourly / $29,610 annually for ophthalmic technicians to $33.20 hourly / $69,050 annually for nuclear medicine technologists.[8]
▸ Work Location	▸ All inpatient and many outpatient facilities.

Glossary

DSM IV: The fourth edition of the Diagnostic and Statistical Manual of Mental Disorders. This work is the gold standard for the clinical treatment of mental health problems.

Fellowship: Typically, a fellowship is a one- to two-year program following residency in which a health care provider trains in a sub-specialty of his or her residency field. For instance, a neonatologist does a fellowship to focus on newborn care after finishing a residency in pediatrics.

References

1. Career Guide to Industries, 2010-2011 Edition: Healthcare. http://www.bls.gov/oco/cg/cgs035.htm. U.S. Bureau of Labor Statistics. Accessed Feb 4, 2012.
2. The ACGME at a Glance. http://www.acgme.org/acWebsite/newsRoom/newsRm_acGlance.asp. Accreditation Council for Graduate Medical Education. Accessed Aug 5, 2011.
3. Shetty KD, Bhattacharya J. Changes in hospital mortality associated with residency work-hour regulations. Annals of Internal Medicine. 2007;147(2):73.
4. Singh H, Thomas EJ, Petersen LA, Studdert DM. Medical errors involving trainees: a study of closed malpractice claims from 5 insurers. Archives of Internal Medicine. 2007;167(19):2030.
5. Ulmer C, Wolman DM, Johns MME, Institute of Medicine . Committee on Optimizing Graduate Medical Trainee Hours and Work Schedules to Improve Patient Safety. Resident duty hours: Enhancing sleep, supervision, and safety. Washington, DC: National Academies Press; 2009.
6. AMA Scope of Practice Data Series: Nurse practitioners. http://www.aanp.org/AANPCMS2/publicpages/08-0424%20SOP%20Nurse%20Revised%2010-09.pdf. American Medical Association. Accessed Jan 5, 2012.
7. Occupational Outlook Handbook, 2010-11 Edition. http://www.bls.gov/oco/. Bureau of Labor Statistics. Accessed Aug 7, 2011.
8. Occupational Employment Statistics. http://www.bls.gov/oes/home.htm. Bureau of Labor Statistics. Accessed Aug 7, 2011.
9. 2010 Audiology Survey. http://www.refworks.com/RWSingle/RefList.asp?M=3&T=Last Imported. American Speech-Language-Hearing Association. Accessed Aug 7, 2011.
10. Doctor of Audiology. http://pacs.wustl.edu/pacs/pacsweb.nsf/WV/1028F89E4B4FA5BC86257383005E1C46?OpenDocument. Washington University School of Medicine. Accessed Aug 7, 2011.

11. Cadge W, Freese J, Christakis NA. The provision of hospital chaplaincy in the United States: A national overview. Southern medical journal. 2008;101(6):626.

12. Practice Analysis of Chiropractic 2010. http://www.nbce.org/publication/practice-analysis.html. National Board of Chiropractic Examiners. Accessed Aug 7, 2011.

13. Shaw G. Chiropractic Specialties on the Rise. http://www.acatoday.org/content_css.cfm?CID=2323. American Chiropractic Association. Accessed Aug 7, 2011.

14. Survey of Dental Practice. http://www.ada.org/1619.aspx. American Dental Association. Accessed Aug 7, 2011.

15. Compensation & Benefits Survey of the Dietetics Profession 2009. http://www.readexsurvey.com/results/ada/2009/2009ADACompensationSummary.pdf. American Dietetic Association. Accessed Aug 5, 2011.

16. EMS Workforce for the 21st Century: A National Assessment. http://www.hhs.state.ne.us/ems/EMSWorkforceforthe21stCentury.pdf. National Highway Traffic Safety Administration. Accessed Aug 5, 2011.

17. Wisconsin Paramedic Medication List. http://www.dhs.wisconsin.gov/ems/License_certification/Paramedic_SCT_Meds.pdf. Wisconsin Bureau of Local Health Support and EMS.

18. O*NET OnLine. http://www.onetonline.org/. U.S. Department of Labor, Employment & Training Administration. Accessed Aug 7, 2011.

19. Yamada Y. Profile of home care aides, nursing home aides, and hospital aides. The Gerontologist. 2002;42(2):199.

20. Medical Assistants in California. http://www.futurehealth.ucsf.edu/Content/29/2004-05_Medical_Assistants_in_California.pdf. UCSF, The Center for the Health Professions.

21. The American Occupational Therapy Association, Inc. http://www.aota.org/. Accessed Aug 7, 2011.

22. Survey Data. http://www.aoa.org/x4753.xml. American Optometric Association. Accessed Aug 5, 2011.

23. National Physician Assistant Census Report. http://www.aapa.org/images/stories/Data_2009/National_Final_with_Graphics.pdf. American Academy of Physician Assistants. Accessed Aug 5, 2011.

24. Midwest Pharmacy Workforce Research Consortium. 2009 National Pharmacist Workforce Survey. http://www.aacp.org/resources/research/pharmacymanpower/Documents/2009%20National%20Pharmacist%20Workforce%20Survey%20-%20FINAL%20REPORT.pdf. Pharmacy Manpower Project Inc.

25. Knapp KK, Shah BM, Kim HBH, Tran H. Visions for required postgraduate year 1 residency training by 2020: a comparison of actual versus projected expansion. Pharmacotherapy. 2009;29(9):1030-1038.

26. R. Malone. American Physical Therapy Association. Personal Communication.

27. American Board of Physical Therapy Specialties. http://www.abpts.org/home.aspx. Accessed Aug 7, 2011.

28. Executive Summary. http://www.apma.org/. American Podiatric Medical Association, Inc. Accessed Aug 5, 2011.

29. Podiatry Facts and Statistics. http://www.ipma.net/displaycommon. cfm?an=1&subarticlenbr=15. Illinois Podiatric Medical Association. Accessed Aug 22, 2011.

30. Michalski D, Mulvey T, Kohout J. 2008 APA Survey of Psychology Health Service Providers. http://www.apa.org/workforce/publications/08-hsp/report.pdf. American Psychological Association. Accessed Aug 5, 2011.

31. Physician characteristics and distribution in the U.S, 201. Chicago, Ill.: American Medical Association; 2011.

32. Boukus E, Cassil A, O'Malley A. A Snapshot of U.S. Physicians: Key Findings from the 2008 Health Tracking Physician Survey. http://www.hschange.com/ CONTENT/1078/. Center for Studying Health System Change. Accessed Sept 14, 2011.

33. Leigh JP, Tancredi D, Jerant A, Kravitz RL. Physician Wages Across Specialties: Informing the Physician Reimbursement Debate. Archives of Internal Medicine. 2010;170(19):1728-1734.

34. The Physician Workforce: Projections and Research into Current Issues Affecting Supply and Demand. http://bhpr.hrsa.gov/healthworkforce/reports/physwfissues. pdf. Health Resources and Services Administration. Accessed Apr 12, 2011.

35. National Sample Survey of Registered Nurses. http://datawarehouse.hrsa.gov/ nursingsurvey.aspx. Health Resources and Services Administration. Accessed Aug 7, 2011.

36. Ridge R. Nursing certification as a workforce strategy. Nursing management. 2008;39(8):50.

37. 2009-10 AANP National NP Sample Survey. http://www.aanp.org/NR/rdonlyres/ AC773A15-35BA-4AAC-9734-56516ACE8142/0/OnlineReport_Compensation2. pdf. American Academy of Nurse Practicioners. Accessed Aug 5, 2011.

38. G. Hamilton. American College of Nurse-Midwives. Personal Communication.

39. http://www.nacns.org/. National Association of Clinical Nurse Specialists. Accessed Aug 22, 2011.

40. Who We Are. http://www.aana.com/AboutAANA.aspx?id=38. American Association of Nurse Anesthetists.

41. Sipe TA, Fullerton JT, Schuiling KD. Demographic profiles of certified nurse-midwives, certified registered nurse anesthetists, and nurse practitioners: Reflections on implications for uniform education and regulation. Journal of Professional Nursing. 2009;25(3):178-185.

42. Compensation and Benefits Survey 2007. www.midwife.org/Salary-Information. American College of Nurse Midwives. Accessed Aug 5, 2011.

43. Glossary of Statistical Terms - Productivity adjustment. http://stats.oecd.org/ glossary/detail.asp?ID=7163. Organisation for Economic Co-operation and Development. Accessed Aug 5, 2011.

44. 2010 AANA Membership Survey. American Association of Nurse Anesthetists. 2010.

45. Supply, Demand and Use of Licensed Practical Nurses. http://bhpr.hrsa.gov/ healthworkforce/reports/supplydemanduselpn.pdf. Health Resources and Services Administration. Accessed Aug 5, 2011.

46. The Speech-Language Pathology Workforce in North Carolina. http://www.
    shepscenter.unc.edu/data/nchpds/slp.html. North Carolina Health Professions
    Data System. Accessed Aug 5, 2011.

47. Assuring the Sufficiency of a Frontline Workforce: A National Study of Licensed Social
    Workers. http://workforce.socialworkers.org/studies/nasw_06_execsummary.pdf.
    National Association of Social Workers, Center for Workforce Studies. Accessed
    Aug 5, 2011.

48. Clinical Supervision: A Practice Specialty of Clinical Social Work. http://www.
    abecsw.org/images/ABESUPERV2205ed406.pdf. American Board of Examiners in
    Clinical Social Work. Accessed Aug 5, 2011.

Chapter 3
Insurance and Economics

If you want to understand the health care system, it's first essential to understand insurance and economics—but being essential doesn't mean it's easy. We know these topics can be confusing and convoluted, as does anyone who's tried to purchase health insurance or understand why health care costs so dang much. So we've done our best to reduce the abstractions and confusion, because the secret is that the economics of health care is fascinating. Once you begin to understand it, you'll see how patients' and providers' behavior that seems to have nothing to do with money ends up affecting our bottom line and how the way the U.S. health care system is structured influences that behavior.

Everything about health care that we discussed in Chapter 1 costs money, and money changes options, affects behavior, and produces problems. Insurance—the way we pay for care—and economics—the study of the production, distribution, and consumption of that care—helps to piece together what the problems are, what creates them, and how to fix them.

What Is Insurance?

Your auto insurance doesn't pay for tune-ups, but it *will* pay for your car if it's totaled in a wreck. Life involves a certain amount of luck, and accidental events often come with big price tags. Insurance, then, exists to defray the potentially devastating expenses you may or may not find yourself up against in life, vehicular or otherwise.

The logic behind insurance is two-fold. First, money should be set aside in small increments over time to spread out the potential cost of an accident. Second, your money should be pooled with others' to further spread out the cost of accidents. The benefit to insured individuals is that, as long as you make monthly payments, then your accidents are covered—even if you get into a wreck after holding the policy for a week. The benefit to the insurance company is that it gets to keep your monthly payments if that wreck never happens. The benefit to society is that a few car crashes seem more trivial when the costs are spread out amongst thousands of people.

As a metaphor, comparing health insurance to auto insurance is an obvious over-simplification. As we said, health care is complicated! This metaphor ignores two important differences between auto and health insurance. First, having a crappy car doesn't really affect anyone besides you; if it breaks down, you're the only one who has to deal with it. The uninsured individual who ends up in the ICU for two weeks racks up tens of thousands of dollars in bills that the rest of society ends up paying for. Second, having a crappy car is, in some sense, both a choice and not that big of a deal. On the other hand, having an injured or sick body may be due, at least in part, to genetics or how you were raised or the environment where you live. Further, even if one's behavior may have played a role in substandard health, society's values make us wary of simply making people live with the severe consequences of illness and death. Our health is a much bigger deal than any car could ever be.

How Is Insurance Different from Insulation?

Insurance is designed to protect against large, unexpected costs. However, when this protection covers even relatively small, predictable costs, insurance becomes insulation. An analogy would be the difference between a teenager who has to pay for his own car (including gas, oil changes, and tune-ups) but knows that his parents would lend him money if he ever got into a wreck, and a teenager whose parents pay almost all of his car-related expenses. However, most health insurance plans come closer to the latter than the former.

Many critics of rising health care costs claim that our current system of health insurance contains too much insulation, which, in addition to taking the burden of regular costs off of consumers, may also increase costs through moral hazard. Economist Arnold Kling writes, "In the United States, […] about 86 percent of health care spending is paid for by someone other than the patient, usually government or private insurance."[1] When examining arguments that discuss insulation, however, you shouldn't forget the potentially high premiums, co-pays, and co-insurance that most patients pay in exchange for their care. It's simply the direct relationship between price and goods that's obscured.

In addition, health insurance has evolved over time to be considered a right rather than a privilege. When discussing health insurance, it's never simply an economic matter; it also involves values. Ultimately, we're discussing an aspect of the modern liberalization of society, focused on what "membership benefits" all citizens should receive. In most cases, these benefits include basic health services, but some states even mandate the coverage of elective services like in-vitro fertilization.

Health Insurance Basics

Before we delve deeper into the specifics of health insurance, let's cover some of the basic concepts and terms.

An individual enrolled in a health insurance plan or policy is known as a **beneficiary** or **member.** The person who purchases the insurance is the **subscriber** and any other people on the policy (spouse or children) are **dependents**. The insurance company charges the subscriber a monthly fee, called the **premium**. When a beneficiary receives health care services, the insurance company will pay the health care provider, clinic or hospital on behalf of the beneficiary. However, the beneficiary is still required to pay for some of the cost that he or she incurs—this is known as **cost sharing**. Cost sharing comes in different flavors:

▸ The **deductible** is a fixed-dollar annual amount of health care costs that the beneficiary must pay entirely out of pocket. For example, if the deductible is $500, the first $500 in medical costs incurred each year is paid by the beneficiary; for costs beyond $500, the insurance company may pay completely or require a co-payment or co-insurance.

- A **co-payment** (or "co-pay") is a fixed-dollar amount that the beneficiary must pay for certain services. For example, the policy might say that the beneficiary pays $15 out of pocket for each primary care visit and $25 for each specialist visit, while the insurance company pays the rest of the bill.

- **Co-insurance** is similar to co-payment, but it's a percentage of the bill rather than a fixed amount. For example, the beneficiary might pay 20% of the cost of a primary care visit and 25% of the cost of a specialist visit, and the insurance company pays the rest.

- Some insurers used to set annual and lifetime **limits** on the total amount of costs they would cover for an individual beneficiary. For example, a plan might pay up to $100,000 in costs in any given year and $5 million over the course of a patient's life. After the limit has been reached, any additional medical costs must be paid by the beneficiary out of pocket. Lifetime maximums have already been eliminated by the ACA, and annual maximums will be prohibited after 2013.

- The **out-of-pocket max** is the total amount that the beneficiary must pay in a given year. This includes what the beneficiary pays toward the deductible, any co-pays or co-insurance. After that total amount has been reached, the insurer pays 100% of the costs for all covered services.

Legal regulation of health insurance is a bit messier. Some insurance plans, like self-insured employers and Medicare, are federally regulated. Others, such as plans bought individually, are governed primarily by state law. Insurance regulations vary significantly state by state, so while we'll discuss the fundamentals of health insurance here, keep in mind that the specifics depend on the state where the beneficiary lives.

What Types of Insurance Are There?

Coverage and Organization Formats

In all types of insurance, the following parties exist: patients (or consumers, depending on your perspective), providers, and payors. These three parties have varying incentives in regard to cost, access, and quality, and these incentives may not always align. The different insurance plan structures themselves can modify these incentives, leading to changes in the way that these three parties act and interact.

Indemnity plans were both the simplest and the most popular type of insurance plans for most of the 20th century. The best known of these plans were those offered by Blue Cross/Blue Shield. In an indemnity (or "conventional") plan, the beneficiary has a fixed amount of cost-sharing regardless of which physician or hospital he or she visits. Beneficiaries are responsible for paying premiums to the insurer and co-insurance (after the deductible has been reached) to the provider or facility, while the insurance company reimburses the provider or facility for the majority of the bill.

As health care spending skyrocketed throughout the 1980s, many insurance companies moved to a new model—the **Managed Care Organization (MCO)**—in an attempt to constrain costs. As the name implies, these insurers take a more active role in managing the *care* their beneficiaries receive, rather than focusing solely on premiums and reimbursements. Indemnity plans have little leverage to influence provider prices or what care their beneficiaries receive. Managed care plans stress the integration of insurance and medical care, especially by exerting more control over providers and patients in regard to reimbursements and care utilization.

The original MCO is the **Health Management Organization (HMO)**, the most tightly integrated insurance plan. Beneficiaries of HMO plans can only receive covered care from physicians in the HMO "network."[a] In some plans, such as Kaiser Permanante, these physicians are directly employed by the HMO; in others, the physicians are still in private practice (page 18)

---

a   Patients can still visit providers, clinics, or hospitals that aren't in the HMO network, but must pay the bill out-of-pocket.

or part of another sort of clinic or hospital-based group but sign contracts with the HMO, becoming "participating providers." HMOs also emphasize primary and preventive care. HMOs help control costs by asking the primary care physician (PCP) to coordinate all the services the member receives, so the HMO usually requires the member to get a referral from his or her PCP for covered services, a practice known as "gatekeeping." Some hospitalizations and costly outpatient procedures will only be covered if the insurance company "pre-authorizes" them before the fact.

In many HMOs plans, physicians have a financial interest in keeping the patient healthy, which further constrains costs. In "capitated" reimbursement systems, the PCP is paid a certain amount per patient each month, and the PCP is then financially responsible for all of the patient's primary care. In larger multispecialty groups, the physician group may be capitated for all professional services, and sometimes the capitation includes even more services, such as labs, radiology, and outpatient surgery, for instance. Some practices accept "full risk," which means their capitation covers all covered services, including hospital charges. The healthier the patient and the fewer medical services needed, the more money the physician or medical group makes.

HMOs were successful in bringing down health care spending in the 1990s but faced a major backlash from patients, providers, and lawmakers who felt that the insurance companies had gone too far in restricting patient and provider choice. Thousands of state laws were passed to regulate HMOs, which reduced some of their power to restrain utilization and spending. Nationwide, the number of individuals enrolled in HMOs has decreased significantly in the past 15 years.

The most popular MCO plan today is the **Preferred Provider Organization (PPO)**. These plans also negotiate contracts with physicians, who form the plan's network. These physicians agree to charge discounted rates to the plan's beneficiaries in exchange for the increased flow of patients from participating in the network. Beneficiaries can receive care from providers who aren't in the network, but when the services are obtained out-of-network, the beneficiary has a higher deductible, and has higher co-insurance and co-payments to make. The insurer's goal is to create incentives to keep the beneficiary using in-network providers. PPOs place less emphasis on coordination of care and don't employ gatekeeping or capitation. Without gatekeeping, and with the ability of members to receive covered care out-of-network, PPOs offer beneficiaries more choices but the insurers don't have as much power as HMOs to constrain spending.

The final MCO plan is the **Point of Service (POS)**, which combines features of HMOs and PPOs. POS plans were very popular in the 1990s but have largely been supplanted by PPOs, because requirements for authorization before seeing a specialist have proven to be highly unpopular.

See the table below for more about the three types of MCO plans.

	HMO	PPO	POS
▸ Primary Care	Emphasizes overall wellness and preventive care. PCP usually serves as "gatekeeper" (i.e., you can't see a specialist unless your PCP refers you).	PCP less emphasized, not used as gatekeeper.	Uses PCP as gatekeeper but allows patients to pay extra to see specialists without a referral.
▸ Physician Payment	Historically, capitated payments that increase risk sharing with the provider. Today, some plans use annual salary or discounted fee-for-service.	Network providers offer discounted fee-for-service to the PPO, often 25-35% for primary care and up to 50-60% for specialists. Hospitals often bundle payments.	Similar to HMO.
▸ Coordination of Care	Ranges from owning its own hospitals to contracting with groups of providers in individual offices. Tight coordination of services allows increased interaction among providers as well as lower overhead.	Less than with HMOs.	Similar to HMO.
▸ Restrictions	Tend to limit choice of physician as well as type of services reimbursed.	Less restrictive than HMOs; allow patients to use out-of-network providers for an extra fee.	Similar to PPOs.

Consumer-Driven Health Plans are a relatively new type of coverage that give beneficiaries more choice and control over their health care spending. Think of these as tax-free bank accounts that can only be used for medical expenses (non-medical withdrawals incur penalties). They come in several formats—health savings accounts (HSA), flexible spending accounts (FSA), and health reimbursement accounts (HRA). HSAs were first developed in 2003 as a way for individuals to opt out of traditional insurance. Patients who use these are partially saving for their own health needs rather than just paying insurers monthly; however, all who enroll in an HSA must also enroll in an insurance plan with high deductibles (between $1,200 - $5,950 for individuals and $2,400 - $11,900 for families).[2] HSAs are of primary benefit to patients who are young, healthy, and expect a steady source of income, and the plans allow members of this population to lower their spending to match their low risk.

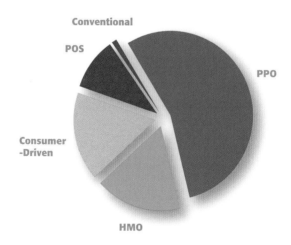

Distribution of Health Plan Enrollment for Covered Workers, by Plan Type

Conventional

POS

PPO

Consumer-Driven

HMO

The Henry J. Kaiser Family Foundation & Health Research and Educational Trust, "Employer Health Benefits 2011 Annual Survey," September 2011. Used by permission.

Note: HDHP/SO = Consumer-Driven Plan

How Do Insurers Set Premium Prices?

Let's take a look at the basic finances for an insurance company over one year. Expenses will equal the amount of care the company will have to pay for plus administrative costs. To stay solvent, the amount the company takes in from monthly premiums will have to equal these expenses. The company can choose from different strategies when deciding how to divvy up the premium cost among its subscribers.

- ▶ **Community Rating:** All subscribers pay the same monthly premium. The premium cost is calculated by dividing the total expenses by the number of beneficiaries.
- ▶ **Medical Underwriting:** Subscribers are charged different monthly premiums depending on how much medical care they're likely to need. Insurers estimate likely future care needs by considering members' age, sex, location, self-reported health status, and personal medical history as well as past claims costs.
- ▶ A mix of the two, known as **Community Rating By Class** or **Modified Community Rating.**

Keep in mind that not all members will require the same amount of care. In America, the sickest 5% of the population accounts for half of total health care spending, while the healthiest 50% of the population only accounts for 3% of health care spending.[3] This leads to problems for both types of premium pricing. In medically underwritten plans, premiums become incredibly expensive for the sickest members of the community. Therefore the people who most need health insurance can't afford it. In community rated plans, you have to deal with the problem of adverse selection, which we detail later in this chapter.

In the U.S., different plans use different rating methodologies, depending on the insurance laws of the state where the insurance is being offered.

And Just What Are Your Premiums Paying For?

The medical loss ratio (MLR) is the percentage of insurance premiums that the insurance company spends on clinical services and activities to improve quality.[4] Put in plain English, this is the percentage of your insurance premium that actually pays for health care. The rest of the revenue goes to pay for administrative costs, marketing, overhead, and company profits. For understandable reasons, insurance companies do consider paying for health care to be a loss.

As of 2009, the MLR for the five largest for-profit insurance companies was in the 70% range for individuals and in the 80% range for small and large groups.[5]

Ways to Get Insurance

Health Insurance in the U.S.

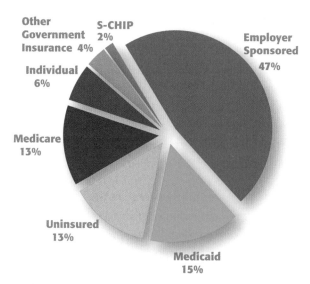

Other Government Insurance 4%
S-CHIP 2%
Employer Sponsored 47%
Individual 6%
Medicare 13%
Uninsured 13%
Medicaid 15%

Centers for Medicare & Medicaid Services, "National Health Expenditure Data," January 2012.

THROUGH EMPLOYMENT

The current relationship between health insurance and employment arose during World War II after the federal government enacted a freeze on wage increases in private industry. In response, employers improved their non-wage benefits, including health insurance for employees and their families. This arrangement of employer-sponsored insurance (ESI) spread even more rapidly when the IRS ruled that employer payments for insurance weren't taxable.[6] ESI has since become the predominant method of obtaining insurance in the U.S.; in 2009, 70% of all insured non-elderly Americans had ESI, either through their own employer or through a family member.[7]

ESI comes in one of two types, depending on who's ultimately footing the bill.

Fully-Insured: The employer buys insurance from a private insurance company for its employees. In this arrangement, the insurance company is the payor and takes the risk for future medical costs for the beneficiaries. The employer usually works with a broker to price different insurance options—different kinds of plans and from different insurers—and the employee can select from one of these employer-approved plans.

Employees can sign up for individual coverage, or, for a higher price, cover their spouses and children on the same plan. Premiums are not risk-adjusted per employee (e.g., all employees who pick the PPO family plan are charged the same amount).[b] The employer contributes 50-90% of the monthly premium, and the employee pays the rest. Employees see reduced wages, as employers must pay less in wages to maintain this benefit; however, neither employees nor employers have to pay income tax on benefits. Thus, though employees have reduced wages, they receive a larger total compensation package.

Self-Insured: The employer acts as the payor and assumes the risk of future medical expenses for its own employees. A private insurance company is contracted to handle the day-to-day administration of the plan. The employer also usually purchases what's called "stop loss insurance" from a private insurer, which protects the employer from unexpectedly high costs from employees' medical care. Employees are still required to contribute monthly fees for the cost of their insurance coverage, but the payments go primarily to the employer rather than the insurance company. Today, three in five Americans who have ESI are covered by a self-insured plan.[8]

These different arrangements are often a source of confusion. For instance, large employers which self-insure usually contract through companies like Aetna to administer their plans. Thus, while you might pay the same monthly premium as your neighbor and have the same Aetna insurance

---

b   ESI premiums may (depending on state law) be adjusted by the insurer to account for the claims history of the employer, so an employer with a track record of employees who need lots of medical care may have to pay a higher premium. This is why insurance for employees of mining companies is usually higher than those of a health food store.

card, you don't actually have the same plan or the same coverage. Self-insured plans, for example, do not have to follow state law about what insurance should cover.

Key differences between fully and self-insured plans include:

▸ In a fully insured plan, the insurance company foots the bill after an employee receives medical care; in a self-insured plan, the employer does.

▸ In a fully insured plan, the insurance company usually makes a profit from insuring the employees; in a self-insured plan, those dollars stay with the employer.

▸ Fully insured plans are regulated primarily by state law while self-insured plans are regulated by federal law, which is much less oner-ous. This means that fully insured plans have to include all of their state's mandated benefits but self-insured plans have no such obli-gation. The fewer medical services you have to cover, the less you'll spend—this is one reason why employers choose to self-insure.

▸ Large companies are more likely to offer self-insured plans than small companies. Big companies have more financial resources to cover medical costs, and the risks of insurance can be spread out better over a greater number of employees.

Pros and Cons of ESI

From the employee's standpoint, ESI provides both advantages and disad-vantages. The advantages are reduced premiums (due to both the contri-bution of the employer as well as the economy of scale), reduced income taxes, and the fact that employer plans will cover pre-existing conditions if the employee is coming from another job where he/she has had health insurance, or had prior individual insurance. The disadvantages are that it decreases mobility (it's harder to change jobs if you have to change insur-ance plans too) and may constrict choice (since you can only choose an insurance plan that's been selected by your employer).

From the insurance company's standpoint, ESI reduces both the need for marketing and adverse selection. A group of employees is likely to be both large (meaning a dependable stream of revenue as long as they maintain a relationship with the employer) and relatively healthy[c] (meaning they

---

c   Compared to a similar-sized group of unemployed individuals.

won't require as much pay-out on their premiums). While employers do have the clout to reduce premiums from what individual consumers pay, this is still a profitable trade-off for the insurers.

From the employer's standpoint, the advantages of ESI increase with the size of the business. For a large business, the economy of scale means they have to pay less, as a percentage of payroll, to provide the benefit. The opposite is true for small employers. You can see this reflected in the number of large companies (>200 workers) vs. small companies (<200 workers) who provide health insurance: 99% vs. 59%.[10] No matter the employer's size, benefits get increasingly difficult to provide as health costs rise faster than wages. Between 1999 and 2010, health premiums rose by 138%, and wages rose 42%.[11] As a result, ESI has been on the decline: from 2001-05, the number of employers providing health insurance decreased from 84% to 80%,[12] and, from 2004-06, the number of working-aged adults receiving ESI decreased from 63% to 59%.[7]

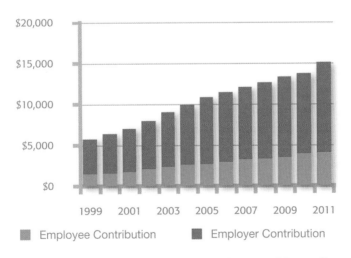

Family Coverage Through ESI: Average Premium Contributions for Employee and Employer

The Henry J. Kaiser Family Foundation, "Employer Health Benefits 2011 Annual Survey" (8225), September 2011. Used by permission.

From society's standpoint, ESI is beneficial in that it can insure a large number of citizens without the government directly insuring them. It's problematic, though, because it reduces the amount of income tax paid (since workers don't have to pay taxes on their benefits, only on their wages)—and it increases employees' dependence on their employers.

PUBLIC INSURANCE PROGRAMS

Here's a quick roundup of the key public insurance programs:

- **Medicare:** A federal program that provides health insurance coverage to people 65 years or older and to those younger than 65 and permanently disabled, regardless of financial status.
- **Medicaid:** A joint federal-state program that insures certain low-income adults and children.
- **State Children's Health Insurance Program:** (Variably called S-CHIP or CHIP; we'll use CHIP) Operates as part of a state's Medicaid program and makes health insurance available for children with no insurance and for those from low-income families.

Please see Chapter 5 for an in-depth look at Medicare, Medicaid, and CHIP.

- **Veterans Health Administration:** A component of the U.S. Department of Veterans Affairs (VA) that provides medical care to veterans and their families at low or no cost. The VA operates numerous outpatient clinics, hospitals, and long-term health care facilities.
- **TRICARE:** A Department of Defense program that provides insurance to the dependents of active-duty military members and to military retirees and their dependents.
- **Consolidated Omnibus Budget Reconciliation Act (COBRA):** Those who have recently lost their jobs can keep their ESI for up to 18 months through this program. However, the individual or family has to continue their previous monthly fee and pay for the share that the employer had been contributing, so the out-of-pocket cost is often three to four times greater than before.

INDIVIDUALLY, ON THE MARKET

Millions of Americans can't obtain insurance through their employers or the government—think of the unemployed, self-employed, early retirees, and those working for companies that don't offer ESI—and must turn to the individual market for coverage. The cost of insurance in this market is almost always more expensive because insurers can't spread the risk among a larger group, and because they risk-adjust the premium by age, sex, and health status. Furthermore, there's no employer to defray the costs of insurance. Those with significant medical histories and/or pre-existing conditions often find that the cost of premiums on the individual market are far beyond what they can afford, or, in some cases, the insurer may decide the risk isn't worth it and decline to even offer coverage at any price. Not surprisingly, relatively few Americans purchase their insurance through the individual market.

NO INSURANCE

We would be remiss in discussing the ways people get insurance if we didn't also talk about those who *don't* get insurance. As of 2010, the uninsured numbered 47 million, which is more than 15% of the U.S. population.[13] See the "Issues" section later in this chapter for more information about this demographic.

One other category you'll need to know about is the "underinsured"—these are individuals who do have some health insurance coverage, but not enough to adequately cover their medical expenses.[14] Calculating the total number of underinsured Americans isn't easy, but one well-accepted 2007 study pegged it at 25 million, a 60% increase since 2003.[15]

Reimbursement Types

Insurers negotiate contracts with individual health care facilities as well as with providers. These contracts may include any of the following reimbursement systems, or even multiple ones (e.g., different rates for outpatient vs. inpatient services).

Reimbursement Systems[16]		
Physician	**Hospital**	**Explanation**
Fee-for-Service	Fee-for-Service	Set reimbursements for specific procedures or actions
—	Per Diem	Set reimbursement for each day hospitalized
Episode of Illness/ Bundled Payment	Per Diagnosis	Set reimbursement for the entirety of care during an illness or procedure (could include hospital, physician, post-acute care setting, home care, and more)
Capitation	Capitation	Set reimbursement per patient, regardless of services rendered
Salary	Global budget	Set reimbursement per year, regardless of services rendered

Pay for Performance: Another reimbursement system that's become increasingly popular over the past 10 years is "pay-for-performance (P4P)." P4P reimburses providers and facilities based on measures of clinical quality, safety, efficiency and patient satisfaction.[17] Many experts have concluded that fee-for-service systems are inefficient because they reward providers for how *much* they did, not how *well* they did it or how it impacted the patient's health. Pay-for-performance systems are instead structured to reward quality, not volume. However, measuring quality is tough (page 169), and there's a lot of variation between different P4P systems in the specific measures that are used, and how those measures are converted to dollars.

P4P is often combined with other reimbursement systems; for example, a single provider might receive 70% of his or her compensation via fee-for-service and 30% from his or her performance on quality measures (e.g., percentage of female patients receiving mammograms), and patient satisfaction. Pay-for-performance is also an integral part of new health care delivery models, especially the Accountable Care Organization (page 206).

Diagnosis-Related Group: In addition, perhaps the most important hospital reimbursement system to know is the diagnosis-related group

(DRG). DRGs were instituted by Medicare in the early 1980s as a way to reduce costs—they were revolutionary: DRGs shifted reimbursement from *retrospective* to *prospective* payment. This means that Medicare pays a flat rate based on the diagnosis[d,e] (there are about 500 DRGs in total) and, as the Department of Health & Human Services puts it, "In this DRG prospective payment system, Medicare pays hospitals a flat rate per case for inpatient hospital care so that efficient hospitals are rewarded for their efficiency and inefficient hospitals have an incentive to become more efficient."[18]

Relative Value Unit: The corresponding system for physicians is known as the relative value unit (RVU). This is the way that Medicare and other insurers and institutions can convert the wide variety of medical diagnoses, treatments, and procedures into a common fee-for-service payment system. Each action a physician undertakes is rated on three factors:
1. Work of the physician
2. Expense to the practice
3. Cost of malpractice insurance[19]

For example, a diagnostic colonoscopy is worth 4.96 RVUs, while removing part of the colon surgically is 1900 RVUs.[20] The RVU value is multiplied by a conversion factor to determine the amount of money the physician receives for the service. RVU values are constantly updated by a national committee, and they're adjusted for geographic differences in cost. The number the formula computes is the RBRVS (resource-based relative value scale). Private insurers jumped on Medicare's bandwagon with RBRVS, and usually pay their contracted doctors a percentage (higher or lower) from RBRVS, as well.

If this seems simple and unimportant to you, think again. Before, providers had all the power to set the cost of reimbursement; DRGs and RVUs allow payors (specifically, the government) a way to gain the upper hand and influence provider behavior. Note, too, that DRGs may control the payment

---

d Diagnoses, diseases, symptoms and the like are all classified according to a mind-numbing system known as the International Classification of Diseases (ICD). The U.S. is currently transitioning between the 9th version of the ICD to the 10th, which will include 140,000 codes, including gems like V9542XA—"Forced landing of spacecraft injuring occupant."
e Medicare does make allowances for cases that are unusually complicated and expensive. These "outlier cases" are billed separately and at a higher reimbursement rate than a typical DRG.

for services but have no control over what types of services are offered, and how often.

Please keep in mind that health insurance in the U.S. will be undergoing some major changes as the ACA is implemented over the next decade. See Chapter 5 for the details.

Now that we've looked at what insurance is and how it's administered, let's look at how much U.S. health care costs and then move to the REALLY big question…**why** does it cost so much?

How Much Does U.S. Health Care Cost?

According to the Center for Medicare & Medicaid Services (CMS), in 2010, national health expenditures reached $2.6 trillion, which is $8,402 per person and 17.9% of the nation's gross domestic product (GDP), far more than any other developed country. CMS expects spending to grow by around 6% per year, reaching 19.8% of GDP by 2019.[13] Per capita spending varies widely by state, from 74% of the national average in Utah to 136% in Massachusetts.[21]

Where Health Care Dollars Come From . . .

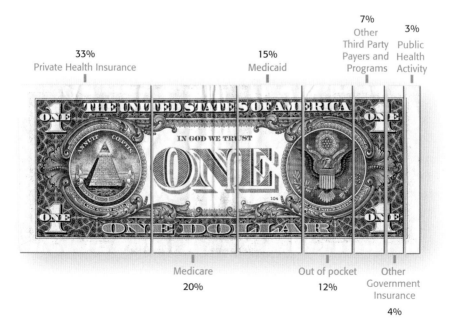

33%
Private Health Insurance

15%
Medicaid

7%
Other Third Party Payers and Programs

3%
Public Health Activity

Medicare
20%

Out of pocket
12%

Other Government Insurance
4%

. . . and Where They Go

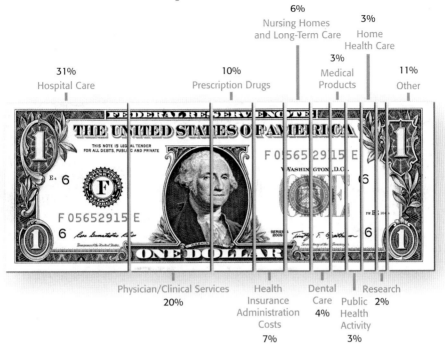

6%
Nursing Homes
and Long-Term Care

3%
Home
Health Care

31%
Hospital Care

10%
Prescription Drugs

3%
Medical
Products

11%
Other

Physician/Clinical Services
20%

Health
Insurance
Administration
Costs
7%

Dental
Care
4%

Research
Public 2%
Health
Activity
3%

Centers for Medicare & Medicaid Services, "National Health Expenditure Data," January 2012. Note: Does not include Investment, Research, Structures & Equipment.

The bottom line is that U.S. health care is very, very expensive. Which leads us to our next question....

Why Does U.S. Health Care Cost So Much?

This question has a lot of answers.[f] We'll examine them by category: those that are common to any system of insurance or health care ("Universal"), those that are specific to the current U.S. system ("Unique"), and those that are issues in society that affect medicine ("Societal"). After looking at these issues, we'll examine methods used to defray costs as well as the consequences of high costs.

---

f   Unfortunately, it's not simply "Because the health care system is so good"—see pg 179 for more.

Universal	Unique	Societal
Economic Concepts:	**Organizational Issues:**	▸ Unhealthy behaviors
▸ Information asymmetry	▸ Lack of coordination	▸ Poverty
▸ Moral hazard	▸ Administrative overhead	▸ Constraints of rural or urban life
▸ Adverse selection	▸ Overtreatment	▸ Lack of patient education
▸ Supply-induced demand	▸ Loose governmental regulation	
▸ Behavioral economics	**Expensive Elements:**	
Inherent Issues:	▸ High physician wages	
▸ Chronic care	▸ Iterative reimbursements	
▸ End-of-life care		
▸ Lack of transparency	▸ Pharmaceuticals & technology	
	▸ Medical malpractice	

Universal Reasons

These issues fall into two categories: (1) economic concepts and (2) inherent issues of health and knowledge (e.g., bodies are designed to wear out, and some medical concepts are inherently confusing). Let's go through them.

ECONOMIC CONCEPTS

(Note: Please see the end of this section for a comment on the limitations of traditional economic concepts as applied to health care.)

Information Asymmetry

As a concept, this is as simple as it sounds: one side of a transaction has more information than the other side, which is usually the case for patients and providers, or patients and insurers. Information asymmetry influences a wide swath of the interactions in the health care system. It often involve situations in which one side wants the other side to act on its behalf (termed the "principal-agent conflict" in economics). For example, the insurance company wants the policyholder to incur fewer costs (whether through good health or through foregoing medical services) so that the insurer won't have to pay.

Information asymmetry can cause adverse selection, moral hazard, conflict of interest, and supply-induced demand, all of which are explained below.

Moral Hazard

Let's say you fall in love with a house on the beach, but it happens to sit on a stretch of the coast known for getting beaten in hurricane after hurricane. "That's too bad," you think, "but I guess insurance would pay for it," and you buy it anyway. That's moral hazard: the trend toward more risky behavior when you know you won't end up having to cover the full cost.

In terms of medicine, examples of moral hazard would be continuing unhealthy or risky habits, such as smoking or neglecting to get regular check-ups, because you know that large cost consequences down the line will be covered by insurance. Many think that moral hazard plays a big role in rising health care costs, and things like co-pays, deductibles, and lifetime limits exist to reduce its effects (though lifetime limits will be a thing of the past as of 2014; see Chapter 5).

Percent of Health Care Costs Paid Out of Pocket

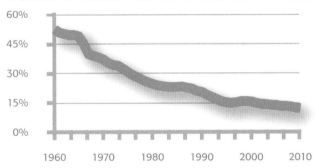

Centers for Medicare & Medicaid Services, "National Health Expenditure Data," January 2012.

Moral hazard plays a particularly intractable role, considering how much some conditions cost. Imagine a teenage girl who goes to the tanning salon each week, claiming blithely that she doesn't care if she gets cancer when she's old as long as she's beautiful now. Granted, she may not develop cancer, and, if she does, it may not be for decades. Yet she clearly is taking a risk without any thought to the costs of the consequences. Even if someday she has large co-pays and deductibles, her out-of-pocket cost will still be far below the actual costs of melanoma treatment. In such cases, in which the damage is already done, aside from requiring patients to pay more than they have funds to cover—or denying care altogether—it's not clear how the problem of moral hazard can be minimized.

Adverse Selection

Contrast a healthy 22-year-old who runs 20 miles a week with a 45-year-old diabetic who had a heart attack five years ago. Which one is more likely to desire health insurance?

Insurance exists to spread costs among even those who don't end up incurring them. The law mandates that those who have cars must get auto insurance, so it's easy to spread costs among the population, but the same hasn't historically been true with health insurance. Young, healthy people have low enough risk that they can reduce their costs entirely by not purchasing insurance. The risk-spreading purpose of insurance is thus compromised, as the total number of people paying premiums goes down while the number of people making claims stays the same. Thus, premiums grow untenably high for remaining policyholders. That's adverse selection.

Supply-Induced Demand

In normal market economics, supply will rise to meet demand. For example, sometimes people want to buy flower bouquets for their girlfriends (the demand comes first), so entrepreneurs open florist shops (supply comes second). This is demand-induced supply. On the other hand, picture a couple sitting in a restaurant. The boyfriend probably isn't considering buying flowers at that moment, yet some intrepid salesperson is walking around selling flowers to these innocent couples. Suddenly, when someone is standing in front of the girlfriend extending a rose, the situation seems to call for an opening of the boyfriend's wallet. That is supply-induced demand.[g] In the first case, demand comes first; in the second, supply does.

Supply-induced demand arises as a problem in health care because health care involves economics in addition to medicine—there are diseases to be cured, but there is money to be made in the process. The normal model of medicine is that, if more people need heart surgeries, then more physi-

---

g   Some might call this girlfriend-induced demand, as well.

cians will choose cardiothoracic surgery as a field, more hospitals will build cardiac surgery suites, and more device companies will devote research to developing cardiac devices.

Yet it's not so simple—the split between physicians and patients complicates matters. As we explained in the Information Asymmetries section, patients and physicians don't always have the same level of information, so the demand for medical services doesn't come purely from the patient side. Procedures, tests, and pills may be offered that aren't strictly necessary, but, in the hospital, it's the physician, not the patient (i.e., the supplier, not the demander) who makes most decisions, and patients rarely question the physicians. Thus, tests are ordered, and costs rise.

Behavioral Economics

Humans are not perfectly rational beings. What's more, unlike models of behavior used in classical economics, we aren't motivated solely by money. We make imperfect risk-benefit analyses, respond to the heat of the moment, and ignore evidence to the contrary of our beliefs and desires—so a person might end up gambling instead of saving for retirement, punching his best friend during a brief argument, and buying a gas guzzler despite gas prices. Behavioral economics takes this irrationality into account as a combination of both economics and psychology, a study of how humans actually behave in the world.

To illustrate this point, let's look at a study of rice subsidies in rural China. Poor families will often list hunger as their chief complaint and may have reduced work productivity as a result, so we might expect that cheaper rice would mean these families would buy and eat more rice. However, studies show that this isn't the case. Instead, when given rice subsidies, these poor Chinese families eat the same or less rice and use the extra savings to buy meat instead, meaning their caloric intake remains the same or even decreases.[22] This decision may seem irrational in an economic model, but keep in mind these families are now eating what they consider better-tasting food. While we might view their caloric intake and work productivity (and attending wages) as having the highest value, they might view having tasty meals as even more important to their well-being. Whether such decisions are right or wrong, behavioral economics recognizes that non-financial incentives need to be taken into account.

The main areas of study for behavioral economics are heuristics (rules of thumb), framing (mental context), and market inefficiencies. Here's a short list of some concepts in these areas:

▸ **Anchoring Fallacy:** People may weigh one piece of information too heavily when making decisions (e.g., This hospital has nicer décor, so it must be better).

▸ **Cognitive Framing:** Cultural background, family, and personal experience help us understand how information fits as part of a whole, but it can lead us to adhere to anecdotal evidence and stereotypes rather than scientific evidence or expert judgment (e.g., "I don't know anyone who got sick from using steroids, so I'll be fine").

▸ **Time Inconsistency:** Personal preferences change over time—sometimes even very quickly—so as to be inconsistent with past or future preferences. (For instance, a smoker wants to put off quitting until tomorrow—but when tomorrow finally comes, he may wish he'd quit years before.)

Behavioral economics can help us understand and design incentives for getting people to eat healthier, exercise more, seek preventative care, quit smoking, get vaccinated, and take their medications regularly, to name a few examples.

The Limits of Economic Concepts

Traditional economic concepts arose as a way of explaining how humans behave, specifically when their behavior involves money, goods, and services. Yet, as seems obvious with any attempt to explain human behavior, economics is neither an exact nor an all-inclusive science. Economics offers an explanation, not *the only* explanation, for behavior. Thus, we cannot present the above economic concepts without discussing the counterpoint, which suggests that traditional economics falls short of explaining health care.

There are two general categories of such critiques: first, that the human body is so different from market goods and services that traditional economics fails on a philosophical level, and, second, that, regardless of philosophy, research indicates people don't behave as traditional economics would predict. An in-depth discussion of these critiques isn't possible here, so instead we will just briefly illustrate with an example.

First, the discrepancy between market goods and health care. In March of 2012, the Supreme Court heard testimony on the Affordable Care Act, during which Justice Scalia compared purchasing health insurance to purchasing broccoli. When you buy groceries, all the costs are known in advance, but that's not the case with health care. The two are not analogous. It would be like calling up Whole Foods to ask how much your mushrooms are going to cost, but not only do you not know how many you'll be buying, you also don't know if your recipe requires button mushrooms or truffles.

As for purchasing health care services (for instance, surgery to remove an inflamed gallbladder), there are many factors, some of them unpredictable, which produce the total cost. How long will you be in the hospital? What other medical conditions do you have? Will you have a difficult recovery? What drugs are you going to need, and for how long? What tests will be run, and how many? These aren't things that a hospital administrator is going to be able to tell you before the fact. There's a huge variance in how much the same procedure costs for different individuals, and it's hard to see how that could change.

Second, even if you could know the cost ahead of time, would that change your behavior? Would you decide not to have the gallbladder surgery? Would you go to another hospital? Would you nickel-and-dime the imaging and tests down, or would you trust your doctor to know what's best? And what if the services you turned down were preventive, so your costs increased in the long run?

The point is that your health is subject to forces outside of your control, and it's also an emotionally and psychologically laden subject. You can choose not to buy a pound of truffle mushrooms. You can't choose not to have heart disease or breast cancer, and you can't expect someone in that position to make choices based solely on money.

INTRINSIC HEALTH AND KNOWLEDGE ISSUES

Chronic Care: Once upon a time, humans died mostly from infectious diseases, but then the advent of sanitation, refrigeration, and vaccination put a damper on such mortality and morbidity. In industrialized nations, at least, the bugs have moved to the back of the bus, leaving room for chronic conditions to step forward. Diabetes, heart disease, high blood pressure, and cancer are ongoing, very expensive chronic conditions that plague the U.S. now, and there is no vaccine or quick cure for them. Diabetes may not be as deadly as smallpox, but it's not curable, and it costs more to treat.

In 2010, six out of the top 10 leading causes of death were from chronic diseases (the bold diseases in the table)—and 50% of American adults live with a chronic disease diagnosis.[23] According to the Centers for Disease Control and Prevention (CDC), the best way to deal with chronic diseases is through prevention. This is worth repeating: most chronic conditions are preventable through healthy eating and living. Thus, unless the U.S. population begins trending toward healthier lifestyles, chronic conditions will continue— and perhaps grow—as a driver of increased health care spending.

Leading Cause of Death, 2010	
Cause	**Deaths**
Disease of the heart	595,444
Cancer	573,855
Chronic lung diseases	137,789
Stroke	129,180
Accidents	118,043
Alzheimer's	83,308
Diabetes mellitus	68,905
Kidney diseases	50,472
Influenza and pneumonia	50,003
Suicide	37,793

Murphy et al., "Deaths: Preliminary Data for 2010," National Vital Statistics Reports, January 2012.

End-of-Life Care: The cost of end-of-life health care greatly outstrips those of any other time; a full quarter of Medicare spending goes to care in the last year of life.[24] Patients, physicians, and families often "pull out all the stops" to treat those near death, even if the tests and procedures have little chance of succeeding. The bioethicist Arthur Caplan states, "What would you do if your mother needed an expensive, painful operation that had only a one in a million chance of saving her? [...] Most Americans would say 'do it.' In this country, we are all about hope."[25]

Unfortunately, you rarely know ahead of time that it's your last year of life. It's obvious that death is inevitable, and, in hindsight, it seems odd to spend hundreds of thousands of dollars to extend lives by only a few months. Yet, for patients and their families in the moment, impending death may not feel obvious. Just as inevitable as death is the fact that health care will always be mediated by emotion. As long as death doesn't come quickly by sudden accident or illness, patients and families will seek to pull out all the stops to prolong life. And that's expensive.

Lack of Transparency: As mentioned in the "Insurance Reimbursement" section, Medicare uses DRGs to make prospective—rather than retrospective—payments to providers. Such a payment system is possible because Medicare is vast enough to have the data needed to set reimbursement amounts as well as to have the power to make providers accept it.

Non-governmental insurers may not use prospective payments, but they do have access to research about the costs and quality of providers across the nation as well as the average reimbursements of any particular provider and are able to negotiate contracts and payments with providers.

For Medicare and other insurers, then, costs are at least slightly transparent, and they're able to take cost into account when deciding what treatments to cover. No such transparency exists for individual patients, though. Individuals are often exhorted to account for costs in their medical decision-making; however, many barriers stand in their way:

- Hospitals and physicians don't provide up-front information about billing.
- Patients don't have access to national data or average costs at individual hospitals.
- Even if patients could access the above data, they would need to compare costs at all regional hospitals and be willing to switch hospitals even if they are in critical condition.
- Patients have no way of knowing whether *their own care* would be comparable (their illness may be more acute, they may have more or fewer co-morbidities, their care may have more or fewer complications, etc.).
- Patients usually don't understand how medical billing works.
- Patients usually don't have time to hassle with billing forms and learn about coverage rules.
- Patients lack the clinical knowledge in comparing the added value of a more expensive treatment.

The fact is not just that medical costs aren't transparent—it's also that costs never can be fully transparent. Patients have no idea what their care is going to end up costing, and thus their ability to make cost-effective decisions is inherently compromised.

Unique Reasons

The U.S. health care system is pretty unique. Some problematic issues may be shared by other countries' systems but these issues are certainly not inherent to all. We'll examine these issues in two categories: organizational issues and expensive parts.

ORGANIZATIONAL ISSUES

Lack of Coordination: Health care in the U.S. arose not as a coordinated system but rather as an organic response to diverse and growing needs over time. As seems natural with such development, some parts don't overlap when they should, and some parts duplicate the same work needlessly; in a word, the U.S. system is inefficient. A good example of this lack of coordination is that medical billing is done separately at every doctor's office and hospital across the country.

The more diversity there is in payment forms, systems, rules, and payors themselves, the more work time must be devoted to billing. For example, the Department of Surgery at Washington University School of Medicine in St. Louis employs 15 medical coders and four coding supervisors (serving 90 clinical physicians), for whom salaries total about $750,000 per year—and that's just one department. Since insurance payments reimburse not just for supplies, but also for wages of physicians, nurses, and, yes, medical billers, then any increase in the billing or coding workforce entails an increase in costs that the patient ends up paying. This billing workforce cost has played a role in the decreasing ability of physicians to maintain private practices.[h]

---

h   Many offices and hospitals outsource their billing services to a specialized business, like the Medical Billing Service, and, as is a trend in other areas of health care, some of this outsourcing is going abroad in an attempt to reduce costs. Interestingly, privacy concerns have both increased billing needs (by increasing the amount of paperwork required by law) and constrained cost-reduction (by raising concerns about privacy in outsourcing).

Lack of coordination increases the need for medical billing in two ways: first, because each health care facility must pay for its own dedicated billing department or pay to outsource it (unlike, say, in England, where billing is a centralized organization); second, because each billing department must master different forms and reimbursement rules for each of many different insurers and plans. And this is just looking at billing! You can just imagine the other ways in which a similar lack of coordination in other departments increases costs.

Administrative Overhead: Health care professionals and health-related businesses (e.g., hospitals, insurance companies, and pharmaceutical companies) need administrative support to make things run. Administrative support inherently increases prices, since billing must cover these indirect costs in addition to any direct costs. The U.S. system has, overall, greater administrative costs than any other industrialized country. Lack of centralization is one reason; another is that spending of premium money has not historically been regulated, though this will change in 2014, as the Affordable Care Act mandates the medical loss ratio at 85%.

Overtreatment: Overtreatment occurs when patients receive treatments or procedures that aren't medically necessary. As you might imagine, this raises costs.

Perhaps you've already heard about this issue; after all, in 2009, Atul Gawande, a surgeon, public health researcher, and writer, wrote a much-discussed article in *The New Yorker* about regional differences in Medicare expenditures. The idea is relatively simple. The idea behind overtreatment is just that providers may order—and patients may demand—more expensive tests and procedures than are necessary, and they may diagnose and treat diseases that either aren't there or don't really need *treatment*, per se. As Gawande puts it:

"Between 2001 and 2005, critically ill Medicare patients received almost fifty per cent more specialist visits in McAllen than in El Paso and were two-thirds more likely to see ten or more specialists in a six-month period. In 2005 and 2006, patients in McAllen received twenty per cent more abdominal ultrasounds, thirty per cent more bone-density studies, sixty per cent more stress tests with echocardiography, two hundred per cent more nerve-conduction studies to diagnose carpal-tunnel syndrome, and five hundred and fifty per cent more urine-flow studies to diagnose prostate troubles. […] The primary cause of McAllen's extreme costs was, very simply, the across-the-board overuse of medicine."[26]

Since newer, more complex tests, procedures, and drugs are expensive, and since health care dollars are limited, it's legitimate to ask how much quality improvement is worth how much cost. Might you, as a patient who suspects abdominal obstruction, be willing to have a $300 X-ray instead of an $1,800 CT scan if the CT scan is only 3% more sensitive? Most patients wouldn't know what the range of diagnoses might be or how to evaluate such a calculation.

They might be likely to either:

▸ Reflexively go with the cheaper one (if paying out-of-pocket) or
▸ Reflexively go with the most state-of-the-art (if insured).

Physicians, who know both the range of diagnoses as well as the benefits of different diagnostics, may be best suited to make the decision, but they, too:

▸ May not be up-to-date on evidence or
▸ May reflexively go with the state-of-the-art imaging if they know their patient is insured.

Policymakers could set a particular cost-benefit calculation for decisions, but this would fail to account for outliers (those whose bodies and experiences don't fit the average) and patient choice. (See "Comparative Effectiveness Research" in Chapter 4.)

Another difficult issue with overtreatment is physician conflict of interest. Let's say you're a gastroenterologist in a private practice. Because you send so many patients for CT scans, you decide that it would be more efficient to buy one yourself for the office. This may be more convenient for both you and the patient, but it also means that you are now the person who both decides when a patient uses the CT *and* the person who benefits monetarily when they do. Even if you have nothing but the best intentions, this is an obvious conflict of interest.

Regulating this conflict of interest faces powerful opposition. First, while the conflict of interest is clear in the hypothetical, physicians may be offended at the thought that their decision-making capabilities could be compromised and, therefore, may oppose attempts at regulation. In addition, device manufacturers benefit monetarily when physicians buy separate devices instead of sharing them and may further oppose attempts at regulation. Thus, both authority and money bolster the status quo.

Loose Governmental Regulations: Governments in Japan, Germany, and England strictly regulate payments in health care. For instance, in Japan, the government decides what physicians may charge for any service. In Germany, physicians go to school for free but then are salaried. In England, the government negotiates down the price of pharmaceuticals.

Certainly, the U.S. government regulates the health care industry on cost, access, and quality. But our checks on costs are nowhere near those of other industrialized nations. Whether this relative weakness of regulation is good or bad (and there are strong arguments for the benefits of minimal regulation), it does contribute to higher costs for patients in the U.S.

EXPENSIVE ELEMENTS

High Physician Wages: Let's face it: physicians in the U.S. make a lot of money. In 2009, the median income was $49,777 for all U.S. workers,[27] but $186,044 for primary care physicians and $339,738 for specialists.[28] Those high incomes are reflected in high health care costs.

Obviously, you can offer many reasons why physicians' wages are and should be high (they work long hours, their jobs are important to society, they spend many years in training for little or no pay, they have a lot of debt to pay off, etc.), but let's focus on the economic, market-based explanation: physician supply is limited. And when supply is limited (as with diamonds or scalped concert tickets), price goes up.

It's certainly possible to take either side of this issue. You may be for or against limits on physician numbers, and you may be for or against high wages for physicians. What is clear, though, is that limiting physician numbers limits competition. Limited competition contributes to high physician wages, and high physician wages drive up health care costs.

And yet...it's not that simple. Areas of the U.S. with the most physicians per capita actually have higher health care spending than average[29] (and the quality isn't any better either).[30] While economic principles tell us that competition should drive costs down, the facts indicate that other factors, like supply-induced demand and overtreatment, may be more powerful in this case. Just another reminder that, when it comes to health care, it's always more complicated than it first appears.

Iterative Reimbursements: A large insurer like Blue Cross/Blue Shield gets billed a lot of money by any given hospital, and owing that much means the insurer has leverage (because the hospital needs its payment). The insurers use this leverage when negotiating contracts with hospitals; typically, the insurers only reimburse a percentage of the bill charged by the hospital. This gives hospitals an incentive to simply increase the prices of their services, thereby increasing the amount, if not the percentage, they get reimbursed. The ugly underbelly of this tug of war is that patients who are uninsured or underinsured (that is, those who must pay out-of-pocket) get handed a bill much higher than any insurer would ever actually pay. This undiscounted bill is known in the industry as the "rack rate."

Pharmaceuticals & Technology: Research, development, marketing and use of new drugs and devices account for a large and growing share of U.S. health care spending. See Chapter 4 for more information about these industries and their financial impact.

Medical Malpractice: See the "Malpractice" section later in this chapter.

SOCIETAL REASONS

Unhealthy Behaviors

Maybe you've heard, but Americans aren't the healthiest people around. An astounding 75% of Americans are either overweight or obese (nearly twice as many as 50 years ago),[31] an epidemic that accounts for more than one-tenth of U.S. health spending.[32,33] Similarly, 20% of American adults smoke tobacco, which causes an array of diseases that rack up $157 billion annually.[34] And those who undergo medical treatment don't always do so perfectly: less than half of all prescriptions are taken as directed, a lack of adherence that is estimated to cause 10% of all hospital admissions.[35]

The point of this section isn't to heap blame on those who smoke, don't exercise enough, or miss a pill every once in a while (and by no means to suggest these are uniquely American failings, either). The point is that personal behavior and lifestyle affect health, and health itself is the major determinant of health care costs. Health care providers can treat illness and injury, screen for disease, and emphasize healthy behaviors, but, short of following patients home to make sure they eat right and work out, there's only so much providers can do.

Due to unhealthy behaviors (i.e., a lack of prevention), a large component of health care costs isn't subject to the control of medical professionals. However, as indicated in the next three sections, it is much more complicated than simply exhorting people to live healthier lives.

Poverty

The U.S. government defines the federal poverty level (FPL) by family size, as shown in the table on the right with data from 2012.[36] (These thresholds are the same throughout the nation, excluding Alaska and Hawaii, and don't account for cost of living variations.) The thresholds are used to determine eligibility for most government welfare programs, including Medicaid.

Household#	Income Threshold
1	$11,170
2	$15,130
3	$19,090
4	$23,050

In 2010, 46.2 million people—15.1% of the population—were living in poverty in the U.S.[37] While poverty may not always directly worsen health or increase health care spending, it does have far-ranging indirect effects. Living in poverty may affect a person's ability to get proper care as a child, leading to unchecked conditions later in life. It may affect the ability to get off work for appointments or to find work that even offers health insurance. It may correlate with education and ability to understand health information. It may affect the ability to afford needed prescriptions or to buy healthy, nutritious food.

You get the idea. All of these examples and more adversely affect the health of millions, and poor health increases the health care costs needed for treatment. The U.S. health care system feels the effects of poverty in two ways: first, as an effect on health that physicians address without any ability to change; second, by swelling the ranks—and increasing the costs—of public insurance programs.

Constraints of Rural and Urban Life

Rural individuals' ability to access care and maintain positive health status can be compromised by outside forces. A higher percentage of rural Americans are uninsured, and there are fewer physicians per capita in rural areas. Similar to those living in poverty, lack of access affects health status, which ultimately affects the cost of care.

Lack of Patient Education (Health Literacy)

Normally, we think of literacy as the ability to comprehend the written word. Certainly, reading ability affects health literacy, but it's about more than that. A person's knowledge of anatomy (e.g., where the stomach is), body functioning (e.g., that the kidneys process urine), and basic medication information (e.g., don't take medicine on an empty stomach) has a huge impact on how she approaches both wellness and disease.

Gap between basic and specialized knowledge:

- ▸ **Clinical:** Low health literacy is quite widespread in society—even PhDs complain about not understanding their physicians—and a large, nationwide study showed that only 12% of Americans had proficient health literacy.[38] In a world of ever-increasing knowledge, it's understandable that those who don't specialize in medicine might not know much about it; in the world of health care, it's understandable that health professionals might forget what their patients don't know. Thus, encouraging both general patient education as well as physician "plain speech" are important goals.
- ▸ **Research:** Biomedical research gets published in science journals, using standards, statistical analysis, and jargon that leave the lay reader scratching his head. Even with good health literacy and plain speaking in appointments, it's unrealistic to expect even the educated patient to know how to evaluate recent medical evidence. Patients must trust that their physicians keep up with the literature, and this has implications for shared decision-making.

Health disparities: Disparities arise in both access and quality of health care, and they're influenced by socioeconomic status, gender, sexuality, geography, ethnicity, language, and culture. All of these categories may influence health literacy as well, but it's interesting to note that low reading literacy is the single best predictor of poor health status.[39] In addition, those with chronic diseases are more likely to have limited literacy.[40] It makes sense that people who have trouble reading their medication labels and understanding their physicians might have difficulty managing their diseases, and this difficulty has implications not just for individual health status, but also for costs and population health.

Misinformation: We live in an era of incredible access to information; however, not all of that information is correct. The media can be misleading ("Carrots Will Kill You," then, six months later: "Carrots Are a Superfood"). And the Internet can be both the best and the worst friend a doctor ever had ("Doc, I have a runny nose, and I read on the Internet that might mean I have lupus!"). Obviously the media and Internet can be an enormous help, but sometimes they function to confuse, too.

Patients may lack understanding of many aspects of health care:

▸ How to stay healthy
▸ What their physicians tell them
▸ Reading instructions
▸ What their diseases are
▸ Evaluating the different options to treat their diseases
▸ Understanding their medicines and how to properly take them
▸ Evaluating medical literature and evidence, technologies and procedures, and medical costs

The lack of understanding on that list can have wide-reaching consequences on behavior. We see them in the following ways:

▸ Over-reliance on physicians, e.g., never getting a second opinion or always taking physicians' orders without sharing your own opinion
▸ Under-reliance on physicians, e.g., believing Jenny McCarthy about vaccines or using crystals to cure cancer.
▸ Mismanagement of health, e.g., eating unhealthily or not using condoms with new sexual partners.
▸ Mismanagement of disease, e.g., skipping pills or eating high-sugar foods as a diabetic

‣ Over-prioritizing innovation, e.g., wanting the newest technology, even when it may not be the actual best

‣ Over-prioritizing cost, e.g., not going to the ED even when you really need to because it costs too much

And these behaviors have consequences for health care and the population at large:

‣ Lack of shared decision-making

‣ Increased costs (through over-prioritizing innovation and mismanagement of health or disease)

‣ Decreased health

It's often stated that increased patient involvement in health care will solve the three above consequences. However, looking at these lists of consequences (ignorance leads to behavior, which leads to increased costs and poorer health outcomes) should indicate that it's not so simple. As ThinkProgress commentator Matthew Yglesias puts it, "People have been earning a living as medical professionals for a *long* time. And yet everybody knows that the invention of actually useful medical treatments is a pretty recent development. Surely this tells us something about the nature of the health care consumer's ability to find and purchase cost-effective treatments."[41]

We can see that it's not so simple to ask someone who doesn't understand what an MRI does or how to read a prescription to play a larger role in health care decisions. The information revolution does pose solutions, like being able to email physicians, check WebMD.com for symptoms, or see lab results online, but these may entail difficulties of their own. It's also unclear what coordinated effort it might take to solve the widespread problems of lack of patient education and poor health literacy.

Issues

Defraying Costs

There are, of course, many ways to keep costs low, ranging from using fewer services to paying physicians less to shifting costs onto patients to eliminating avoidable bureaucracy. We're just going to look at two economic concepts you might not be familiar with.

QUALITY-ADJUSTED LIFE YEARS

When researchers are studying new drugs and procedures, they often look to see if these treatments increase life expectancy—if patients live longer, that's undoubtedly a good thing. However, most people would prefer eight years without medical problems to 10 years in a coma; thus, the introduction of quality-adjusted life years (QALY), which adjust total life expectancy by the quality of those years. For example, a year of perfect health would rank as 1 QALY as a baseline while a year of blindness might be 0.5 QALYs. The use of QALY is an attempt to turn medical outcomes into a clear-cut equation, allowing prioritizing of decision making. The QALY is then used as a measure of analyzing effectiveness (in medicine) and of determining how to prioritize treatment (in policy).

QALYs are used in comparative effectiveness research and will be used by the newly established Patient-Centered Outcomes Research Institute (PCORI), though PCORI is banned from using dollars-adjusted QALYs as some other nations do. (See Chapter 5 for more information about PCORI.) For instance, the UK has a threshold of acceptable costs-per-QALY which is used in evaluating new drugs for coverage.

Consequences of High Costs

RATIONING

Health care is a limited resource: there are restrictions on money, on providers, on time, on supplies, on technology. While it would be ideal for everyone in America to receive the kind of care that Bill Gates must receive, it simply isn't possible. Unless all world resources are devoted to health care, rationing must exist.

We already do it. The current U.S. system rations by restricting access based on ability to pay. All suggested, potential reform plans include rationing, too—even if they simply preserve the current practice.

The real question is how to choose a method that is most fair and efficient. Different ways to arrange a system of rationing may be:

- By how much a given treatment will extend a patient's life (e.g., prioritize expensive, lifesaving measures for the young or otherwise healthy rather than for the elderly or very ill)
- By a patient's ability to pay (e.g., high deductibles for patients or low reimbursements for providers)
- By first come, first served (e.g., a waiting list, like those for transplants)
- By comparative effectiveness (e.g., prioritize treatments that have been proven to work well)

Rationing often gets criticized by pundits and politicians as an erosion of our rights, and certainly it feels appalling to prioritize some lives over others. However, as the ethicist Peter Singer notes,[42] "For every patient we hear about in Britain who has to wait three months for a hip replacement or cannot get an experimental cancer treatment funded, there are thousands of Americans who cannot afford a wheelchair or the standard-of-care chemotherapy medication." Every system rations in some way, and each system has pros and cons. To understand health care, you must acknowledge and comprehend the ways that care is rationed and the effects of that rationing.

MEDICAL BANKRUPTCY

In 2001, a study showed that half of all U.S. bankruptcies were medical bankruptcies.[43] A medical bankruptcy means that medical bills and income lost due to illness were a significant (but not necessarily the only) contributor to a person or family going broke.

In 2007, the same authors released an updated study showing that the percentage of medical bankruptcies had increased to 62.1%.[44] The authors suggest that the percentage growth was due to increasing medical costs and increasing numbers of uninsured and underinsured citizens.

Considering that 727,167 people filed for bankruptcy that year,[45] this means that just under half a million people did so at least in part because they had so much medical debt they could no longer survive economically. As the study states, "Most medical debtors were well-educated, owned homes, and had middle-class occupations. Three-quarters had health insurance."[44] This may challenge many people's ideas about bankruptcy and those who file for it, though it becomes easier to understand in context of annual or lifetime limits on what most insurance policies will pay. Annual and lifetime limits will no longer be permitted with the implementation of the ACA.

Some critics, such as Megan McArdle of *The Atlantic Monthly*, argue that the authors' definition of medical bankruptcy used to determine those figures is too inclusive and that the magnitude of the problem is somewhat overstated.[46] However, no matter what you think of the researchers' methods, and no matter your politics, everyone agrees that it's a problem when people are forced to go bankrupt due to medical problems. Therefore, if an increasing number of people are forced down that path, then it can be an argument for increasing funding for a heath care safety net (and perhaps even increasing the already astronomical percentage of GDP the U.S. spends on health care). But not only would different ideologies differ on what the safety net measures should be, they may also differ, as McArdle does, on whether medical bills are truly creating a large enough bankruptcy issue to call for reform.

BEING UNINSURED

A few years ago, we were talking to an acquaintance about health care and the uninsured. She didn't see the big deal: "If a poor person gets cancer, they just go to a free clinic and it's covered, right? I mean, it's not like anyone's dying because they don't have insurance." Sadly, this mistaken view is held by far too many people. While there's some truth to this argument (free clinics, hospital charity care, and public programs *do* exist and help many uninsured folks), it's so simplistic as to be completely off the mark.

A lot of research has been done on the uninsured: who they are, how they access care, how they do or don't pay for it, what the financial impacts are for society, and what the health impacts are for these individuals. An excellent resource is the Kaiser Family Foundation's *The Uninsured: A Primer*,[7] which is published yearly. All of the following facts are taken from that document (which you really should read in full).

Characteristics

- 61% of the uninsured are from families with at least one full-time worker, and 16% are from families with at least one part-time worker. 90% have a family income below 400% of the federal poverty level.
- Young adults (age 19-25) have the highest uninsured rate of any age group: 30%.
- 60% of uninsured, nonelderly adults have no education past high school.
- 81% of the uninsured are U.S. citizens. They comprise 32% of Hispanics, 14% of Whites, and 22% of African-Americans.
- They are more than twice as likely to report being in fair or poor health as those with private insurance. Almost half of all uninsured, nonelderly adults have a chronic medical condition.
- More than 70% have gone without health coverage for over a year.

Access to Care

- About 26% of uninsured adults have forgone care in the past year (with more than 25% not filling a drug prescription) because of cost, compared to 4% of the insured.
- The uninsured are diagnosed in later stages of diseases, including cancer, and die earlier than those with insurance. They are also more likely to be hospitalized, where they receive fewer diagnostic and therapeutic services, and are more likely to die in the hospital than the insured.
- When uninsured patients turn 65 and gain Medicare coverage, their access to care improves, their use of preventive care increases, and their overall health improves.

Finances

- Hospitals frequently charge uninsured patients two to four times what insurers actually pay for services. Less than half of low-income uninsured adults report that they have received free or reduced-cost care in the past year.
- In 2010, 27% of uninsured adults used up all or most of their savings paying medical bills. Half of uninsured households had $600

or less in total assets, compared to median assets of $5,500 for insured households.

Care Compensation

▸ In 2008, the average uninsured individual incurred $1,686 in health costs (compared to $4,463 for the nonelderly insured).

▸ The uninsured paid for about a third of this care out of pocket. About 75% of the remaining, uncompensated cost was paid by federal, state, and local funds appropriated for care of the uninsured, which accounts for about 2% of total health care spending.

▸ 60% of uncompensated care costs are incurred by hospitals. Most government dollars are paid indirectly based on the share of uncompensated care each hospital provides.

▸ The percent of all physicians who provide charity care fell from 76% in 1996-97 to 68% in 2004-05.

Hospital-Specific Issues

Certificate of Need

Certificate of Need (CON) laws require a new facility, usually a hospital, to prove that there is a need for such services in the area before construction can be approved by the city or region. Thus, they allow local governments to have some control over the planning of and access to new services and facilities. These laws first appeared in the 1960s and remain today, to varying degrees, in 36 states.[47] The regulations may apply not just to new hospitals, but also to new centers in old ones (e.g., a new cardiac clinic). There are arguments both for and against them.

CON Laws Help	CON Laws Hurt
▶ Market solutions are flawed for health care, and thus regulatory measures are necessary to control cost	▶ Other regulatory measures, such as payment streamlining in Medicare, could control cost just as well or better
▶ Regulation maintains competition while blocking the concentration of limited resources on one location or specialty	▶ CON laws actually hamper competition and may keep costs higher
	▶ These laws are inconsistently applied
▶ Increase quality due to the regulatory oversight of current hospitals	▶ Political influence is not the best measure for planning health facilities; it should be left up to institutions who survey the markets they wish to enter
▶ The laws allow policymakers to distribute care to all demographic and geographical areas; they can give preference to requests that maintain equal access throughout an area	

Aggregate Hospital Payment-to-cost Ratios for Private Payers, Medicare, and Medicaid, 1989–2009

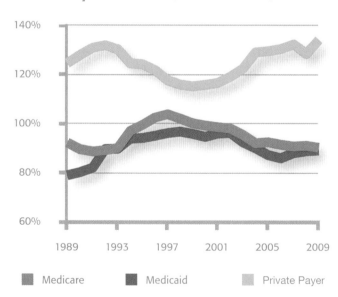

American Hospital Association Chartbook, "Aggregate Hospital Payment-to-Cost Ratios for Private Payers, Medicare, and Medicaid, 1989 – 2009," March 2011.

Note: Includes Medicaid Disproportionate Share payments.

Underpayment

Uncompensated care and undercompensated care are major problems for many hospitals. Uncompensated care includes both charity care (which the hospital gives away for free and doesn't expect to recover) and debt (which the hospital tries to recover from patients, who are often uninsured, and may end up covering by charging insurers more). In 2010, 4,985 hospitals reported $39.3 billion in uncompensated care, which made up 5.8% of their total expenses. This amount has increased tenfold, from $3.9 billion, in the past 20 years, though the percentage has remained steady.[48]

As the American Hospital Association (AHA) states, "Payment rates for Medicare and Medicaid, with the exception of managed care plans, are set by law rather than through a negotiation process as with private insurers. These payment rates are currently set below the costs of providing care, resulting in underpayment."[49] In 2009, the AHA found, Medicare compensated only 90% of costs, and Medicaid compensated only 89% of costs; combined, this made up $36.5 billion in lost revenue.[49] Some of this lost revenue is made up by charging private insurers a higher rate, a process that is known as "cost shifting."

This means that nearly 12% of hospital care goes uncompensated (though keep in mind this is an average—the amount will differ for different hospitals). That is clearly a problem and must be considered when evaluating downsizing, cutting costs, merging, or opening lucrative centers and closing charitable ones.

Emergency Department Issues

In the late 1980s, as health care costs and levels of uninsured patients were rising, there were concerns about EDs turning away patients who couldn't afford care. To combat this, Congress passed the Emergency Medical Treatment and Active Labor Act (EMTALA) for all Medicare-participating hospitals.[50] EMTALA requires that EDs screen all presenting patients to determine whether they have an emergency condition and stabilize patients who are deemed to have one. (Some may be transferred without stabilization, but this can only be with a signed physician's explanation under certain conditions.)

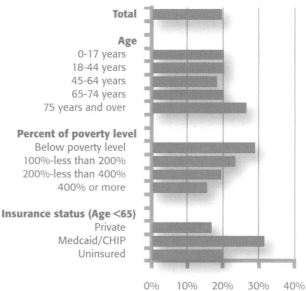

Percentage of Population Who Visited the ED One or More Times in the Past Year

Garcia, et al. "Emergency Department Visitors and Visits: Who Used the Emergency Room in 2007?," National Center for Health Statistics, May 2010.

Note: Private, Medicaid, and uninsured categories are mutually exclusive. Persons with both private and Medicaid coverage are categorized as having private coverage. Poverty status is based on family income and family size and composition using U.S. Census Bureau poverty thresholds.

The groups with the largest ED usage rates are Medicaid recipients, individuals under the federal poverty limit, and the elderly,[51] though we should note that these groups may overlap. These groups have higher-than-average rates of chronic medical conditions,[52] which often require expensive, ongoing care in an environment that is already very expensive. And all three groups tend to be insured by the government, which, as we have seen, reimburses hospitals under cost. Thus, EDs are very expensive and money-losing enterprises for hospitals to maintain. (At the same time, they're a major point of entry for inpatients and will always be necessary.)

This may contribute to why the number of EDs declined from 5,108 to 4,564 between 1991 and 2010. During the same period, though, ED visits rose from 88 million to 127 million.[53] As such, some EDs in large urban areas operate on "diversion" (meaning they turn away all but the most severe cases to other hospitals) and have hours-long wait times.

Some suggested solutions to overcrowded, costly EDs have been to reduce the utilization of tests and procedures (which some claim is due to defensive medicine) or to increase the availability of community-based outpatient care centers like urgent care or retail clinics (page 20), which can attend to medical issues that may be urgent to the patient but are not otherwise necessary to handle in an ED. For instance, the CDC reports that nearly one-third of ED visits are semi-urgent or non-urgent and could be handled in other facilities.[53]

Medical Malpractice

Patients who believe they have been injured in some way by a health care provider can file a medical malpractice claim. To prove malpractice, the patient must show that the injury was caused by the provider's negligence, meaning that he or she didn't practice medicine consistent with the accepted standard of care. If a patient wins a case or a favorable settlement, the health care provider may have to compensate the patient for loss of income due to injury and for noneconomic losses, such as pain and suffering. Although most malpractice claims are made against physicians, claims can be brought against any health care provider, including students. To protect against the financial risk of future malpractice lawsuits, most physicians purchase malpractice insurance. Hospitals and health care networks often purchase insurance for their employees, while independent physicians typically purchase their own policies.

Why Have It?

As discussed in Chapter 1, the 1999 Institute of Medicine report *To Err is Human* estimated that between 44,000 and 98,000 Americans die in hospitals due to medical errors every year.[54] Obviously, this is a serious problem. One way to tackle it is by improving quality internally—ranging from hiring more nurses to instituting checklists for surgical safety—and another way is by external discipline of those who err. Medical malpractice claims are a way both for individual patients to recover damages as well as for society to censure physicians who have erred.

A few key facts about medical malpractice:

- More than 75% of physicians will have at least one malpractice claim brought against them by the age of 65. For those in high-risk specialties such as general surgery, the rate is 99%.[55]
- The cost of malpractice insurance varies dramatically by location and specialty. Premiums for a general internist in rural California run around $3,500 per year, while those of OB/GYNs in Miami cost $150,000 or more.[56,57]
- The overwhelming majority of patients who receive negligent care don't file malpractice claims.[58]
- Only one-fifth of malpractice claims result in payment to the patient, and the average payment is $275,000. However, proving that there's no liability isn't cheap either—averaging $110,000 for a successful trial defense, and $22,000 even if the claim is dropped, withdrawn, or dismissed before making it to the courtroom.[59]
- As shown below, Americans are much more likely to file malpractice claims than patients in other countries—four times more than Canadians, for example.

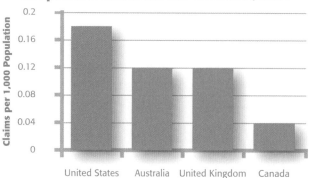

Malpractice Claims in Four Countries, 2001

Data from Anderson et al. "Health Spending in the United States and the Rest of the Industrialized World," Health Affairs, Jul/Aug 2005.

Problems It Creates

Costs to Providers: These costs are both economic and psychological. Some physicians pay exorbitant rates for their malpractice insurance. Economically, this may inhibit a physician's ability to maintain a private practice and affect what field she chooses to enter. Many physicians think malpractice insurance premiums are a major problem, and their feelings on this matter may be extrapolated from their behavior: when Texas passed tort reform in 2003, the state saw medical license applications jump from 2,561 in 2003 to 4,041 in 2007, an unprecedented increase.[i,60]

Defensive Medicine: The fear of litigation has caused a shift in the way that physicians provide care to patients, which is known as "defensive medicine." There are two types of defensive medicine: positive, in which physicians overuse services to "cover their bases" in case of a lawsuit, rather than to practice good medicine; and negative, in which physicians avoid high-risk patients and procedures they fear could be a higher risk for litigation. This isn't just a theoretical problem—in recent surveys, more than four out of five specialist physicians report practicing positive defensive medicine.[61,62]

- ▸ **Quality:** Positive defensive medicine leads to the use of tests and procedures, such as MRIs or colonoscopies, when not medically necessary. Not only can this expose patients to procedural risks for very little possibility of a finding, but it also may turn up benign findings, leading to more procedures and more risks—providing no increased, and perhaps even decreased, health benefit.
- ▸ **Cost:** Defensive medicine is how medical malpractice indirectly raises health care costs, as the above-mentioned tests and procedures tend to be very expensive. Although calculating the true cost of defensive medicine is an inexact science, a recent study by researchers at Harvard estimated that the total cost in 2008 was $38 billion in hospital services and $6.8 billion in physician and clinical (outpatient) services,[63] accounting for 5.2% and 1.3% of total spending in those categories.[13]

---

i   Opinions vary on the true effect of tort reform and the increase of license applications. A group of legal researchers concluded in 2008 that "[Tort reform] does not appear to have had a large effect on the supply of Direct Patient Care physicians. A delayed effect remains possible. There is also no dramatic upswing in specialists in high lawsuit-risk areas, but some evidence of a modest upturn, relative to the immediate pre-reform period."[68]

Costs to Patients: Patients without good insurance coverage will often end up paying very large bills, in part due to defensive medicine (for instance, the average cost of an ED visit was $1,265 in 2008).[64] In addition, if patients do encounter medical errors, it's extremely unlikely that they will receive a malpractice pay-out. Several barriers are in their way:

▸ A patient has to convince a lawyer to take on his or her case. Considering that most malpractice plaintiffs' lawyers are paid via a percentage of the settlement, and considering the high costs of litigating malpractice lawsuits regardless of the victor, patients must have clear-cut cases with large damages to entice most lawyers. This means that most patients who experience medical errors face difficulties in establishing lawsuits and thus have no recourse for compensation.

▸ Patients must convince juries to find in their favor. Regardless of the reasons, right or wrong, this just isn't likely: most claims are settled, withdrawn or dropped before making it to trial, and 90% of those that do go to a jury trial are found in favor of the physician.[59]

In addition, many feel that the psychological environment created by our current system of medical malpractice erodes the trusting relationship necessary for good medicine—which is bad for both physicians and patients.

Potential Solutions

General Fund/No Fault: In his book, *Better*, Atul Gawande suggests replacing the tort system with the system used for vaccines. He writes, "American vaccines now carry a seventy-five-cent surcharge (about 15 percent of total costs), which goes into a fund for children who are injured by them. The program does not waste effort trying to sort those who are injured through negligence from those who are injured through bad luck. An expert panel has enumerated the known injuries from vaccines, and, if you have one, the fund provides compensation for medical and other expenses. If you're not satisfied, you can sue in court. But few have."[65] New Zealand has such a system for medical errors, though it limits pay-outs to rare and severe outcomes to limit costs. If we adopted this system, we would need to either rely on professional organizations or develop some other method to censure and dismiss bad physicians.

Arbitration: A growing trend among clinics and hospitals is to require mandatory arbitration agreements, meaning that patients can't sue for damages but must enter into arbitration instead.

The benefits of this system are that costs are kept low for both parties, arbitrations can happen more quickly than lawsuits, and patients don't need "rainmaker" cases to convince lawyers to represent them. The draw-backs of this system are that patients must sign binding arbitration agreements before receiving care, arbitration pay-outs are often capped at levels that may be low (i.e., $250,000), and providers may reject arbitrators who decide in favor of patients too often (i.e., skewed decision-making).

Health Courts: Philip Howard, a New York attorney and founder of the legal reform organization Common Good, suggests keeping the courts but bypassing the juries. In Howard's conception, "Expert judges with special training would resolve health care disputes. They would issue written rulings providing guidance on proper standards of care. These rulings would set precedents on which both patients and physicians could rely. As with existing administrative courts in other areas of law—for tax disputes, workers' compensation, and vaccine liability, among others—there would be no juries. Each ruling could be appealed to a new medical appeals court."[66]

Tort Reform: In general, tort reform seeks to cap damage pay-outs and block frivolous lawsuits. California was the first to enact tort reform, in 1975, when it passed the Medical Injury Compensation Reform Act. This act contains five stipulations:

- Noneconomic damages are capped at $250,000
- Attorney's fees are capped
- The statute of limitations on medical errors is shortened
- Arbitration is binding
- Physicians can pay damages in installments rather than in a lump sum

Many other states have enacted tort reform in varying ways, including 21 that limit non-economic damages.[57] Proponents of these reforms claim that they reduce the number of frivolous lawsuits as well as the emphasis on defensive medicine. Opponents claim that, in addition to punishing patients whose damages truly are higher than the cap, they're ineffective in reducing medical errors and costs.

Medical malpractice and how to fix it appears to be a mess—a crucially important mess, based on how often it comes up in society. Which raises the question: Is the problem overstated?

Health services researcher Aaron Carroll made the graph shown below to illustrate the costs of medical malpractice in the context of total health spending.[67] While the costs of defensive medicine—$45 billion—are nothing to sneeze at, it's also clearly not the primary driver of high health costs. Accordingly, Carroll indicates that tort reform will do little to reduce costs.

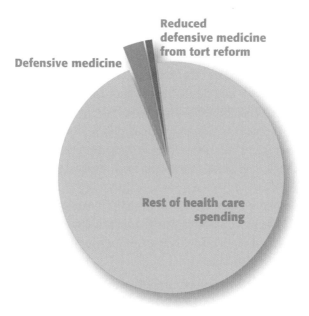

Costs of Defensive Medicine

Reduced defensive medicine from tort reform

Defensive medicine

Rest of health care spending

Aaron Carroll, "Meme-busting: Tort reform = cost control"
The Incidental Economist, June 2011. Used by permission.

Glossary

Catastrophic Insurance: An insurance plan that has a minimum of insulation. Such plans have low premiums with high co-pays or deductibles and cover costly, unexpected medical services, but not routine care.

Centers for Medicare & Medicaid Services (CMS): A Department of Health & Human Services (HHS) agency that oversees Medicare, Medicaid, CHIP, Health Insurance Portability and Accountability Act (HIPAA) regulations, nursing home accountability, quality improvement programs, and more.

Physician Shortage Area: The Health Resources and Services Administration and the National Health Services Corps within HHS work to define, locate, and help Health Professional Shortage Areas (HPSAs). For primary care physicians (PCPs), a shortage is defined as a population to PCP ratio of greater than 2000:1. See where these shortage areas are located by visiting http://bhpr.hrsa.gov/shortage/.

Pre-Existing Condition: A medical condition that was present before enrollment in an insurance plan. Today, regulations about pre-existing conditions vary by state, but many insurers can charge higher premiums for customers with such conditions. Also, patients already enrolled in insurance plans may have cost reimbursement denied if the company determines the care was necessary for a pre-existing condition.

Sensitivity and Specificity: Statistical methods of measuring the effectiveness of any test. In a screening test for a medical condition, the sensitivity is the percentage of people with the condition who are detected by the test, and the specificity is the percentage of people without the condition who are not detected by the test. A perfect test is 100% sensitive (no false negatives) and 100% specific (no false positives).

Urgent Care: Outpatient care for patients with conditions that require prompt attention but are not true emergencies. Urgent care is for patients who cannot wait to make an appointment with a PCP but don't need to visit the ED. Many urgent care centers are open later than regular physicians' offices but aren't open 24/7 like hospital emergency departments.

Suggested Reading

Crisis of Abundance: Rethinking How We Pay for Healthcare, by Arnold Kling. *This book, written by a libertarian economist, proposes a specific reform plan; however, he spends much of the book discussing the trade-offs that must be dealt with in any health care system.*

Health at Risk: America's Ailing Health System – And How to Heal It, by Jacob Hacker, et al. *This text combines several papers, including the Elizabeth Warren article referenced in this chapter, displaying research on a range of subjects. It doesn't really give a specific plan for "healing."*

Mama Might Be Better Off Dead, by Laurie Kaye Abraham. *This author followed a poor Chicago family with a host of medical and financial problems for a year in 1989. Though some of the obstacles presented are now outdated (and more will be outdated after 2014), a surprising number are still relevant. It gives an excellent view into what it's like to be sick and on Medicaid.*

The Incidental Economist, http://theincidentaleconomist.com/. *A fantastic blog that's regularly updated with crucial insights and analysis of health economics and health policy.*

The Social Transformation of American Medicine and ***Remedy and Reaction***, by Paul Starr. *The former is a history book, not strictly on insurance or economics, which describes how the issues in this chapter arose in the U.S., and which will likely forever affect how you view them. Also, it was written in 1980 but is still the definitive text and completely worth reading. The second book listed was written in 2011 and details the history of health care reform— including the ACA—in America.*

The Wall Street Journal Health Blog, http://blogs.wsj.com/health/. *This isn't so much a blog as it is a directed news source for health care and politics.*

References

1. Kling AS. *Crisis of abundance: Rethinking how we pay for health care.* Cato Inst; 2006.
2. Publication 969 - Main Content. http://www.irs.gov/publications/p969/ar02.html#en_US_2011_publink1000204020. Internal Revenue Service. Accessed May 5, 2012.
3. Health Care Costs: A Primer. http://www.kff.org/insurance/7670.cfm. Kaiser Family Foundation. Accessed May 5, 2012.
4. Medical Loss Ratio: Getting Your Money's Worth on Health Insurance. http://www.healthcare.gov/news/factsheets/2010/11/medical-loss-ratio.html. U.S. Department of Health & Human Services. Accessed Apr 7 2012.

5. Iglehart JK. Defining Medical Expenses — An Early Skirmish over Insurance Reforms. *N Engl J Me*d. 2010;363(11):999-1001. http://dx.doi.org/10.1056/NEJMp1008571.

6. Blumenthal D. Employer-Sponsored Health Insurance in the United States — Origins and Implications. *New England Journal of Medicine*. 2006;355(1):82-88. http://dx.doi.org/10.1056/NEJMhpr060703.

7. Streeter S, Howard J, Licata R, Garfield R, Lawton E, Chen V. The Uninsured: A Primer. http://www.kff.org/uninsured/upload/7451-07.pdf. Kaiser Family Foundation. Accessed Apr 12, 2012.

8. Employer Health Benefits 2011 Annual Survey. http://ehbs.kff.org/. The Kaiser Family Foundation and Health Research & Educational Trust. Accessed May 5, 2012.

9. Mandated Benefits, Offers, and Coverages for Accident & Health Insurance and HMOs. http://insurance.illinois.gov/healthinsurance/mandated_benefits.asp. Illinois Department of Insurance. Accessed May 5, 2012.

10. Employer Health Benefits : 2007 Summary of Findings. http://www.kff.org/insurance/7672/upload/Summary-of-Findings-EHBS-2007.pdf. Kaiser Family Foundation. Accessed Sept 14, 2011.

11. Snapshots: Employer Health Insurance Costs & Worker Compensation February 2011. http://www.kff.org/insurance/snapshot/Employer-Health-Insurance-Costs-and-Worker-Compensation.cfm. Kaiser Family Foundation. Accessed Aug 5, 2011.

12. Snapshots: Trends in Employer-Sponsored Health Insurance Offer Rates for Workers in Private Businesses, September 2010. http://www.kff.org/insurance/snapshot/chcm091610oth.cfm. Kaiser Family Foundation. Accessed Aug 5, 2011.

13. National Health Expenditure Data https://www.cms.gov/NationalHealthExpendData/. Centers for Medicare & Medicaid Services. Accessed Apr 7, 2012.

14. Gold J. The 'Underinsurance' Problem Explained. http://www.kaiserhealthnews.org/Stories/2009/September/28/underinsured-explainer.aspx. Kaiser Health News. Accessed Apr 12, 2012.

15. Schoen C, Collins SR, Kriss JL, Doty MM. How Many Are Underinsured? Trends Among U.S. Adults, 2003 And 2007. *Health affair*s. 2008;27(4):w298-w309.

16. Bodenheimer TS, Grumbach K. *Understanding health policy.* 5th ed. New York: McGraw-Hill; 2009.

17. Rosenthal MB, Dudley RA. Pay-for-Performance. *JAMA: The Journal of the American Medical Associatio*n. 2007;297(7):740-744.

18. Gottlober P. Medicare hospital prospective payment system: How DRG rates are calculated and updated. *Office of the Inspector Genera*l. 2001.

19. Relative Value Units. http://www.nhpf.org/library/the-basics/Basics_RVUs_02-12-09.pdf. National Health Policy Forum. Accessed Aug 26, 2011.

20. CodeManager: cpt Code/Relative Value Search. https://ocm.ama-assn.org/OCM/CPTRelativeValueSearch.do. American Medical Association. Accessed Aug 26, 2011.

21. Cuckler G, Martin A, Whittle L, et al. Health spending by state of residence, 1991-2009. *Medicare & medicaid research revie*w. 2011;1(4):10.5600/mmrr.001.04.a03.

22. Jensen RT, Miller NH. Giffen behavior and subsistence consumption. *The American Economic Revie*w. 2008;98(4):1553.

23. Chronic Diseases and Health Promotion. http://www.cdc.gov/chronicdisease/overview/index.htm. Centers for Disease Control and Prevention. Accessed Aug 5, 2011.

24. Hogan C, Lunney J, Gabel J, Lynn J. Medicare Beneficiaries' Costs Of Care In The Last Year Of Life. *Health affairs*. 2001;20(4):188-195.

25. Duncan D. What Price For Medical Miracles? High Costs At End Of Life Still Part Of National Health Debate. http://www.kaiserhealthnews.org/Stories/2010/March/09/fiscal-times-end-of-life.aspx. Kaiser Health News. Accessed 08/05, 2011.

26. Gawande A. The Cost Conundrum. http://www.newyorker.com/reporting/2009/06/01/090601fa_fact_gawande?currentPage=all. The New Yorker. Accessed Aug 5, 2011.

27. Income, Poverty, and Health Insurance Coverage in the United States: 2009. http://www.census.gov/prod/2010pubs/p60-238.pdf. US Census Bureau. Accessed Aug 5, 2011.

28. Physicians and Surgeons. http://www.bls.gov/oco/ocos074.htm. Bureau of Labor Statistics. Accessed Aug 5, 2011.

29. Fisher ES, Wennberg DE, Stukel TA, Gottlieb DJ, Lucas FL, Pinder ÉL. The Implications of Regional Variations in Medicare Spending. Part 1: The Content, Quality, and Accessibility of Care. *Annals of Internal Medicine*. 2003;138(4):273-287.

30. Goodman DC, Fisher ES. Physician Workforce Crisis? Wrong Diagnosis, Wrong Prescription. *N Engl J Med*. 2008;358(16):1658-1661. http://dx.doi.org/10.1056/NEJMp0800319.

31. Ogden C, Carroll M. Prevalence of Overweight, Obesity, and Extreme Obesity Among Adults: United States, Trends 1960–1962 Through 2007–2008. http://www.cdc.gov/NCHS/data/hestat/obesity_adult_07_08/obesity_adult_07_08.pdf. National Center for Health Statistics. Accessed Sept 14, 2011.

32. Cawley J, Meyerhoefer C. The medical care costs of obesity: an instrumental variables approach. *Journal of Health Economics*. 2011.

33. Finkelstein EA, Trogdon JG, Cohen JW, Dietz W. Annual Medical Spending Attributable To Obesity: Payer-And Service-Specific Estimates. *Health Affairs*. September/October 2009;28(5):w822-w831.

34. Dept. of Health and Human Services, Centers for Disease Control and Prevention, National Center for Chronic Disease Prevention and Health Promotion, Office on Smoking and Health. *The health consequences of smoking: A report of the surgeon general.* Washington, D.C.: U.S. G.P.O.; 2004.

35. Haynes RB, McDonald H, Garg AX, Montague P. Interventions for helping patients to follow prescriptions for medications. *Cochrane database of systematic reviews (Online)*. 2002;(2)(2):CD000011.

36. 2012 HHS Poverty Guidelines. http://aspe.hhs.gov/poverty/12poverty.shtml#guidelines. Department of Health & Human Services. Accessed Apr 13, 2012.

37. Poverty. http://www.census.gov/hhes/www/poverty/about/overview/index.html. US Census Bureau. Accessed Apr 12, 2012.

38. National Assessment of Adult Literacy (NAAL) - Health Literacy - Highlights of Findings. http://nces.ed.gov/naal/health_results.asp. National Center for Education Statistics. Accessed Aug 5, 2011.

39. Lagay F. Reducing the Effects of Low Health Literacy. *Virtual Mentor*. 2003;5(6).

40. Health Literacy Fact Sheet. http://www.chcs.org/usr_doc/Health_Literacy_Fact_Sheets.pdf. Center for Health Care Strategies, Inc. Accessed Aug 5, 2011.

41. Yglesias M. Adventures in 18th Century Health Care. http://thinkprogress.org/yglesias/2011/06/07/238890/adventures-in-18th-century-health-care/. ThinkProgress. Accessed Aug 5, 2011.

42. Singer P. Why we must ration health care. *New York Times*. Jul 15, 2009 Accessed Aug 5, 2011.

43. Sullivan TA, Warren E, Westbrook JL. *The fragile middle class: Americans in debt.* New Haven: Yale University Press; 2000:380.

44. Himmelstein DU, Thorne D, Warren E, Woolhandler S. Medical bankruptcy in the United States, 2007: results of a national study. *The American Journal of Medicine*. 2009;122(8):741-746.

45. Jones K. Ada vs Wall Street. http://www.thedailybeast.com/newsweek/2008/09/25/ada-vs-wall-street.html. Newsweek. Accessed Apr 12, 2012.

46. McArdle M. A Little More About Medical Bankruptcy. http://www.theatlantic.com/business/archive/2010/02/a-little-more-about-medical-bankruptcy/35919/. The Atlantic. Accessed Apr 12, 2012.

47. Yee T, Stark L, Bond A, Carrier E. Health Care Certificate-of-Need Laws: Policy or Politics? http://www.nihcr.org/CON_Laws.pdf. National Institute for Health Care Reform. Accessed Apr 11, 2012.

48. Uncompensated Hospital Care Cost Fact Sheet. http://www.aha.org/content/12/11-uncompensated-care-fact-sheet.pdf. American Hospital Association. Accessed Apr 12, 2012.

49. Underpayment by Medicare and Medicaid Fact Sheet. www.aha.org/aha/content/2010/pdf/10medunderpayment.pdf. American Hospital Association. Accessed Aug 5, 2011.

50. Thorne J. EMTALA: The Basic Requirements, Recent Court Interpretations, and More HCFA Regulations to Come. http://www.aaem.org/emtala/watch.php. American Academy of Emergency Medicine. Accessed Aug 5, 2011.

51. Garcia T, Bernstein A, Bush M. Emergency Department Visitors and Visits: Who Used the Emergency Room in 2007? http://www.cdc.gov/nchs/data/databriefs/db38.htm#ref1. National Center for Health Statistics. Accessed Apr 12, 2011.

52. Newton MF, Keirns CC, Cunningham R, Hayward RA, Stanley R. Uninsured adults presenting to US emergency departments. *JAMA: the journal of the American Medical Association*. 2008;300(16):1914.

53. TrendWatch Chartbook. http://www.aha.org/research/reports/tw/chartbook/index.shtml. American Hospital Association. Accessed Aug 5, 2011.

54. Kohn LT, Corrigan J, Donaldson MS. *To err is human: Building a safer health system.* Vol 6. Natl Academy Pr; 2000.

55. Jena AB, Seabury S, Lakdawalla D, Chandra A. Malpractice Risk According to Physician Specialty. *N Engl J Med*. 2011;365(7):629-636. http://dx.doi.org/10.1056/NEJMsa1012370.

56. Medical Malpractice Insurance Rates by State. http://www.mymedicalmalpracticeinsurance.com/medical-malpractice-insurance-rates.php. . Accessed Apr 11, 2012.

57. Lowes R. Regional Variation in Malpractice Premiums Defies Tort Reform. http://www.medscape.com/viewarticle/731833. . Accessed Apr 11, 2012.

58. Studdert DM, Thomas EJ, Burstin HR, Zbar BIW, Orav EJ, Brennan TA. Negligent care and malpractice claiming behavior in Utah and Colorado. *Medical care*. 2000;38(3):250.

59. The Case for Medical Liability Reform. http://www.ama-assn.org/ama1/pub/upload/mm/-1/case-for-mlr.pdf. American Medical Association. Accessed Aug 5, 2011.

60. Sorrel A. Texas liability reforms spur plunge in premiums and lawsuits. http://www.ama-assn.org/amednews/2008/09/08/prl20908.htm. American Medical News. Accessed Aug 5, 2011.

61. Studdert DM, Mello MM, Sage WM, et al. Defensive Medicine Among High-Risk Specialist Physicians in a Volatile Malpractice Environment. *JAMA: The Journal of the American Medical Association*. 2005;293(21):2609-2617.

62. Investigation of Defensive Medicine in Massachusetts. http://www.massmed.org/AM/Template.cfm?Section=Research_Reports_and_Studies2&TEMPLATE=/CM/ContentDisplay.cfm&CONTENTID=27797. . Accessed Apr 7, 2012.

63. Mello MM, Chandra A, Gawande AA, Studdert DM. National Costs Of The Medical Liability System. *Health affairs*. 2010;29(9):1569-1577.

64. Medical Expenditure Panel Survey. http://www.meps.ahrq.gov/mepsweb/data_stats/tables_compendia_hh_interactive.jsp?_SERVICE=MEPSSocket0. Agency for Healthcare Research and Quality. Accessed Aug 5, 2011.

65. Gawande A. *Better: A surgeon's notes on performance.* 1st ed. New York: Metropolitan; 2007:273.

66. Establish Health Courts. http://www.commongood.org/pages/establish-health-courts. Accessed Apr 12, 2012.

67. Carroll A. Meme-busting: Tort reform = cost control. http://theincidentaleconomist.com/wordpress/meme-busting-tort-reform-cost-control-2/. The Incidental Economist. Accessed Sept 15, 2011.

68. Silver C, Hyman D, Black B. The Impact of the 2003 Texas Medical Malpractice Damages Cap on Physician Supply and Insurer Payouts: Separating Facts from Rhetoric. http://papers.ssrn.com/sol3/papers.cfm?abstract_id=1139190#. Social Science Research Network. Accessed Apr 13, 2012.

Chapter 4
Research, Pharmaceuticals, and Medical Devices

Many books about health care and health policy skip over information on research, pharmaceuticals, and medical devices. However, these industries form the backbone of the practice, cost, and experience of health care. In this chapter, you'll gain an overview of these important topics. Keep in mind, though, that this entire book is designed to be an overview rather than an in-depth study—many, many books have been filled with what we omit—which is especially true of this chapter.

The worlds of research, pharmaceuticals, and devices intersect and blur together. Let's look at what they are, how they work, and what issues arise from them as a whole.

Authors' note: This chapter focuses on a number of problems and issues in the world of research, pharmaceuticals, and devices but doesn't devote the same space to the incredible advancements in knowledge and practice that these areas have been able to achieve. We prioritize the problems in the limited space of this book because they're less likely to be familiar to the average reader. For a more complete picture of the positives and negatives of these industries, please see the Suggested Reading at the end of this chapter.

Research

BASIC RESEARCH

You can think of basic scientific research as the pure quest for knowledge. This quest covers an enormous range, from cellular components to organ structure and function, and from the interactions between organ systems to behavioral science. Being pre-clinical, basic research tends to take place in a lab and often involves living cells and tissue from both humans and animals. (It may involve live insects and larger animals as well.) Some examples of basic research include stem cell research, visualizing the structure of a viral envelope, sequencing a section of DNA, and finding the cellular mutations that cause cancer.

Some basic research may end up without any practical application; some—like the discovery of penicillin's bactericidal effects—may revolutionize medicine. The famous biologist Richard Dawkins wrote that basic science research "might be no use for anything at present, but it has great potential for the future."[1]

APPLIED RESEARCH

Applied research is similar to basic research, but with a practical end goal in mind. You can think of applied research as science with a direct purpose or application, or a quest for knowledge to solve problems we already know about. Examples include the development of gene therapies, testing potential cancer drugs, and the development of vaccines.

One type of applied research, known as translational research, focuses specifically on the application of basic science to human illness. Translational research usually includes multidisciplinary teams of researchers in medicine who work on different aspects of guiding the research process "from bench to bedside."

Basic and applied research necessarily overlap and feed into each other. For instance, the Human Genome Project involved a lot of research that is rapidly being applied in terms of diagnosis and disease processes, but many applications from the project remain to be discovered. Though immediate aims may not be obvious for all of genetics research, the impetus for sequencing the human genome is that it will someday be useful for developing new therapies.

CLINICAL RESEARCH

Clinical research is any scientific research that involves humans as subjects. This type of research is most commonly seen in clinical pharmaceutical trials, which test potential new drugs and treatments on humans to check for both efficacy as well as safety. The research question is no longer, "How does this compound interact with cancer cells?" nor even "Can this compound possibly block the growth of cancer cells?" but "Is this compound safe and useful enough to give to cancer patients?"

The scope of clinical research is not just the effect of drugs, though. It also looks at behavioral science. Behavioral research focuses on humans as well as on other animals in controlled examinations of decision, communication, and behavior processes within a social system. (It's similar to but distinct from social science, which focuses on the social framework itself and how it affects these processes.) For example, a clinical researcher may examine how patient-provider communication affects birth control choice and usage.

PUBLIC HEALTH RESEARCH

Public health research focuses on the health of a population. It also tends to focus more on prevention and wellness than other types of research. Public health research encompasses many disciplines including:

▸ **Epidemiology:** Uses statistics about a population to investigate the relationship between exposure or experience and disease processes (e.g., smoking and lung cancer).
▸ **Biostatistics:** The study design, data collection, and analysis processes of studies focused on living organisms (e.g., collecting data about smokers and lung cancer).
▸ **Population or Community Health:** Looks at what things affect the health of a community. A community is often defined geographically but may be, for instance, an ethnic or socioeconomic

community (e.g., why do African-Americans have higher rates of heart disease?).

▸ **Other Public Health Research:** Environmental health, behavioral health, and occupational health—all as they sound.

Another important subset is health services research, which focuses on the effectiveness of health systems, institutions, and delivery models and their resulting effects on cost, access, quality, and health outcomes. Examples may include examining how the adoption of electronic health records changes nursing behaviors, how the availability of generic drugs affects the treatment of uninsured patients, and what practices most reduce hospital-acquired infections.

You can think of these types of research as moving from looking at the trees (or even at the cells in a single leaf) to looking at the forest.

Institutions and Funding

Scientists perform research at a variety of public and private institutions. Funding for their activities may be provided by their own institution or by an outside group. Many for-profit corporations and government agencies keep everything in-house, employing scientists and funding their research. Things get more complex when more than one institution is involved; for example, a single scientist employed at a public university may pursue a project that draws on funding from the federal government, a non-profit organization, the host university, and private industry. Let's discuss the major players in the research world.

ACADEMIC

A large percentage of research scientists are employed by universities and medical colleges, where they educate students as well as conduct research. However, only 20% of research and development (R&D) completed at academic centers is funded by the host institution; the remainder is provided by federal, state, and local governments, and private industry.[2]

PUBLIC

Federal, state, and local government agencies are involved in all areas of the research process. Most medical research falls under the federal Department of Health & Human Services (HHS), which controls the National Institutes of Health (NIH), along with agencies that focus on health services research (Agency for Health Research and Quality), basic research (National Science Foundation), and public health research (Centers for Disease Control and Prevention), among others. A variety of other federal agencies also participate in research, including the Department of Defense and the National Institute of Food and Agriculture. Each of these agencies employs its own researchers as well as funds projects at other institutions. The NIH alone has nearly 6,000 scientists on staff and provides grant funding for another 325,000 researchers at outside institutions.[3]

INDUSTRY

Pharmaceutical, biotechnology, and medical technology companies often conduct research in their own institutions, with their own employees and labs. They also fund research performed at academic institutions.

PRIVATE NON-PROFIT

Private non-profit organizations in the research field usually fund outside scientists using a grant system similar to the NIH. However, some conduct research in-house as well. One example is the RAND Corporation, a relatively small organization that conducts health services research. An example of a much larger organization is the World Health Organization (WHO), part of the United Nations, which conducts public health research globally.

FUNDING

Research accounts for 1.9% of the total spending on health care in the U.S.[4] Here are the top funders of health research in 2010, according to the research advocacy group Research!America[5] (see next page):

Source	Funds	▶	Primary Research Focus
	Industry		
Pharmaceutical R&D	$37,371 Million	▶	Basic, Applied, and Clinical Research
Biotechnology R&D	$30,029M	▶	Basic and Applied Research
Medical Technology R&D	$9,122M	▶	Basic and Applied Research
	Federal Government		
National Institutes of Health	$34,829M	▶	All types
National Science Foundation	$2,914M	▶	Basic Research
Department of Defense	$2,667M	▶	Basic and Applied Research
Department of Agriculture	$1,265M	▶	Basic and Applied Research
Department of Energy	$1,037M	▶	Basic and Applied Research
Environmental Protection Agency	$596M	▶	Basic and Public Health Research
Department of Commerce	$588M	▶	Applied Research
Department of Veterans Affairs	$581M	▶	Applied Research
Centers for Disease Control and Prevention	$363M	▶	Public Health Research
Food and Drug Administration	$248M	▶	Clinical Research
Department of Homeland Security	$207M	▶	Basic Research
Department of the Interior	$205M	▶	Basic Research
NASA	$182M	▶	Basic, Applied, and Clinical Research
U.S. Agency of International Development	$158M	▶	All types
Centers for Medicare and Medicaid Services	$27M	▶	Clinical and Health Services Research
Health Resources and Services Administration	$8M	▶	Health Services Research
	Other Sources		
Universities (Institutional Funds)	$11,198	▶	All types
State and Local Governments	$3,647	▶	All types

Source	Funds	▶	Primary Research Focus
Independent Research Institutes	$1,259M	▶	All types
Philanthropic Foundations	$1,127M	▶	All types
Voluntary Health Associations	$877M	▶	All types
Total	$140 Million		

Research!America, "2010 U.S. Investment in Health Research," August 2011.

The Research Process

After completing a project, researchers summarize their methods, findings, and conclusions in a short article (a "paper") and submit this for publication in a scientific journal. At the journal, the article undergoes peer review, and the submission can be accepted, returned with a request for resubmission after changes, or denied. If the article is denied, the researchers can resubmit the paper to other journals. Today, there are over 20,000 active scientific journals publishing 1.35 million articles each year.[6] However, in private industry, some research is proprietary and not shared publicly.

Peer Review System

Richard Haldane was a British politician in the early 20th century who thought that research funds should be distributed according to what researchers, not politicians, thought most important. This mode of thinking (called the Haldane Principle) influenced British research policy throughout the 20th century, and, though there is no such official policy in the United States, the same sentiment helped to establish our current system of peer review. Peer review refers to the concept that medical or scientific practice and research should only be judged by others in the field—peers—who have a greater understanding of the material than the lay public.

Medical peer review encompasses both scientific research and clinical behavior. Articles submitted to scientific journals are judged by a committee comprised of researchers whose expertise is in the same field as the article. Each reviewer is given an advance copy of the article and may accept it as is, request revisions to the manuscript, or reject the article. Reviewers are expected to recuse themselves if they are working on the same project, so that conflict of interest will not bias the review.

Peer review is also used in clinical practice. Hospital discipline committees and expert witnesses at medical malpractice trials employ peer review to judge physicians' decisions. Who makes up the "peers" varies by situation and institution, but health professionals are usually evaluated by other members of their discipline (e.g., physical therapy) and specialty (e.g., cardiology).

The peer review system has many problems—in research, the veracity of the data is assumed (thus, the system is not designed to detect fraud), and scientists are often asked to objectively judge the work of their competitors. In clinical practice, the physicians who make up discipline committees are often co-workers, and the physician you are judging today may be judging you next week. Such practices can lead to leniency rather than rigorous challenges.

REGULATION AND OVERSIGHT

Anyone who has had to do HIPAA training knows at least some of the background of why research is regulated today. Many atrocities have been perpetrated in the name of medicine and science, and so individual governments and international organizations have developed laws and codes of ethics to regulate research. Depending on the type of research and how it's being funded, research may be regulated by the government, the institution where it's being conducted, or both.

Let's look at some of the regulators and ethical principles more closely.

Office of Research Integrity (ORI): This is a branch of the federal Department of Health & Human Services, which is charged by Congress with maintaining regulatory oversight on research. It regulates all research with the exception of that subject to the FDA (U.S. Food and Drug Administration). ORI monitors institutional investigations of research misconduct and reviews policies involving such misconduct.[7]

Institutional Review Boards (IRB): These peer review bodies of medical professionals, often multidisciplinary, are charged with protecting the safety and welfare of human subjects in medical research and clinical trials. IRBs focus primarily on legal issues and must approve protocols, consent forms, etc. You'll find these at every institution that conducts medical research, and all research that involves humans (even if only collecting data from their medical records) requires approval from an IRB.

Health Insurance Portability and Accountability Act (HIPAA): This doesn't sound like it has much to do with research regulation, and that's because the 1996 law's main purpose was to allow employees who lost their jobs to maintain insurance coverage. However, the law also enacted the first universal code in the U.S. to protect patient privacy—a pretty nifty development—and set forth a multitude of regulations that have increased the time and cost for many research studies. If you work in the health professions, you will most certainly have to learn more about HIPAA. We won't go into it here but will simply state that it's the law protecting patient confidentiality and informed consent, and it regulates how patients' information can be viewed, stored, and used in research and all aspects of clinical care and management.

Basic Ethical Tenets: These tenets are patient autonomy, beneficence (do good), non-maleficence (don't do harm), justice, and dignity. These values, unlike those described above, aren't regulatory but rather provide an ethical framework with which to approach medical practice and its dilemmas.

Pharmaceuticals

A pharmaceutical is a chemical substance used to prevent, treat, or cure a disease. In the 1920s, there weren't many drugs beyond aspirin, codeine, morphine, digitalis, nitroglycerin, quinine, and insulin. Today, the more than 3,600 prescription drugs in the U.S. represent a $250 billion industry.[8] The average American fills more than 12 prescriptions per year.[9]

Pharmaceuticals are usually divided into two groups:

1. **Small molecule** drugs are chemically synthesized molecules that are often derived from naturally occurring products. Most of the prescription drugs available, from Valium to Vicodin to Viagra, fall into this category.
2. **Large molecule** drugs, also known as "biologics," are produced by

living cells rather than through chemical synthesis. They're larger and more complex than small molecule pharmaceuticals and, not surprisingly, usually cost a whole lot more. Examples of biologics include insulin, vaccines, and the anti-cancer drug Avastin.

The Industry

So far, the research we've talked about has been in terms of intellectual inquiry and the social good, which seems quite lofty and academic. However, treatment—and research—is also a business. Pharmaceutical companies invest lots of money in R&D to identify, develop, and test potential therapeutics, and they're heavily regulated by the government. Don't feel too bad, though, as they end up with quite a nice financial reward from the drugs that do make it to market.

The five largest pharmaceutical companies, by revenue[10] are:

Company	Country	Annual Revenues	Employees	Top Seller
Pfizer	USA	$58.5 Billion	110,500	Lipitor
Novartis	SWI	$44.4B	119,500	Diovan
Merck	USA	$46.0B	94,000	Singulair
Sanofi	FRA	$37.4B	100,000	Lantus
GlaxoSmithKline	UK	$36.2B	96,500	Advair

Contract Pharma, "The Top 20 Pharmaceutical Companies," July 2011.

Note: "Annual Revenues" refer to total revenue from sales of all pharmaceuticals.

Critics of the pharmaceutical industry call it "Big Pharma." This is a biased term, and we won't use it here. However, it's easy to see why people might use this term for the industry.

Government Regulation

The mission of the FDA is to regulate and ensure the safety of goods that affect individual and public health. It regulates food and nutritional supplements, drugs, vaccines and biotechnology, radiation-emitting devices, cosmetics, tobacco products, and veterinary products. To give an idea of its scope, the FDA regulates about 25% of all consumer goods sold in the

United States.[11] However, it approves very few pharmaceuticals—for example, only 30 new drugs passed muster in 2011.[12]

The path to approval for a new pharmaceutical agent is long and stringent. A manufacturer can apply for a new drug if it's a "new molecular entity" or a previously used molecular entity used in a new way. The FDA requires several stages of clinical testing before allowing a new drug on the market. The entire process looks something like this:

1. A pharmaceutical company identifies a promising molecular compound. Testing begins on individual cells, and, if successful, proceeds to testing on live animals. The company can then submit an **Investigational New Drug (IND)** application to the FDA. The FDA has 30 days to review the IND, and, if approved, trials on human subjects can begin.

2. **Phase I:** The drug is tested on a small group (20-100) of healthy volunteers to make sure it's not immediately toxic and to determine some basic information about how the drug is absorbed and excreted from the body.

3. **Phase II:** The drug is tested on a larger group (100-500) of volunteers, all with the disease the drug targets (e.g., diabetes for insulin). This phase continues the experiments from Phase I and starts to assess the drug's safety and efficacy at different doses.

4. **Phase III:** Randomized controlled trials, usually double-blinded and multicenter, of a large group (1,000-5,000) of patients with the disease of interest. Half of the patients receive the new drug and half receive a placebo or current gold standard treatment. After a sufficient amount of time, the outcomes of the two groups are compared. Phase III trials are the most expensive and time-consuming part of the approvals process.

5. The manufacturer submits a **New Drug Application (NDA)** to the FDA, which contains all information known about the drug, both negative and positive, in all circumstances.

6. The FDA has 10 months to review the application. It may approve it, approve it on condition of Phase IV trials, or reject the application. Once the FDA has approved an NDA, the drug may be sold immediately.

7. **Phase IV:** Post-approval monitoring of a group of patients on the drug to determine side effects and drug interactions.

8. For every drug approved by the FDA, the manufacturer must survey the population and report all new drug interactions quarterly, though serious and fatal drug effects must be reported to the FDA within 15 days. After three years, manufacturer reports switch from quarterly to annually.[13]

There are several variations to be aware of:

▸ **Treatment IND:** This is an exception to the typical NDA process that the FDA uses to make promising new drugs available to desperately ill patients even before the drug has been formally approved.

▸ **Supplemental NDA:** After a drug is approved, if the manufacturer wishes to change the dose, strength, manufacturing process, or labeling of that drug, it must submit a supplemental NDA. This is the pathway by which drugs are approved for new indications and for pediatric patients, both of which require new clinical trials.

▸ **Abbreviated NDA:** This is the pathway used for approval of a generic version of an already approved medication. It's faster and cheaper than a typical NDA because the molecular compound had already been proven safe and efficacious in the original application.

▸ **Orphan drugs:** To stimulate research into rare diseases, the federal government gives special incentives to "orphan drugs," whose potential market is less than 200,000 individuals. These incentives include tax credits, expedited reviews, research grants, market exclusivity, and fee exemptions.

Intellectual Property

A new drug, like any other invention, receives intellectual property (IP) protection from the U.S. government. This is achieved in two ways:

1. **Patents:** Many aspects of a pharmaceutical can be patented, including the molecular structure, method of use, and manufacturing process. These patents last for 20 years but most drugs are patented early in development, years before they're approved by the FDA. The duration of a patent on a new drug can be extended by up to five years to compensate for time lost to clinical trials and FDA review. By the time a drug is released to market, it typically has eight to 14 years of patent protection left.

2. **Data Exclusivity:** For a period of time after a new drug is approved,

the safety and efficacy data from its Phase I, II, and III trials cannot be used by generic manufacturers. Small molecule drugs have data exclusivity for five to seven-and-a-half years after approval (the specific duration depends on review times and legal challenges),[14] while biologics have 12 years. Data exclusivity can be extended by filing a supplemental NDA for a new indication (adding three years)[a] or a pediatric indication (adding six months).

An FDA-approved drug represents a culmination of years of research, development, and clinical trials—not to mention hundreds of millions of dollars. IP protection is meant to ensure that the drug is protected from competition for some time, allowing the manufacturer to recoup its investment. However, finding the right duration for patent protection and data exclusivity is tricky: longer IP protection keeps low-cost generics off the market, translating to higher prices for patients and insurers, while a shorter duration would decrease the financial reward for the manufacturer and reduce the incentive to develop new drugs in the future.

Generics and Biosimilars

After the patent for a small molecule drug has expired,[b] other manufacturers can make their own version of the same molecule; these are dubbed "generic" pharmaceuticals. Generic manufacturers must conduct trials to show that their version of the drug is absorbed and distributed in the body in the same way as the original, "brand-name" drug—that it is "bioequivalent." If bioequivalence is proven, the generic can be approved via the Abbreviated NDA pathway and sold openly on the marketplace alongside the original drug. Generic drugs are much cheaper than brand-name drugs because generic manufacturers don't have to invest in research, development, testing, or marketing pharmaceuticals. In several states, pharmacies can automatically substitute a generic for any bioequivalent prescription unless the provider or patient specifically requests the brand-name drug. Today, 78% of all prescriptions are written for generics.[15]

---

a   Not available for biologics.

b   There are *many* more legal issues here but we'll just mention one important point: Four years after a new small molecule drug is approved, any other manufacturer can file a lawsuit claiming that the drug's patents are invalid. If the court agrees, the company that filed suit is allowed to start making generics immediately. Take home message: patent protection for new, small molecule drugs may be cut off after four years due to legal challenges.

The generic version of a biologic drug is known as a "biosimilar." Biosimilars are much more difficult to create than generics because the manufacturing and purification process for biologics is far more complex than for small molecule drugs. Nevertheless, the ACA mandates a process for the FDA to approve and regulate biosimilars, so expect to see more on the market in the next decade.

Payment and PBMs

The way pharmaceuticals are paid for in the U.S. is similar to the general health care payment systems outlined in Chapter 3, with a few extra layers of complexity thrown on top. Two terms you'll need to know: a **formulary** is a list of the prescription drugs available at a health care institution, and a **pharmacy benefits manager** (PBM) is a for-profit company that manages pharmaceutical sales for a health care plan. Pharmaceutical delivery and payment differ significantly in the inpatient and outpatient settings.

In the hospital, the formulary is regulated by the hospital's Pharmacy & Therapeutics (P&T) committee (page 11). Drugs that are approved by the P&T committee are purchased and stocked by the hospital pharmacy. Providers may prescribe any drug on formulary for a patient while she is in the hospital. In most cases, one organization (e.g., private insurance, Medicare, Medicaid) pays for all of the costs incurred, including pharmaceuticals, during a patient's hospital stay. These drugs aren't paid separately but are bundled into the payment for the entire episode of care, as with a DRG (page 92).

Outside the hospital, most insurance plans contract PBMs to handle all aspects of outpatient pharmaceuticals for their beneficiaries. PBMs negotiate drug prices and purchase drugs from pharmaceutical manufacturers and manage the distribution of those drugs to patients, either through contracts with retail pharmacies (e.g., Walgreens) or via their own mail-order pharmacies. Formularies for outpatient medicines are established by PBMs and/or insurance plans. In contrast to hospital formularies, these lists also indicate how much a patient will have to contribute as a co-payment for any approved drug. PBMs and insurance plans try to keep their costs low by steering patients to use generics and other cheaper drugs, so they set lower patient co-payments for those drugs; this system of classifying drugs by co-pay is known as a "tiered formulary." In a typical plan, a generic statin prescription requires a $10 patient co-pay (tier 1) while the co-pay for Crestor, a brand-name statin, is $40 (tier 3).

Pharmaceuticals and payments are shuffled between manufacturers, pharmacies, hospitals, wholesalers, PBMs, private insurers, government programs, third-party administrators, patient assistance programs, employers, and, finally, patients.[16] As you might imagine, any system this complex has many issues. In one all-too-common scenario, a sick patient is hospitalized and his physicians start him on several different medicines to control his disease and symptoms. Over the course of a week, the dosages and formulations of the medicines are adjusted until a good regimen is found and the patient is well enough to go home. Sounds simple enough, until you remember that the patient's inpatient formulary (determined by the hospital) and outpatient formulary (tiered, determined by the PBM) are different. So, at the time of discharge, the patient's prescriptions have to be switched and he goes home on a completely different medication regimen that may or may not work. This example is just another reminder that the way the U.S. health care system is structured—although it may seem abstract and removed from day-to-day clinical care—can, and often does, directly impact the health of patients.

Medical Devices

Both pharmaceuticals and medical devices are real-world applications of research. While pharmaceuticals allow for chemical manipulation of the body, medical devices allow for mechanical manipulation. Medical devices can improve health and treatment through:

- Better diagnostics (e.g., CT scans)
- Safer and less invasive procedures (e.g., laparoscopic surgery)
- Longer lives (e.g., pacemakers)
- Easier lives (e.g., full joint replacements)

The number and complexity of available medical devices has increased significantly over the past 25 years. Today, more than $110 billion is spent on medical devices in the country each year.[17]

The Industry

The U.S. has the world's largest medical device industry. The five companies with the greatest revenues are:[18]

Company	Country	Annual Revenues	Employees
Johnson & Johnson	USA	$24.6 Billion	114,000
GE Healthcare	USA	$16.9 B	46,000
Siemens Healthcare	GER	$16.7 B	49,000
Medtronic	USA	$15.8 B	40,000
Baxter	USA	$12.8 B	48,000

MPO Magazine, "The Top 30," July/August 2011.

Note: The revenue and employee numbers for Johnson & Johnson, GE Healthcare and Siemens Healthcare refer only to their medical device and product divisions.

Government Regulation

The FDA is the government agency that regulates the approval and sales of medical devices in the U.S. The specifics of the approval process for each device depend on the level of risk to the patient. The FDA categorizes every device as low (Class I), intermediate (Class II), or high risk (Class III), and the requirements to prove safety and effectiveness vary accordingly. This makes sense—complicated, high-risk devices such as pacemakers ought to go through more testing than simple, low-risk devices such as tongue depressors. New devices can be approved by the FDA in one of three ways:[19]

1. **Registration:** Class I and low-risk Class II devices don't have to undergo a true approval process. Manufacturers of these products simply have to register new devices with the FDA when they enter the market.
2. **Substantial Equivalence/510(k):** Intermediate-risk Class II devices that can demonstrate "substantial equivalence" to an FDA-approved medical device that's already on the market are cleared by the 510(k) process. Substantial equivalence originally referred to new versions of previously approved devices with minor modifications, but the 510(k) pathway also is now used for new devices with a

similar intended use and safety profile as a previously approved product, even if the new device has a different mechanism of action and/or is constructed of different materials.[20] Clinical trials aren't required for the 510(k) process. More than 3,000 products are approved by this pathway each year.[21]

3. **Premarket Approval:** Class III devices are approved by the FDA via a process known as a Premarket Approval (PMA), which is similar to the method used for new pharmaceuticals. Clinical trials demonstrating safety and efficacy of the new product are required before the device can be approved through the PMA pathway. This process is much more expensive and time-consuming than the 510(k) pathway.[c] Fewer than 50 devices are approved by the PMA pathway each year.[21]

The FDA also maintains a system for tracking adverse events for products that have been approved and released into the market. Manufacturers are required to report to the FDA any serious device-related adverse events that caused or could have caused serious injury or death, and similar requirements exist for hospitals and other health care facilities. The FDA receives tens of thousands of these reports each year.[19]

After receiving reports about a specific device, the FDA has a range of options, from further study to mandatory recall of the device. The FDA recalled 42 medical device models in 2011, including products from vascular stents to lubricating jelly.[22] Some of these products were very popular—one of these recalls involved more than 300 million strips for testing blood glucose.[23]

Health Information Technology

While the technology used in medical devices continues to improve, health care communication and organization systems at most institutions are stuck in the pagers-and-faxes era. (Unfortunately, they've ditched the acid-washed jeans.) Health information technology (IT) is a simple concept: the application of electronic systems to organizing and using health data, from writing prescriptions to transmitting MRI results digitally. However,

---

c   The law requires all Class III devices to go through the PMA process. However, due to time and funding constraints, the FDA has used the much less rigorous 510(k) pathway for more than half of these high-risk devices instead.[69] It has been admonished for this by other government agencies several times and is currently working with the Institute of Medicine to improve its approvals process.

as with many aspects of health care, this simple concept quickly becomes extremely complicated when put into practice. For one, health IT goes by many different names, such as electronic health records (EHR), electronic medical records (EMR), and personal health records (PHR). Different software systems may all call themselves EHR, which would suggest they are comparable; however, they may not perform the same functions or have the ability to communicate with each other. The best definition and system may not be clear for those who are actually using it to provide care.

What is clear is that health IT has the potential to significantly improve the efficiency and error rate of health care systems. (Spell check is pretty great and all, but ending the tyranny of physicians' messy handwriting is a true feat: now 25% of prescriptions are issued electronically.)[24] Of course, potential doesn't necessarily equal results—the largest study to date failed to show any improvement in quality of care, cost, length of stay, or readmission rates for hospitals that have implemented EHRs.[25] Health IT penetration is still relatively low in the U.S.[44]—only 1.5% of hospitals have comprehensive EHR systems, while 7.6% operate a basic EHR. Nevertheless, the federal government has prioritized health IT and has unveiled a range of measures to encourage the adoption of EHRs across the country. Interestingly, the one area in which health IT has already been implemented quickly and universally is medical billing—99% of hospitals have computerized patient billing systems.[26] Money has an uncanny ability to speed anything along, doesn't it?

Issues

So far, we've looked at how research, pharmaceutical, and technological progress is made. This progress has arguably been the greatest improvement for human life in all of history. The story of medical science is an amazing one, and many books have been filled with that story; however, as stated at the beginning of the chapter, we don't have the space to do the same in this book. Now let's focus on issues and problems within these industries not because they're more important than the positives in the system—they aren't—but rather because they're less obvious and thus more instructive.

The issues themselves are complicated and deep: the more you learn, the more shades of nuance appear. We can't fully explore those issues here but we'll introduce some of the major issues facing these vitally important industries. (Please see the Suggested Reading at the end of the chapter if you would like to explore them in depth.)

Utility of Research Findings

PLACEBO EFFECT

The typical way for a new drug to be approved by the FDA is to prove that it leads to a statistically significant health improvement over a placebo. So to truly understand the pharmaceutical system, you must understand the importance of placebos. A placebo is a medical treatment that has no direct physiological effect; i.e., a sham treatment. The effect of a placebo is psychological, though studies show that the psychological can become the physiological.

Placebo drugs may be active (such as antibiotics given for a viral infection) or inactive (such as a sugar pill). Placebos also may be surgeries (some of the most effective placebos!) or clinically unrelated procedures (such as sham acupuncture). In addition, the physician-patient relationship itself may even establish a placebo effect. The placebo effect can work even when patients know they're receiving a placebo.

The placebo effect is a mixture of both expectations and conditioning,[27] the idea being that people experience what they expect to (whether positive or negative—a "nocebo"). This effect isn't just a theoretical concern; in fact, it's real and surprisingly large. For example, placebos are an effective treatment for 32% of patients with depression (compared to 48% for SSRIs, the most popular type of antidepressants).[28] And, weird but true, the placebo effect seems to be growing more potent over time.[29] As you can imagine, the placebo effect is a major concern for those involved in developing new drugs.

VALIDITY CONCERNS

Scientific research is susceptible to many problems:

- Researchers may frame their questions in a way that points to conclusions.
- They may choose a poorly-representative population sample.
- They may make a mistake in data analysis.

- A journal may publish or reject articles for reasons other than the validity of the science.
- The media may report conclusions that weren't truly there.
- The study may be later invalidated but never retracted in the eyes of other researchers and the public.

Further, science barrels forward, and studies may quickly go out of date as new methods and materials are introduced. We aren't suggesting that scientists and the media are motivated by malice; to the contrary, they're simply human. No matter how exacting and hard-working scientists may be, there's no perfect research study. Thus, a growing number of scientists have begun to analyze not only biomedical questions, but rather the research world itself and how it's affected by the problems listed above. Some of their findings are startling:

- Many studies end up being refuted. Eighty percent of non-randomized studies (the most common type), 25% of gold-standard randomized trials, and as much as 10% of "platinum," large randomized controlled trials end up being refuted by later studies. In fact, of the 49 most influential studies of the last 13 years, 41% have been shown to be wrong or significantly exaggerated.[30,31]
- Researchers are more likely to submit, and journals are more likely to publish, experiments with positive results.[32,33] This is termed "publication bias." Five identical experiments may only produce the desired result once; but if that one trial is the only one submitted and published, the general public would have the false impression that 100% of the experiments were successful.[d]
- Conflict of interest may arise. New medical and pharmaceutical products are subject to multiple trials to prove efficacy and safety. Yet many of these studies are funded by the very same company that produces the product in question. Not surprisingly, trials funded by a private company are more likely—four times as much, in one major study[34]—to have results that benefit the sponsoring company than are trials funded by others.
- Researchers sometimes don't challenge or retest each other's results. This is in part because unoriginal or repeat questions are

---

d To counteract publication bias, the NIH has created a publicly available trial registry at www.ClinicalTrials.Gov. There, researchers can prospectively catalog their trials and report basic results after completion, even if the research isn't published in a journal. The FDA and several consortiums of medical journals now require many trials to be registered at ClinicalTrials.Gov.

less likely to be funded, published, or acclaimed, so peer review may end up falling short of a full-on investigation.

▶ The research system lacks a consistent way to retract published research that is later determined to be invalid. Researchers often continue to cite the results of invalid papers as correct for many years after they have been retracted, and, even more surprising, many papers found to be fraudulent are never retracted at all.[35]

You may argue with any of the above claims. However, these claims are generally accepted and lauded within the research community, and we present them here as the contrarian view of established practices.

Wouldn't it be something if this research got refuted someday, though?

Evidence-Based Medicine

Evidence-based medicine (EBM) is the movement to base clinical practice on our best understanding of the safety, effectiveness, and cost of medical practices. The key is that our "best understanding" comes from evidence and research, not historical precedent or anecdote. EBM relies on primary research, systematic review of research, and expert analysis to determine best clinical practices. Although this idea seems rather obvious—basing medical decisions on the best possible evidence—the commitment to EBM is relatively new.

The Centre for Evidence-Based Medicine at the University of Oxford lists five steps of EBM:[36]

1. **Asking Focused Questions:** Translation of uncertainty to an answerable question
2. **Finding the Evidence:** Systematic retrieval of the best evidence available
3. **Critical Appraisal:** Testing evidence for validity, clinical relevance, and applicability
4. **Making a Decision:** Application of results in practice
5. **Evaluating Performance:** Auditing evidence-based decisions

Despite the process steps listed above, EBM isn't intended to be formulaic. Scientific evidence and clinical guidelines can enhance but never replace individual clinical expertise. Health care professionals must decide what evidence, if any, is applicable to each individual patient. It's often said that medicine is both a science and an art; EBM is meant to bolster the science without diminishing the art.

CLINICAL PRACTICE GUIDELINES

One widespread application of EBM to everyday clinical care is the Clinical Practice Guideline (CPG). CPGs serve as reference guides for what the best available evidence indicates health practitioners should do in a given situation, and all practitioners will consult some of these guidelines during their careers. You can see from the graphic below how these guidelines come to be, moving from what is seen in individual cases to what provides the best outcomes for the greatest number of patients.

Preclinical Research

Case Studies

Small Trials

Randomized Controlled Trials

Meta Analyses

Expert Committee

Clinical Practice Guidelines

Guidelines are created by many organizations and professional societies, and CPGs are available for thousands of conditions and illnesses. One well-known example is the Ottawa Ankle Rules. These guidelines help physicians determine whether an X-ray should be taken for ankle and foot injuries. The rules state:

> "X-rays of the foot should only be ordered if there is pain in the midfoot zone AND any one of the following:
> Bone tenderness at the base of the fifth metatarsal
> OR

Bone tenderness at the navicular bone
OR
An inability to bear weight both immediately after injury and in the
emergency department for four steps."

Despite the utility of CPGs (the Ottawa Ankle Rules are correct for nearly all ankle and foot injuries and can reduce the number of unnecessary X-rays by at least one-third),[37] not all physicians use them all the time. Fewer than one-third of American emergency physicians use the Ottawa Ankle Rules most of the time,[38] and, in general, a recent study found only 55% of Americans who visited a physician received the recommended care based on available guidelines.[39]

Why don't clinicians use clinical practice guidelines more often? Like many topics we cover in this book, translating the theoretical benefits of EBM to the real world is much more difficult than it would seem at first glance. Many health care professionals have expressed deep-seated concerns about CPGs, and with EBM in general. Some of their concerns include:

▸ EBM is based on evidence from clinical trials, but medical practice in the real world is much more complex than can be represented in trials. Clinical trials often focus on a select patient population (e.g., healthy females between 18-50 in Sweden) that may not apply to a given patient; they usually compare two treatments for a medical condition when, in reality, a range of options are available; and practical considerations like cost and access aren't usually included. If your patient can't afford the treatment that's supported by the evidence, then what?

▸ CPGs focus too much on the "average" patient, so guidelines aren't applicable to patients with unique characteristics or multiple medical conditions. Conversely, creating different CPGs for every conceivable case would be expensive and make it impossible for physicians to wade through them all.

▸ One of the key tools of EBM is the meta-analysis, which combines data from many different clinical trials. Pooling data is intended to make the resulting conclusions more robust, but a meta-analysis is only as good as the trials it draws from. A synthesis of many poor-quality trials will result in a similarly poor-quality conclusion; furthermore, meta-analyses usually don't correct for conflict of interest in the trials they use, which can influence results. Finally, meta-analyses of the same data can come to different conclusions depending on their design and inclusion criteria, so bias among the designers of the meta-analysis is just as important but often overlooked.

▸ Requiring providers to follow guidelines erodes clinical autonomy. Many health professionals feel that "cookbook medicine," as some derisively refer to EBM, underestimates the value of personal judgment gained from years of clinical practice.

▸ Medical innovation requires experimentation of new methods, combinations, and deliveries of treatment. EBM, by definition, only encompasses treatments that have existed long enough to have been studied. A reliance on EBM may stifle clinical creativity and slow the progress of medical innovation.

▸ Many different organizations create CPGs, and multiple guidelines may be available for the same condition. Unfortunately, they often disagree. For example, the American Congress of Obstetrics and Gynecology guidelines recommend routine mammography to screen for breast cancer every one to two years for women age 40-49 years,[40] while the federal U.S. Preventive Services Task Force recommends against routine mammography for women between 40-49 years old.[41]

In short, evidence-based medicine and clinical practice guidelines are key developments in modern medicine that show promise for significant improvements in health care quality. However, substantial barriers exist to the widespread application of EBM to everyday clinical practice. Furthermore, the elephant in the room is that the utility of EBM is limited by how much we still don't know about medicine and the human body. Consider just how many diseases are "idiopathic"—a fancy term for "we have no clue."[e]

Comparative Effectiveness Research

The Institute of Medicine defines comparative effectiveness research (CER) as
"The generation and synthesis of evidence that compares the benefits and harms of alternative methods to prevent, diagnose, treat, and monitor a clinical condition or to improve the delivery of care. The purpose of CER is to assist consumers, clinicians, purchasers, and policy makers to make informed decisions that will improve health care at both the individual and population levels."[42]

---

e   Or, as the old joke goes, an idiopathic disease is one in which the doctor is an idiot and the patient is pathetic.

CER is different from normal clinical research, which tests whether clinical practices and treatments work or not; CER instead pits treatments, diagnosis methods, and delivery models against each other to see what works best when, for whom, at what cost, and under what circumstances.

CER should accomplish the following:

▶ Make variations transparent
▶ Better inform decision-making for physicians and patients
▶ Change practices so as not to waste money on what doesn't produce better outcomes

In 2010, the ACA established the Patient-Centered Outcomes Research Institute (PCORI) with the aim of using CER to develop national treatment recommendations. See Chapter 5 for more information about PCORI.

CRITICISMS OF CER

▶ **Subverts the Traditional Research Process:** The "gold standard" in research is the randomized controlled trial (RCT), which determines causal efficacy of treatment. CER, however, sidesteps the methodology of the RCT in an attempt to make broader—or more broadly relevant—claims. Rather than controlled conditions, CER uses data sets from the real world to compare effectiveness. Critics challenge that CER doesn't provide enough nuance to accurately reflect real-world conditions nor does it establish causal efficacy before comparing treatments.

▶ **No Allowance for Outliers:** CER tends to focus on the average patient, but all bodies are different, and what is best for the average patient won't be best for all patients.

▶ **Too Much Emphasis on Cost, Not Care:** An important element of CER is reducing waste, and this may involve cutting out expensive treatments that don't offer much (relative) benefit to the average patient. Critics of CER think that cost could become the most important factor considered in some studies, and CER panels in the future may rule against effective treatments simply because they are too expensive. Such critics point to Britain's NICE (National Institute for Health and Clinical Excellence), which explicitly takes cost-effectiveness into account (such as cost-per-QALY, see page 113) and which has sometimes generated controversy for prioritizing cost and population health over individual health. That being said, PCORI, unlike NICE, isn't intended to consider cost measures in its research.

GEOGRAPHIC VARIATION

Among the many factors that influence how medicine is practiced in America, local culture is often overlooked. Since 1996, the Dartmouth Atlas of Health Care has been documenting the geographic variation in how medicine is practiced. Patients with the same medical conditions are clinically treated in very different ways depending on their location. In other words, physicians have different practices, and not only are these unequal in quality or cost, but they also may be influenced by concerns outside of health (e.g., pharmaceutical companies). The data from the Atlas has been used to compare patients' clinical outcomes from different types of treatment; the take-home message, according to the writers of the Atlas, is that a higher volume of treatments doesn't produce better outcomes for patients.[43] That is, "more" doesn't equal "better."[f]

PATIENT VARIATION

Two problems with biomedical research in general are that the outcomes 1) are from a patient population that may not match all populations; and 2) are presented in terms most relevant for the "average" patient. In real life, patients' responses to both disease and treatment vary, so individual patients may have different outcomes than the evidence suggests. A good clinician handles this by experimenting with different dosages, drugs, and treatments until finding one that works best for an individual patient. Many clinicians are concerned that too much focus on population health will erode this ability to experiment and find what works best for the individual patient.

Government Regulation

There are many criticisms of the way the government, specifically the FDA, regulates the pharmaceutical and medical device industries. Here are the major criticisms:

---

f   Please note that many researchers feel that the Dartmouth Atlas shouldn't be used to make generalized conclusions about the U.S. health care system because the Atlas relies on Medicare data, which excludes the majority of the American population, and may not adequately adjust for patient characteristics, such as socioeconomic status,[70,71] that affect health care spending.

TOO MUCH REGULATION

- The FDA approvals process for drugs and devices is too expensive. The cost to develop and test a new drug and bring it to market now exceeds a billion dollars,[45] and these astronomical expenses translate to higher prices for consumers.
- The FDA approvals process is too long, which keeps patients waiting for desperately needed treatments. The FDA trial and approval process for a new cancer drug, for instance, takes an average of eight years.[46]
- The FDA approvals process is too rigorous, so drug and device companies cut back on their R&D spending because of the low probability that new drugs will actually make it to the market.
- The approvals process in the European Union is easier and quicker than in the U.S.[47] Manufacturers may simply avoid the FDA approvals process, leading to medical devices that are available in many other countries but not in the U.S.[48]

NOT ENOUGH REGULATION

- The FDA requires two Phase III trials that show that a new drug is efficacious before approval; however, a company can run as many Phase III trials as it needs to get those two. A drug can be ineffective in 98 out of 100 trials and still be approved by the FDA, and these negative trial results are viewed as proprietary and are kept confidential by the FDA.[49]
- Clinical trials of new drugs and devices are too short, and many new products are released to the market without a good understanding of their long-term adverse effects.
- The FDA approves new pharmaceuticals for specific medical indications, but once a drug is released to the market it may be prescribed for any use. Most of these "off-label" prescriptions haven't been proved to be clinically effective. For example, gabapentin (Neurontin) is FDA-approved for the treatment of epilepsy and post-herpetic neuralgia, but more than 80% of nationwide gabapentin prescriptions are for other conditions, from hot flashes to restless leg syndrome.[50]
- Dietary supplements like vitamins and herbal therapies don't have to demonstrate safety or effectiveness before they are marketed and sold; in fact, the burden of proof is on the FDA to prove a product is unsafe before it has to be pulled from the market.

TOO MUCH INDUSTRY INFLUENCE

In 1992, Congress passed legislation (known by the charming acronym PDUFA) to speed up the FDA drug approvals process. This legislation set specific deadlines for the FDA reviews of new pharmaceuticals. To pay for the extra staff needed to meet these deadlines, PDUFA also mandated a fee system for pharmaceutical companies that submit drugs for FDA review. Although PDUFA did succeed in significantly reducing the amount of time that drugs spend in the approvals process, it also has generated a tremendous amount of controversy. Fees paid by pharmaceutical companies now account for 65% of the FDA budget for drug approvals,[51] meaning, essentially, that the FDA is funded by the industry that it regulates. Similar legislation for the medical device industry (called MDUFMA, naturally) was enacted in 2002. It's beyond the scope of this book to determine if PDUFA and MDUFMA have led to worse health outcomes for patients, but the current set-up certainly creates at least the appearance that the FDA has a major conflict of interest in regard to drug and device regulation.

SIGNIFICANCE: STATISTICAL VS. CLINICAL

To be approved by the FDA, a new drug must prove to be significantly more efficacious than placebo or the current gold standard treatment in clinical trials. What constitutes a "significant" improvement is determined by sophisticated statistical methods. However, this improvement may be as small as 1-2%, which is often insignificant in clinical settings. By contrast, the United Kingdom's NICE emphasizes clinical significance, rather than statistical, which assesses the practical relevance of the finding. Clinical significance is determined using metrics like effect size, number needed to treat, and preventive fraction.

Aside from the technical definitions for both statistical and clinical significance, there's the meta-question of what level of significance should be necessary for physicians to prescribe drugs for patients who must pay for them and who may experience side effects.

Why Are Drug Prices So High?

This is a simple question with a very complicated—and only partially explainable—answer. We should be wary of over-simplification, as the situation is complex, but we'll try our best to break it down. First, some background:

Drug Prices in the U.S.: Drug pricing runs the gamut from $48 per year for generics at Walmart to $1,500 per year for the common cholesterol drug Lipitor to $409,500 per year for Soliris, which treats paroxysmal nocturnal hemoglobinuria.[52] Most patients are protected from the full price of drugs by insurance but the uninsured and underinsured feel the full brunt of this pricing. Oddly enough, Medicare patients did too, until Part D was instituted in 2006 (page 184).

2008 Pharmaceutical Expenditure per Capita	
Australia	$502.8
Canada	$684.4
Denmark	$323.9
France	$621.5
Germany	$594.2
Japan	$558.3
New Zealand	$261.2
United Kingdom	$381.4
United States	$919.1

Organisation for Economic Co-operation and Development, "Health Data 2011," June 2011.

Note: Expenditures in U.S.$ purchasing power parity.

What Drugs Cost Elsewhere: The U.S. spends far more than any other industrialized country on pharmaceuticals. Other industrialized countries are able to keep drug prices lower for patients by negotiating with manufacturers for lower prices. In the U.S., some pharmacy benefits managers, insurance plans, and government programs such as the VA negotiate with drug companies, but none has the market share to negotiate prices as low as a nationwide system can. However, in other countries, just as with the U.S., the justification for price-setting is not always transparent.[53]

Now, let's discuss the reasons for high drug prices in the U.S.

REASON #1: RESEARCH AND DEVELOPMENT COSTS ARE HIGH

To get a new drug on the market, companies must either fund or find basic science research, fund continued research on what actually seems to be

useful, apply for a patent, go through FDA approval, and, finally, manu-
facture and sell the drug. Very little of what goes into the first step (basic
science) ends up in the last one (a sellable drug). So not only do you have
to find a needle in a haystack, but then you have to make sure the needle
won't hurt anyone and will actually sew before you can put it to work.
These costs truly are enormous. To give you an idea:

- In 2009, Merck spent $5.8 billion on R&D,[54] was issued 253 pat-
  ents,[55] and had 81 prescription drugs on the market (total, not just
  those approved in 2009).[56]
- The average cost of developing a single drug is $1.3 billion, and only
  1 in 5,000 compounds are successful.[57]
- Only 20% of medications brought to market make a profit.[57]

Clearly, R&D costs *a lot* and productivity has dropped over the past 10
years, decreasing return on investment even further.[58] To recoup their high
up-front costs, manufacturers charge a hefty price for their brand-name
drugs in the few years before generics enter the market.

REASON #2: MARKETING COSTS ARE HIGH

To thrive in the highly competitive drug marketplace, manufacturers
devote a significant portion of their budgets to marketing to providers
and patients. One study estimated the total amount spent by drug companies for promotion in 2004 at $57.5 billion; 36% of the total was spent
on detailing to physicians, 28% on drug samples, and 7% on direct-to-
consumer advertising.[59] (Note that, as of 2009, small personal gifts such as
pens and restaurant meals for physicians are no longer allowed.)[60]

To compare to Reason #1, the same study estimated that the pharmaceutical
industry spends nearly twice as much on marketing as they do on R&D.[59]
Unlike most other industrialized countries, the United States allows pretty
extensive marketing (including directly to consumers). As with any consumer product, advertising costs are high because they pay off.

REASON #3: WE HAVE NO IDEA

Even knowing what we know, how specific drug prices are set is often
totally unclear. As with any capitalist system, prices are, to an extent, sim-

ply what the market will bear. Though we know that competition reduces costs, no one in the public knows the metrics used by drug manufacturers to set prices during patent periods.

This lack of transparency can be upsetting to patients and providers. For example, KV Pharmaceuticals manufactures Makena, a synthetic form of progesterone which helps to reduce premature births in women with a history of them. Until 2011, there was no patent for Makena, and it was prescribed off-label for $15 per dose. In 2011, however, KV Pharmaceuticals won the right to manufacture Makena as an orphan drug, and they set the price at $690 per dose—meaning the entire course of treatment would cost about $13,800. While KV Pharmaceuticals maintains that this price is still lower than the estimated $50,000 that a premature birth costs, it's not clear what could justify this price increase.

Some emphasize that drug prices are high because we're also paying for innovation—between 2000 and 2009, three-fifths of all drug patents came from the U.S.[61]—and that the high prices we pay subsidize the relatively low price of drugs in other countries. This raises several interesting questions:

▸ How much of the pharmaceutical business is truly innovative?
▸ How necessary is the U.S. intellectual property system to maintain that innovation?
▸ Can we reduce America's subsidization of other countries' drug prices without losing pharmaceutical jobs and investment money to international competitors?
▸ To what extent should we be willing to trade access for innovation, or vice versa?
▸ To what extent can we solve the access problem without driving health care costs up even more?

Trying to answer any of these questions breeds even more perplexing questions—each topic can fill (and has!) entire books. Please see the Suggested Reading to learn more.

Direct-To-Consumer Advertising

Once upon a time, purveyors of medicine freely advertised their wares to consumers, making wild claims about the effectiveness of their "snake oil" and other largely useless remedies. In the early 20th century, as scientific research became more advanced and respectable, such advertising came under heavy restrictions, including banning any pharmaceutical advertising directed at patients rather than at providers.

In 1997, though, the U.S. legalized direct-to-consumer advertising (DTCA). (To date, the only other country where it's legal is New Zealand.) The idea behind DTCA is to help patients take more control over their own health by giving them more access to information about medicines. One of the tenets of medical ethics is patient autonomy, for which DTCA provides support.

On the other hand, we cannot and should not expect patients to access and understand all of the medical knowledge necessary to evaluate diagnoses and treatments. Medication and medical treatment are not consumer goods in the same sense that, say, a garden hose is. A consumer is perfectly capable of researching the best garden hose, and, even if he doesn't end up with the best, it's not a huge deal. In medicine, not only is such research a lifelong pursuit, even for experts, but making the wrong decision can be a matter of life and death. Thus, it may be short-sighted to expect market processes to benefit consumers when they're patients.

Another criticism of DTCA is that it raises already high marketing and advertising costs, contributing to the elevated price of drugs in the U.S. This is an area in which marketing costs could be significantly reduced, as DTCA accounts for 7% of drug marketing[59] (a multi-billion dollar industry already). No business in its right mind would voluntarily stop advertising to consumers, since it would be sure to lose market share to competitors who kept it up, but a nationwide ban on DTCA would likely reduce costs across the board.

Intersections and Conflicts of Interest

As we've discussed, the research, pharmaceutical, and device worlds intersect, interact, and blend together. Anytime you have an intermingling of groups with diverse motivations, conflicts of interest are bound to arise. Medical research is no exception. Scientific researchers investigating a new drug or device are often funded by the very same company that makes and sells said product. Pharmaceutical and device companies pay health care providers and researchers to participate in speakers bureaus and conferences and to consult about new products. Many post-graduate fellowships are funded by industry. More than 70,000 pharmaceutical sales representatives are employed to visit physicians' offices to market drugs and distribute free samples.[62]

Frequency of Physician-Industry Relationships According to Benefit Received	
Benefit	Percentage of Respondents
▶ Drug Samples	78%
▶ Gifts	83%
▶ Food or Beverages in Workplace	83%
▶ Tickets to Cultural or Sporting Events	7%
▶ Reimbursements	35%
▶ For Admission to CME Meetings (free or subsidized)	26%
▶ For Meeting Expenses (e.g., travel, food, lodging)	15%
▶ Payments	28%
▶ For Consulting	18%
▶ For Serving as a Speaker or on a Speakers' Bureau	16%
▶ For Serving on an Advisory Board	9%
▶ For Enrolling Patients in Clinical Trials	3%
▶ Any of the Above Relationships	94%

Campbell et al., "A National Survey of Physician–Industry Relationships," New England Journal of Medicine, April 2007.

Note: Percentages were weighted to adjust for the probability of selection within each specialty and for nonresponse.

It should be no surprise, then, that according to a survey in 2007, 94% of physicians reported some kind of connection to industry during the previous year.[63] The level of the relationship was affected by the type of specialty and practice. (For instance, family physicians and solo practitioners are more likely to meet with drug reps.) You can see the types of behaviors constituting these relationships above.

Some of these relationships may even cross legal lines. In 2005, the federal government opened an investigation of the five largest hip and spine implant manufacturers for violation of anti-kickback laws. The government alleged that the "consulting" fees paid to some surgeons by device companies were little more than bribes for surgeons to use a specific product. The investigation was settled without any company admitting guilt, but the manufacturers did agree to pay a $310 million fine, instituted major changes to their business practices, and accepted strict federal oversight of their interactions with physicians.[64]

Publicity about conflicts of interest in medicine led to the Physician Payments Sunshine Act, a federal law passed in 2010 that comes into effect over three years. This act requires companies to report any gift or payment to a physician that is worth $10 or more. A record of these payments will be made publicly available online starting in September 2013.[65]

While expensive dinners with drug reps may seem like an obvious conflict of interest deserving to be eradicated, intersections between physicians, researchers, professors, and industry are more subtle and more controversial than this. Clinicians have generated the ideas behind many of the important medical innovations in the past 25 years, but, as mentioned earlier, the journey from a good idea to an FDA-approved drug or device is long and expensive. Without the support of private industry, many of these innovations would have never reached the market. Furthermore, many feel there's a lack of evidence to demonstrate that relationships between physicians, researchers, and industry actually lead to worse health outcomes for patients.

Politics and Lobbying

We've discussed the intersections among physicians, researchers, and industry. We've also examined government regulation and oversight of research, drugs, and devices. Now let's take a look at the interactions of lawmakers with these groups.

Lobbying is a practice by which businesses, organizations, and advocacy groups try to inform and persuade politicians to vote in ways that protect certain interests. Lobbyists may influence politicians by sponsoring information sessions, helping to draft legislation, and contributing to political campaigns.

Health-related lobbying accounts for more spending than any other industry sector, outpacing even defense and energy lobbying.[66] As you can see below, some pretty large amounts of money get thrown around:

Lobbying Money (2011)[66]		
Sector	**Total Contributions**	**Top Five Contributors**
Pharmaceuticals and Devices	$240 Million	1. Pharmaceutical Researchers and Manufacturers of America: $18.9 M 2. Pfizer: $12.4 M 3. Amgen, Inc.: $10 M 4. Eli Lilly: $9.8 M 5. Merck: $8.2 M
Insurance	$158.7 M	1. Blue Cross/Blue Shield: $12.5 M 2. America's Health Insurance Plans: $9.7 M 3. Aetna: $3.9 M 4. UnitedHealth: 2.9 M 5. eHealth: $2.3 M
Hospitals and Nursing Homes	$100 M	1. American Hospital Association: $20.5 M 2. Alliance for Quality Nursing Home Care: $3.3 M 3. Kindred Healthcare: $3.1 M 4. Federation of American Hospitals: $2.4 M 5. California Hospital Association: $2 M
Health Professionals	$80 M	6. American Medical Association: $21.5 M 7. American College of Radiology: $3.9 M 8. American Academy of Family Physicians: $3.1 M 9. American Dental Association: $2.6 M 10. American College of Cardiology: $2.1 M

The Center for Responsive Politics, www.opensecrets.org/influence/.

Note: $159M refers to the total amount for the insurance industry, but the top 5 includes only insurance companies that focus on healthcare business.

Critics of such contributions suggest that they fuel ideological biases and conflicts of interest. However, just as with the physician-industry relationship, counter arguments may be made that these relationships play an important role in helping the system function.

Quality

Throughout this book, you'll notice that many of the issues facing the health care system today pertain to the quality of care provided to patients, and how it can be improved. Before figuring out how to improve quality, though, we have to decide how to define and measure "quality" as it relates to medical care. This, as it turns out, is not so simple. A growing number of researchers have been focusing their attention on this exact topic, a trend that will only gather steam as the ACA is enacted. Read on to the next chapter for more information about the many provisions in ACA that focus on quality.

Defining Quality

Quality as a general concept is not so difficult to define. The Institute of Medicine (IOM) defines it as "the degree to which health services for individuals and populations increase the likelihood of desired health outcomes and are consistent with current professional knowledge." The IOM lists six aims of quality: patient safety, patient-centeredness, effectiveness, efficiency, timeliness, and equity.

What's more difficult is defining quality in terms of specific behaviors and actions. Depending on your perspective, different behaviors may produce higher quality. Patients, providers, and payors often have differing opinions on what behaviors and actions result in the highest quality of care. This isn't surprising—in the complex, jumbled system that is U.S. health care, your experience and viewpoint will influence the way a vague concept like quality is interpreted in real-world settings. For instance, providers may think that payors focus on the "efficiency" aspect of quality to the detriment of "effectiveness," while patients perceive a lack of interest in "equity" from both.

The bottom line is that an organization's ultimate goals may affect the way it defines quality. Thus, though most may agree on the overall definition, determining concrete, specific quality measures is challenging and a source of controversy.

Measuring Quality

After figuring out what you *mean* by quality, the next hurdle to overcome is how to measure quality in the clinical setting. It's not easy, particularly considering that the causality between providers' actions and patients' health outcomes is not always clear. The University of Michigan health services researcher Avedis Donabedian developed the "Donabedian Triad" as a plan for measuring quality. The triad has three arms: structure, process, and outcomes. The physician Bob Wachter summarizes the Donabedian Triad here:[67]

Measure	Advantages	Disadvantages
STRUCTURE How was care organized?	▸ May be highly relevant in a complex health system ▸ Easiest to measure	▸ May fail to capture the quality of care by individual physicians ▸ Difficult to determine a "gold standard"
▸ *Example: How many patients is each nurse caring for?*		
PROCESS What was done?	▸ More easily measured and acted upon than outcomes ▸ May not require case mix adjustment ▸ No time lag—can be measured when care is provided ▸ May directly reflect quality, if carefully chosen	▸ A proxy for outcomes ▸ All may not agree on "gold standard" ▸ May promote "cookbook" medicine, especially if physicians and health systems try to "game" their performance
▸ *Example: What percentage of patients was given antibiotics before surgery?*		

Measure	Advantages	Disadvantages
OUTCOMES What happened to the patient?	▸ This is what we really care about	▸ May take years to occur ▸ May not reflect quality of care ▸ Requires case mix and other adjustments to prevent "apples to oranges" comparisons

▸ *Example: How many patients are readmitted to the hospital within 30 days?*

The Agency for Healthcare Research and Quality (AHRQ) describes the Donabedian Triad as the "paradigm for quality measurement" because it specifies a universal, consistent process for measuring quality of different types in different realms.[68] That being said, each of the three areas of measurement has significant disadvantages, as mentioned in the table.

Quality of clinical care definitely influences long-term health outcomes, but so do nutrition, exercise, genetics, medication adherence, income, and a number of other patient-specific factors. Measuring quality by outcomes without adjusting for differences in the patient population would be unfair to providers who work in low socioeconomic areas; however, determining exactly how to factor in patient characteristics when interpreting outcomes measures is beyond complicated. Similar difficulties arise when considering structure and process outcomes.

Glossary

Controlled Trial: A method of reducing bias in experiments comparing different treatments by including at least one group of subjects in the experiment receiving a known treatment or no treatment at all. For example, a controlled trial of a new pain medicine would include one group receiving the new medicine (experimental group), and one group receiving aspirin (control group). The results of the two groups are then compared to determine the effects of the new treatment.

Electronic Health Record (EHR): An electronic filing system for all patient records, which also usually includes upgrades such as reminders and warnings. It's similar to the electronic library catalogs that replaced card catalogs.

Gold Standard: The best available treatment that is widely accepted as the standard of care for any medical condition. For example, propranolol is currently the gold standard treatment to prevent migraines; any new treatment will have to prove more effective than propranolol to be approved by the FDA.

Meta-Analysis: A type of research that combines the results of many similar experiments to determine an overall result. For example, there may have been 10 separate experiments of 50 subjects each comparing insulin and metformin for diabetes treatment; by combining the data from each of the trials, a meta-analysis can compare the results with a virtual subject population of 500, which is much more likely to find a statistically significant difference.

National Institute for Health and Clinical Excellence (NICE): A government agency in the United Kingdom that publishes evidence-based management guidelines for that country's nationalized health system. Notably, it considers both efficacy and cost-effectiveness when formulating its recommendations.

Organisation for Economic Co-operation and Development (OECD): An economic consortium of 34 industrialized countries that encourages international governments to share expertise and seek solutions to common problems. It conducts research in many fields, including health care, and OECD data is often used when comparing American health care systems and outcomes with those of other similar countries.

Randomized Trial: A method of reducing bias in experiments comparing different treatments by assigning patients to different treatment groups via a computer randomizer, rather than having the researchers themselves decide.

Statistical Significance: A mathematical method of determining whether differences in outcomes from different treatments are due to those treatments or are simply from chance. A statistically significant difference in outcomes means that there is less than a 5% chance (also written as p <0.05) that the differences detected are due to chance. This is the commonly accepted threshold for accepting the results of an experiment. Likelihood of an experiment reaching statistical significance depends on the difference in efficacy of the treatments studied and the size of the subject group. That's why the most reliable studies have the largest group of subjects.

Systematic Review: A comprehensive review of all of the relevant scientific research concerning a particular subject. The research is then assessed for quality and graded appropriately. Systematic reviews are often used when formulating clinical practice guidelines.

Suggested Reading

"Left to Their Own Devices," The Economist, September 10, 2011, http://www.economist.com/node/21528644. *This article, about medical technology and device companies, indicates some of the challenges and areas of growth for this burgeoning industry.*

"Why Most Published Research Findings Are False," John Ioannidis, August 2005. http://www.plosmedicine.org/article/info:doi/10.1371/journal.pmed.0020124. *We discuss Ioannidis' work in this chapter, so why not hear it straight from the horse's mouth?*

Overtreated, by Shannon Brownlee. *This book deals mostly with The Dartmouth Atlas and problems not just of geographic variation but, in the author's opinion, of how that variation leads to unnecessary treatment.*

Polio: An American Story, by David Oshinsky. *This book tells the story of how the polio vaccine came to be and may be an entertaining introduction to both the historical and present states of scientific research and vaccine production. One of the best things about it is learning how the rivalry of Jonas Salk and Albert Sabin also represented a real scientific question and controversy.*

The Gold Standard: The Challenge of Evidence-Based Medicine, by Stefan Timmermans and Marc Berg. *The gold standard itself of EBM scholarship.*

The Immortal Life of Henrietta Lacks, by Rebecca Skloot. *Similar to the book on polio, this book provides an entirely different perspective on the scientific world and how it affects patients.*

The Truth About the Drug Companies: How They Deceive Us and What to Do About It, by Marcia Angell. *This is an opinionated book. However, the author is the former editor-in-chief of* The New England Journal of Medicine *and has meaningful opinions.*

The Wisdom of Whores, by Elizabeth Pisani. *This book is about public health research (globally, though, not in the U.S.) and also touches on the ways politics can block the best research and treatment policies.*

References

1. Dawkins R. To Live at All is Miracle Enough. http://richarddawkins.net/articles/91. Richard Dawkins Foundation. Accessed Sept 8, 2011.
2. Table 1: R&D expenditures at universities and colleges, by source of funds: FY 1953–2009. Academic Research and Development Expenditures: Fiscal Year 2009. http://www.nsf.gov/statistics/nsf11313/pdf/tab1.pdf. National Science Foundation. Accessed Sept 14, 2011.
3. NIH Budget. http://www.nih.gov/about/budget.htm. National Institutes of Health. Accessed Jan 17 2012, 2012.
4. National Health Expenditure Data https://www.cms.gov/NationalHealthExpendData/. Centers for Medicare & Medicaid Services. Accessed Apr 7, 2012.
5. 2010 U.S. Investment in Health Research. http://www.researchamerica.org/uploads/healthdollar10.pdf. Research!America. Accessed Feb 4, 2012.
6. Björk BC, Roos A, Lauri M. Scientific journal publishing yearly volume and open access availability. Information Research. 2009;14(1):391.
7. About ORI. http://ori.hhs.gov/about/. Office of Research Integrity. U.S. Department of Health & Human Services. Accessed Sept 14, 2011.
8. Table 155: Retail Prescription Drug Sales: 1995-2009. Statistical Abstract of the United States: 2011. http://www.census.gov/compendia/statab/2011/tables/11s0155.pdf. U.S. Census Bureau. Accessed Sept 8, 2011.
9. Lundy J. Prescription Drug Trends. http://www.kff.org/rxdrugs/upload/3057-08.pdf. Kaiser Family Foundation. Accessed Sept 8, 2011.
10. Roth G, Brooks K. The Top 20 Pharmaceutical Companies. http://www.contractpharma.com/issues/2011-07/view_features/the-top-20-pharmaceutical-companies/. Contract Pharma. Accessed Jan 19, 2012.
11. Harris G. The Safety Gap. New York Times. Oct 31, 2008.
12. Mullard A. 2011 FDA drug approvals. Nature Reviews Drug Discovery. 2012;11(2):91-94.
13. Staff Manual Guide: Chapter 53. Post Marketing Surveillance and Epidemiology: Human Drugs. Adverse Drug Effects. http://www.fda.gov/Drugs/GuidanceComplianceRegulatoryInformation/Surveillance/ucm129115.htm. US Food and Drug Administration. Accessed Jan 20, 2012.
14. Grabowski H. Follow-on biologics: data exclusivity and the balance between innovation and competition. Nature reviews. Drug discovery. 2008;7(6):479-488.
15. Gatyas G. IMS Institute Reports U.S. Spending on Medicines Grew 2.3 Percent in 2010, to $307.4 Billion. http://www.imshealth.com/portal/site/imshealth/menuitem.a46c6d4df3db4b3d88f611019418c22a/?vgnextoid=1648679328d6f210VgnVCM100000ed152ca2RCRD&vgnextfmt=default. IMS Institute for Healthcare Informatics. Accessed Sept 14, 2011.

16. Academy of Managed Care Pharmacy. AMCP Guide to Pharmaceutical Payment Methods, 2009 Update (Version 2.0). Journal of Managed Care Pharmacy: JMCP. 2009;15(6 Suppl A):S3-57, quiz S58-61.

17. King R, Donahoe G. Estimates of Medical Device Spending in the United States. http://www.lifechanginginnovation.org/reports/estimates-medical-device-spending-united-states. AdvaMed. Accessed Jan 19, 2012.

18. Delporte C, Barbella M, Stommen J. The Top 30. http://www.mpo-mag.com/articles/2011/07/the-top-30. Medical Product Outsourcing. Accessed Jan 19, 2012.

19. Maisel WH. Medical Device Regulation: An Introduction for the Practicing Physician. Annals of Internal Medicine. 2004;140(4):296-302.

20. Zuckerman DM, Brown P, Nissen SE. Medical Device Recalls and the FDA Approval Process. Archives of Internal Medicine. 2011;171(11):1006-1011.

21. Medical Technology Innovation Scorecard: the race for global leadership. http://www.pwc.com/us/en/health-industries/health-research-institute/innovation-scorecard. PricewaterhouseCoopers. Accessed Apr 12, 22, 2011 Medical Device Recalls. http://www.fda.gov/MedicalDevices/Safety/RecallsCorrectionsRemovals/ListofRecalls/ucm287581.htm. U.S. Food and Drug Administration. Accessed Jan 20, 2012.

23. FDA announces recall of Abbott glucose test strips. U.S. Food and Drug Administration. Accessed Jan 20, 2012.

24. The National Progress Report on e-Prescribing and Interoperable Healthcare. http://www.surescripts.com/pdfs/national-progress-report.pdf. SureScripts. Accessed Sept 14, 2011.

25. DesRoches CM, Campbell EG, Vogeli C, et al. Electronic health records' limited successes suggest more targeted uses. Health affairs. 2010;29(4):639-646.

26. Market Overview: Hospital Revenue Cycle Management (RCM) Applications. 2008 Year End Report. http://www.himss.org/foundation/docs/marketOverviews/2009_MO_RCM_Final.pdf. HIMSS Analytics. Accessed Sept 14, 2011.

27. Stewart-Williams S, Podd J. The placebo effect: dissolving the expectancy versus conditioning debate. Psychological bulletin. 2004;130(2):324.

28. Melander H, Salmonson T, Abadie E, van Zwieten-Boot B. A regulatory Apologia--a review of placebo-controlled studies in regulatory submissions of new-generation antidepressants. European Neuropsychopharmacology. 2008;18(9):623-627.

29. Silberman S. Placebos are Getting More Effective. Drugmakers are Desperate to Know Why. Wired Magazine. Aug 24, 2009. Accessed Jan 17, 2012.

30. Ioannidis JPA. Contradicted and Initially Stronger Effects in Highly Cited Clinical Research. JAMA: The Journal of the American Medical Association. 2005;294(2):218-228.

31. Ioannidis JPA. Why most published research findings are false. PLoS medicine. 2005;2(8):e124.

32. Emerson GB, Warme WJ, Wolf FM, Heckman JD, Brand RA, Leopold SS. Testing for the presence of positive-outcome bias in peer review: a randomized controlled trial. Archives of Internal Medicine. 2010;170(21):1934-1939.

33. Dwan K, Altman DG, Arnaiz JA, et al. Systematic review of the empirical evidence of study publication bias and outcome reporting bias. PLoS One. 2008;3(8):e3081.

34. Lexchin J, Bero LA, Djulbegovic B, Clark O. Pharmaceutical industry sponsorship and research outcome and quality: systematic review. Bmj. 2003;326(7400):1167-1170.

35. Couzin J, Unger K. Cleaning Up the Paper Trail. Science. 2006;312(5770):38-43.

36. What is EBM? http://www.cebm.net/index.aspx?o=1914. Centre for Evidence-Based Medicine. Accessed Sept 14, 2011.

37. Bachmann LM, Kolb E, Koller MT, Steurer J, Riet G. Accuracy of Ottawa ankle rules to exclude fractures of the ankle and mid foot: systematic review. BMJ. 2003;326(7386):417.

38. Graham ID, Stiell IG, Laupacis A, et al. Awareness and use of the Ottawa ankle and knee rules in 5 countries: Can publication alone be enough to change practice? Annals of Emergency Medicine. 2001;37(3):259-266.

39. McGlynn EA, Asch SM, Adams J, et al. The quality of health care delivered to adults in the United States. New England Journal of Medicine. 2003;348(26):2635-2645.

40. American College of Obstetricians-Gynecologists. Practice bulletin no. 122: Breast cancer screening. Obstetrics and Gynecology. 2011;118(2 Pt 1):372-382.

41. U.S. Preventive Services Task Force. Screening for Breast Cancer: U.S. Preventive Services Task Force Recommendation Statement. Annals of Internal Medicine. 2009;151(10):716-726.

42. Institute of Medicine (U.S.). Committee on Comparative Effectiveness Research Prioritization, ebrary I. Initial national priorities for comparative effectiveness research. Washington, D.C.: National Academies Press; 2009:227.

43. FAQ. http://www.dartmouthatlas.org/tools/faq/. The Dartmouth Atlas of Health Care. Accessed Sept 14, 2011.

44. Jha AK, Ferris TG, Donelan K, et al. How common are electronic health records in the United States? A summary of the evidence. Health Affairs 2006;25:w496-w507

45. DiMasi JA, Grabowski HG. The cost of biopharmaceutical R&D: Is biotech different? Managerial and Decision Economics. 2007;28(4 5):469-479.

46. Clinical Trials: What You Need to Know. http://www.cancer.org/Treatment/TreatmentsandSideEffects/ClinicalTrials/WhatYouNeedtoKnowaboutClinicalTrials/index.htm. American Cancer Society. Accessed Sept 14, 2011.

47. Gottlieb S. The FDA is Evading the Law. Wall Street Journal. Dec 23,2010. Accessed Jan 19, 2012.

48. Pollack A. Medical Treatment, Out of Reach. New York Times. Feb 9, 2011. Accessed Jan 19, 2012.

49. Angell M. The Epidemic of Mental Illness: Why? The New York Review of Books. 2011(June 23, 2011). http://www.nybooks.com/articles/archives/2011/jun/23/epidemic-mental-illness-why/. Accessed Aug 5, 2011.

50. Radley DC, Finkelstein SN, Stafford RS. Off-label Prescribing Among Office-Based Physicians. Archives of Internal Medicine. 2006;166(9):1021-1026.

51. Dutton G. 2011 Budget Outlook: Trim, Cut, Then Slash. http://www.genengnews.com/analysis-and-insight/2011-budget-outlook-trim-cut-then-slash/77899360/. Genetic Engineering & Biotechnology News. Accessed Feb 4, 2012.

52. Herper M. The World's Most Expensive Drugs. http://www.forbes.com/2010/02/19/expensive-drugs-cost-business-healthcare-rare-diseases.html. Forbes. Accessed Sept 14, 2011.

53. Pharmaceutical Price Controls in OECD Countries. Implications for U.S. Consumers, Pricing, Research and Development, and Innovation. http://www.ita.doc.gov/td/chemicals/drugpricingstudy.pdf. International Trade Administration. U.S. Department of Commerce. Accessed Sept 14, 2011.

54. Merck Announces Fourth-Quarter and Full-Year 2009 Financial Results. http://www.merck.com/newsroom/news-release-archive/financial/2010_0216.html. Merck. Accessed Sept 14, 2011.

55. Patent Full-Text Databases. http://patft.uspto.gov/. U.S. Patent and Trademark Office. Accessed Sept 14, 2011.

56. Prescription Products. http://www.merck.com/product/prescription-products/home.html. Merck. Accessed Sept 14, 2011.

57. Chart Pack: Biopharmaceuticals in Perspective. http://www.phrma.org/sites/default/files/159/phrma_chart_pack.pdf. Pharmaceutical Research and Manufacturers of America. Accessed Sept 14, 2011.

58. Paul SM, Mytelka DS, Dunwiddie CT, et al. How to improve R&D productivity: the pharmaceutical industry's grand challenge. Nature Reviews Drug Discovery. 2010;9(3):203-214.

59. Gagnon MA, Lexchin J. The cost of pushing pills: a new estimate of pharmaceutical promotion expenditures in the United States. PLoS Medicine. 2008;5(1):e1.

60. PhRMA Code's revised guidelines take effect January 2009. http://abhishekkatiyar.wordpress.com/2008/07/16/phrma-codes-revised-guidelines-take-effect-january-2009/. Accessed Sept 14, 2011.

61. Friedman Y. Location of pharmaceutical innovation: 2000–2009. Nature Reviews Drug Discovery. 2010;9(11):835-836.

62. Rockoff J. Drug Reps Soften Their Sales Pitches. Wall Street Journal. Jan 10, 2012. Accessed Jan 19, 2012.

63. Campbell EG, Gruen RL, Mountford J, Miller LG, Cleary PD, Blumenthal D. A national survey of physician-industry relationships. New England Journal of Medicine. 2007;356(17):1742-1750.

64. Healy W, Peterson R. Department of Justice Investigation of Orthopaedic Industry. The Journal of Bone and Joint Surgery (American). 2009;91(7):1791-1805.

65. Fact Sheet: Physician Payments Sunshine provisions in Health Care Reform. http://www.prescriptionproject.org/tools/sunshine_docs/files/Sunshine-fact-sheet-6.07.10.pdf. Pew Prescription Project. Accessed Jan 27, 2012.

66. Influence and Lobbying. http://www.opensecrets.org/influence/index.php. The Center for Responsive Politics. Accessed Jan 20, 2012.

67. The Quality of Healthcare: How to Measure and Improve It. http://knol.google.com/k/the-quality-of-healthcare#. . Accessed Feb 4, 2012.

68. The Collection: The Definition of Quality and Approaches to Its Assessment. Vol 1. Explorations in Quality Assessment and Monitoring. http://psnet.ahrq.gov/resource.aspx?resourceID=1567. Agency for Healthcare Research and Quality. Accessed Feb 4, 2012.

69. FDA Should Take Steps to Ensure That High-Risk Device Types Are Approved through the Most Stringent Premarket Review Process. U.S. Government Accountability Office. 2009;GAO-09-190.

70. Abelson R, Harris G. Critics Question Study Cited in Health Debate. New York Times. June 2, 2010.

71. Trapp D. What's in a number? Cost variance figure drives policy and courts controversy. http://www.ama-assn.org/amednews/2009/04/27/gvsa0427.htm. American Medical News. Accessed Apr 13, 2012.

Chapter 5
Policy and Reform

The previous chapters have discussed some of the problems, issues, and controversies within health care. You would be hard pressed to find anyone who thinks the U.S. health care system works perfectly as is, so in this chapter we examine laws and guidelines (policy) that address these issues as well as how improvements might be made (reform).

To talk about reform, you have to first understand what it is you're reforming. Thus, the chapter begins by addressing the current state of Cost, Access, and Quality as well as how the three major governmental health insurance programs—Medicare, Medicaid, and CHIP—work. After setting the stage, we move on to the recent reform law in Massachusetts as well as the national Affordable Care Act (ACA). Aside from explaining what these laws entail, we discuss the criticisms, politics, and public opinion of them.

The Lay of the Land

Using our Cost-Access-Quality triad, let's take a brief look at some of the issues facing the American health care system today.

Cost

American health care costs too much, to be succinct. While we may be paying for increased quality, increased innovation, and relatively short wait times in the U.S.—and while we may be willing to pay *more* than other countries for these benefits—it's clear that this rate of increasing costs is unsustainable. Right now, we spend 17% of national gross domestic product (GDP) on health care, a percentage that has consistently increased in recent years.[2] Everyone agrees that we need to change course; we can't just sit back and watch costs rise.

Total Expenditures as a Percentage of GDP

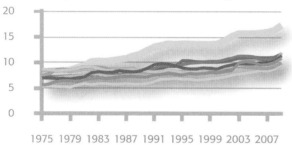

1975 1979 1983 1987 1991 1995 1999 2003 2007

Organisation for Economic Co-operation and Development, "Health Data 2011," June 2011.

Note: Amounts in U.S. $ purchasing power parity.

. . . And in Spending Per Capita

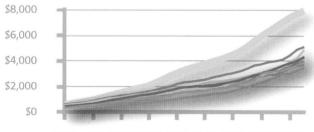

1975 1979 1983 1987 1991 1995 1999 2003 2007

United States vs. various countries: Belgium, Canada, Denmark, France, Germany, Netherlands, Sweden, Switzerland. United Kingdom

We could take some cues from other industrialized nations, all of which spend lower proportions of their GDP on health care.

Access

In the U.S., it can be prohibitively expensive and difficult to get medical care without insurance, so when people speak about the uninsured, they're often using shorthand for lack of access to care. And there's a lot of lack. In 2010, the uninsured numbered about 50 million (16% of the U.S. population). Further, about 20% of non-elderly people living in rural areas were uninsured[4] and 33 million non-elderly lived in physician shortage areas.[5]

Non-elderly Uninsured, 2010

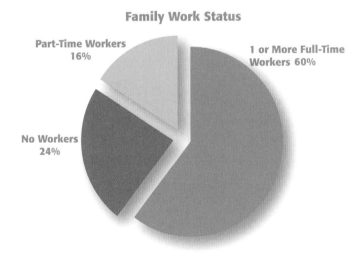

Family Work Status

Part-Time Workers 16%

1 or More Full-Time Workers 60%

No Workers 24%

The Henry J. Kaiser Family Foundation
"The Uninsured: A Primer" (7451-07), October 2011. Used by permission.

Note: Data may not total 100% due to rounding.

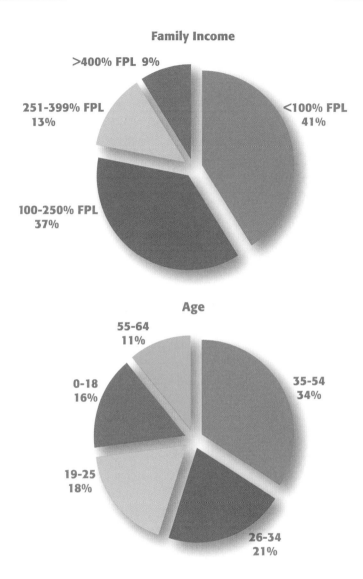

Family Income

>400% FPL 9%

251-399% FPL
13%

<100% FPL
41%

100-250% FPL
37%

Age

55-64
11%

0-18
16%

35-54
34%

19-25
18%

26-34
21%

Lack of insurance severely restricts access to health services—spanning
from preventive care to lifesaving treatment—which adds to the worsened
health status of these individuals relative to the general population. For
more in-depth discussion of the uninsured and access problems, see the
section on the uninsured in Chapter 3.

Quality

As discussed in Chapter 3, health care quality can be defined in many ways, which is why it can be difficult to measure or improve it. The Agency for Healthcare Research and Quality (AHRQ) discusses quality failures in four categories:

‣ Underuse of services: Only 34% of Americans with heart disease receive the influenza vaccine[6] despite evidence that it significantly decreases mortality from heart attack as well as infection.[7]

‣ Overuse of services: Half of all patients diagnosed with the common cold are incorrectly prescribed antibiotics.[8]

‣ Misuse of services: Up to 18% of hospital admissions may result in harm as a consequence of procedures, medications, hospital-acquired infections, diagnostic procedures, and falls.[9]

‣ Variation of services: Medicare patients in Alabama are 18 times more likely to receive epidural steroid injections for low back pain than are Medicare patients in Hawaii.[10]

Clearly, all of these are problems, as quality of care is just as important as access and cost.

Any way you slice it, the U.S. health care system is in trouble. The most recent major international comparison by the Commonwealth Fund ranked our system 7th—which isn't so bad until you realize that the study only included seven countries. It's no surprise, then, that some sort of reform of the U.S. health care system was considered necessary by parties on all sides of the debate.

	AUS	CAN	GER	NETH	NZ	UK	US
OVERALL RANKING (2010)	3	6	4	1	5	2	7
Quality Care	4	7	5	2	1	3	6
Effective Care	2	7	6	3	5	1	4
Safe Care	6	5	3	1	4	2	7
Coordinated Care	4	5	7	2	1	3	6
Patient-Centered Care	2	5	3	6	1	7	4
Access	6.5	5	3	1	4	2	6.5
Cost-Related Problem	6	3.5	3.5	2	5	1	7
Timeliness of Care	6	7	2	1	3	4	5
Efficiency	2	6	5	3	4	1	7
Equity	4	5	3	1	6	2	7
Long, Healthy, Productive Lives	1	2	3	4	5	6	7
Health Expenditures/Capita, 2007	$3,357	$3,895	$3,588	$3,837*	$2,454	$2,992	$7,290

Adapted from Davis, et al., "Mirror, Mirror on the Wall: How the Performance of the U.S. Health Care System Compares Internationally - 2010 Update" The Commonwealth Fund, June 2010. Used by permission.

Government Insurance Programs

Medicare

Medicare is a federal program established in 1965 to insure the elderly and some disabled individuals. It is the largest insurer in the nation—meaning the policies Medicare sets have a large impact on how health care is run in general.

ELIGIBILITY

The primary purpose of Medicare is to cover the elderly, though it has been slightly expanded over the years. To be eligible for coverage, a person must:

▸ Be at least 65 years old, have been a U.S. citizen or permanent resident for over five years, and have (or have a spouse who has) paid Medicare taxes for at least 10 years;

▸ Be under age 65, be permanently disabled, and have received Social Security disability benefits for at least the previous two years;

▸ Be under age 65 and receive Social Security disability benefits for amyotrophic lateral sclerosis (ALS or Lou Gehrig's disease); or

▸ Be under age 65 and need continuous dialysis or a kidney transplant.

COVERAGE

Medicare has four parts:

▸ **Part A:** Inpatient insurance, covering stays in hospitals and nursing homes, home health visits, and hospice. These benefits, however, have a limit on the number of days they will pay for in a facility, and they are subject to co-pays and deductibles.

▸ **Part B:** Outpatient insurance, including coverage for physician visits, preventive services, and home health visits. These benefits are also subject to co-pays and deductibles.

▸ **Part C:** Also called Medicare Advantage, it allows beneficiaries to enroll in a private insurance plan (like an outside HMO), which will cover all regular Medicare benefits and may cover more or require reduced co-pays and deductibles. Medicare pays these private insurers a fixed amount per month, per beneficiary. About 25% of Medicare beneficiaries are enrolled in a Medicare Advantage plan.[11]

▸ **Part D:** Prescription drug benefit; this is voluntary and operates through contracted private insurers. The program is subsidized, particularly for low-income beneficiaries. There is, however, a coverage gap called the "donut hole." This donut hole exists because Medicare covers 75% of annual prescription costs up to $2,700, and it pays 95% of prescription costs over $6,154. If a beneficiary's prescriptions cost between $2,700 and $6,154, however, Medicare pays nothing, and the individual has to pay entirely out of pocket. (Those who are also eligible for Medicaid don't fall into this hole.)

LACK OF COVERAGE AND SUPPLEMENTAL INSURANCE

Medicare requires somewhat high co-pays and deductibles, doesn't have a limit on out-of-pocket costs, and doesn't pay for long-term care (e.g., a permanent nursing home), eye services, or dental services. Thus, many beneficiaries want additional insurance to reduce their out-of-pocket expenses. Options include:

▸ Employer-sponsored retirement benefits
▸ Medigap: Voluntary insurance offered by Centers for Medicare & Medicaid Services (CMS) in addition to Medicare Parts A and B (you can't have this with Medicare Advantage)
▸ Medicaid

FUNDING

The main sources of Medicare funding are general federal revenues (43%), payroll taxes (37%), and beneficiary premiums (13%).[12]

PHYSICIAN PAYMENTS

The Sustainable Growth Rate (SGR) is a formula established in 1997 that is used by Medicare to determine how payments to physicians should be adjusted year-by-year to control costs. The SGR formula has recommended a reduction in Medicare physician reimbursement 11 times. With one exception, Congress has passed a temporary stay to avoid the cut each time. However, the government hasn't made any permanent changes in the SGR program. CMS announced that the 2013 cuts in Medicare physician reimbursement will be 32% unless Congress acts again.[13]

Medicaid

Medicaid is a joint federal-state program established in 1965 to insure the poor.

ELIGIBILITY

These criteria are a little more complicated than those for Medicare, since they depend on the state and the type of person covered. Contrary to popular belief, Medicaid doesn't simply cover those in poverty. To be eligible, a person must belong to one of the following "categorically eligible" groups:

▸ Children
▸ Parents with dependent children
▸ Pregnant women
▸ People with severe disabilities
▸ Seniors (meaning that many Medicaid recipients are "dual eligibles;" that is, they receive both Medicare and Medicaid)

States must cover citizens in these groups who have incomes below defined thresholds (which is where the wiggle room for states comes in). There are no enrollment limits—if a state happens to have an unusually high number of residents who fit in these groups, the state must cover them all regardless.[14]

The income thresholds are based on the federal poverty level (FPL, page 109). All states are required to cover categorically eligible individuals whose incomes are 20% or more below the FPL, but states have authority to allow eligibility at higher incomes. For example, coverage of working adults is available in Minnesota for those with an annual income below $24,015, while in Arkansas the limit is $1,900 per year.[15]

COVERAGE

Medicaid programs are required to offer minimum benefits, though some states choose to offer more. Required coverage includes:

▸ Inpatient and outpatient hospital services
▸ Physician, midwife, and nurse practitioner services
▸ Laboratory and X ray services
▸ Nursing facility services and home health care for individuals age 21 or older
▸ Early and periodic screening, diagnosis, and treatment for children under age 21
▸ Family planning services and supplies
▸ Rural health clinic and federally qualified health center services

FUNDING

The federal government pays a sizable portion of Medicaid costs (the Federal Medical Assistance Percentage, or FMAP), with states covering the rest. FMAP is at least 50% in all states, though it's increased:

▸ In poorer states, up to 76% at the highest, and
▸ Temporarily in all states, due to the 2008 economic stimulus package, up to 85% at the highest.

To receive stimulus funding, states were required to maintain the same eligibility requirements they had previously (so they couldn't drop beneficiaries to save money). The funding expired at the end of 2010; however, the eligibility requirements must be maintained until 2014.

As a side note, an optimal place to cut spending is on fraud. According to a 2009 article in *The New England Journal of Medicine*, 18.6% of Medicaid,

10.4% of Medicare, and 6.8% of Medicare Advantage spending is due to "waste, fraud, and abuse."[3]

CHIP

CHIP (sometimes referred to as S-CHIP, for State Children's Insurance Program) is a joint federal-state program established in 1997 to insure low-income children.

ELIGIBILITY

Low-income children are often covered by Medicaid. At a minimum, Medicaid requires coverage of children up to age 6 with family incomes less than 133% FPL and up to age 18 with family incomes of or less than 100% FPL. (States may choose to cover children at higher family incomes.)

CHIP's purpose is to expand insurance to children who aren't eligible for Medicaid coverage. However, there are no hard-and-fast rules for eligibility; states have broad authority to set their own eligibility rules. As of February 2011, about six million children in the nation were covered by CHIP, and more than eight million children were uninsured.[16]

COVERAGE

Coverage varies by state, and benefits are similar to those under Medicaid. States are allowed to limit coverage below the thresholds for Medicaid, and, further, they may require premiums and deductibles on a sliding scale based on family income level.

FUNDING

The federal government offers matching funds, as with Medicaid, but with CHIP, federal money makes up a larger percentage of the total funding. Each state receives a capped, maximum allotment.

Reform

History was made when Congress passed the Patient Protection and Affordable Care Act (ACA) and Health Care Education and Reconciliation Act (HERA), and they were signed into law by President Barack Obama on March 23, 2010. These laws represent the most sweeping changes to the government's role in the U.S. health care system since 1965.

Because the ACA was modeled after an earlier Massachusetts health care reform law, let's start this section by summarizing the Massachusetts reform and its effects.

State-Based Reform: Massachusetts

Massachusetts passed a comprehensive state health insurance reform law in 2006. The law included an individual mandate to purchase health insurance, expansions of Medicaid and CHIP, the creation of health insurance exchanges, subsidies for individuals below 300% federal FPL, reforms of the insurance markets, and new insurance requirements for employers, among other provisions.[28] The Massachusetts law has been in place for only a few short years; however, intensive research has already been done to track the effects of the law on cost, access, and quality of health care within the state.[29] Here's a quick run-down.

Access: The new laws have dramatically increased health insurance coverage in the state. A large study concluded that the percentage of non-elderly Massachusetts adults who are uninsured has dropped from 13.4% in 2006 to 5.8% in 2010, and that the proportion receiving coverage through ESI has slightly increased since the reform was enacted. Visits to ERs have dropped,[a] while those for specialist and preventive care have risen.[30] The increase in newly insured patients has put a strain on the primary care workforce, and wait times of one month or more for new patients are common.[31,32] The number of non-elderly adults that report not receiving needed medical care has decreased but remains high at 23%.[30]

---

a   Emergency room data is somewhat controversial. Initial studies didn't show any impact of reform on ER visits,[42,43] but the most recent data shows a modest decrease.[30,44] It remains to be seen if this trend will continue in the future.

Cost: Assessing the effect of reform on the costs of care is difficult because of the paucity of state-level cost data, the fact that costs for Medicaid expansion and other provisions of the law are shared between Massachusetts and the federal government, and the confounding effect of the financial crisis and recession that occurred at the same time reform was implemented. The weight of the evidence thus far has shown that, though care has become somewhat more affordable for patients,[30,33] there has been no appreciable reduction in the overall growth in health care spending.[34]

Quality: Defining health care quality is difficult even in ideal circumstances (page 168), and robust data about the changes in quality in Massachusetts after reform is scarce. Several researchers have conducted surveys of Massachusetts adults about health status, which have shown improvements in self-reported health[30] overall, along with other measures of physical and mental health and exercise.[35] However, we would advise reserving judgment on the effect of reform on health care quality until more detailed research is completed.

National Reform: The Patient Protection and Affordable Care Act

To understand the basics of the ACA, let's now look at how it will affect major groups (the federal government, state governments, insurers, hospitals, employers, individuals, and businesses) and how the law will be financed. For a more in-depth look, move to the next section, which answers FAQs about the details of the ACA.

SUMMARY OF CHANGES

Federal Government

The primary changes for the federal government center on Medicare, the establishment of a number of new organizations, and increased government spending on health care (with hopes of reaping savings on increased prevention and quality).

The major Medicare changes are:

▸ Providing more preventive care without co-pays and deductibles
▸ Closing the Part D coverage gap (the "donut hole") through rebates and subsidies

- ▸ Freezes payments to some facilities and providers at 2010 levels for several years, while providing bonuses to primary care providers
- ▸ Testing delivery programs such as Accountable Care Organizations and medical homes
- ▸ Increasing the number of beneficiaries who pay higher premiums due to income
- ▸ Decreasing support for Medicare Advantage plans

Numerous new institutes and boards also have been created—too many to list in a summary—but they mainly focus on national quality and prevention strategies, greater coordination between institutions, comparative effectiveness research, and health workforce research.

The federal government will make more payments for Medicaid, CHIP, and in subsidies to those with low incomes who purchase insurance through Health Insurance Exchanges. These Exchanges establish a marketplace for individuals and small employers to purchase insurance from qualified plans. The federal government also will fund the newly created institutes, grants for states and businesses to develop innovative delivery systems, and tax breaks for small businesses that promote wellness.

State Government
The two major changes for state governments are:
- ▸ They are required to develop and administer the Health Insurance Exchanges.
- ▸ States that accept federal money to expand eligibility for Medicaid and CHIP have additional requirements for how to administer these programs.

For information on the Exchanges, see "What Exactly Is an Exchange?" on page 200.

States may decide whether or not to accept federal money in order to expand their Medicaid programs. If they do accept the money, then they must comply with the changes to Medicaid dictated by the ACA. These are:
- ▸ Expanded eligibility to include childless adults up to 133% of the federal poverty level
- ▸ No federal matching payments for care related to hospital-acquired infections

- Increased federal funding for long-term care, preventive care, and testing new delivery systems
- Increased provider payment rates to equal Medicare rates for the years of 2013 and 2014

Insurers

A number of restrictions are placed on insurers, most of which involve consumer protections:

- Insurers can no longer deny coverage for pre-existing conditions, end coverage when policyholders get sick, or charge higher premiums based on current or projected health status. Rating risk groups can now only focus on age, geographic location, family composition, and tobacco use.
- Insurers must keep their medical loss ratios (see Chapter 3) at 85% for large group and 80% for small group insurers, or else they must provide rebates to policyholders.
- Insurers must allow dependents up to age 26 to be covered under their parents' policies.
- Insurers may not place annual or lifetime limits on the amount they will pay out for policies.

In addition, high-cost and consumer-driven insurance plans have new restrictions, most of which end tax breaks that individuals in these plans have enjoyed previously. Insurance companies get a deal, too: a huge increase in customers.

Employers

The requirements on employers are different for large and small employers, so we'll look at those requirements separately.

- **Small employers (≤50 employees):** Receive tax credits if they offer insurance, and they will be allowed to purchase insurance through the Exchanges. They also will be able to apply for grants to establish employee wellness programs.
- **Large employers (51-200 employees):** Required to offer health insurance and penalized monetarily if they don't. Employers that do offer insurance may be penalized if premiums cost more than 8% of any full-time employee's income. (The point is that employers should be providing affordable insurance.)

> ▸ **Very large employers (>200 employees):** Must automatically enroll employees in the company's health insurance plan, though employees may opt out.

All employers may offer certain rewards to their employees for participating in wellness programs and meeting health benchmarks.

Hospitals

Hospitals will be affected mostly by changes to the Medicare payment structure (including a pilot program for bundled payments), decreased payments associated with hospital-acquired infections (and thus a bigger push for quality), and new requirements for not-for-profit hospitals (including quality measures).

Individuals

The number one change is that now everyone (aside from undocumented immigrants) who wants health insurance will be able to get it. Whether through their employment, on the individual market, or through an Exchange; whether they pay for themselves or get subsidies; whether they have pre-existing conditions or are as healthy as can be—if they want insurance, they'll be able to get it. On the flip side, those who don't want insurance will be taxed if they don't purchase it (with some exceptions).

The law does a little bit of Robin Hood redistribution, too. There is a new tax on income above $200,000, and fewer out-of-pocket medical expenses can be deducted from taxes. On the other hand, Medicaid eligibility criteria widen, and those who aren't eligible but make less than 400% of the federal poverty level can still get subsidies to purchase insurance through Exchanges.

Finally, for those who found insurance unaffordable or very difficult to qualify for based on their health status, things should get easier. Insurers can no longer discriminate based on pre-existing conditions or projected health status, and they can't limit the amount policies pay out in a year or in a lifetime. In addition, young adults will be able to stay on their parents' insurance until they're 26.

Businesses

Health care reform places some haphazard regulations on business. This includes a 10% tax on indoor tanning and a tax on medical device and pharmaceutical companies. Biologics developers can now get generics approved through the FDA. Chain restaurants must post caloric content on menus. And pharmaceutical companies that participate in Medicare will be required to offer discounts to beneficiaries who fall into the Part D coverage gap.

Financial Impact

This is quite possibly the most confusing topic of this book, for many reasons. First, it's hard to find projections of costs that give hard numbers. Then, it's hard to figure out what those numbers are based on. Finally, different organizations have different projections that often disagree. A lot of that discussion is based on somewhat controversial projections and requires a fair amount of financial background. The truth is, no one really knows what the financial consequences of the ACA will be, though a thorough reading of the projections may get you somewhat closer to that knowledge. As such, we won't get into an in-depth discussion here. (But if that's your cup of tea, please see the Suggested Reading section.)

We do want to provide an idea of the financial impact, though. Here's a visual depiction of the broad financial changes caused by health care reform, with estimates from the Congressional Budget Office (CBO).

Estimated Budgetary Effects of Health Care Reform

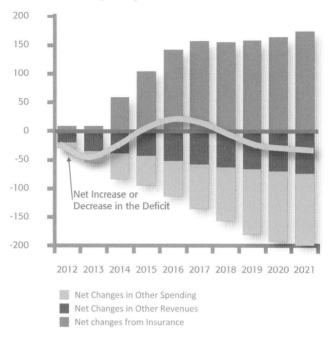

Net Increase or
Decrease in the Deficit

2012 2013 2014 2015 2016 2017 2018 2019 2020 2021

Net Changes in Other Spending
Net Changes in Other Revenues
Net changes from Insurance

Congressional Budget Office, "CBO's Analysis of the Major Health Care Legislation Enacted in March 2010," March 2011.

The CBO projects that the total financial impact of health care reform will be to reduce the federal deficit by $210 billion from 2012 to 2021.[b]

Some critics take issue with these estimates. The CBO has a history of significantly underestimating the future costs of health care programs, including Medicare and Medicaid,[17] and a June 2010 article in *Health Affairs* projected that the ACA would increase the deficit by $500 million from 2010-2019.[18] Whether such challenges are correct or not, it's obvious that the prediction process is pretty tricky, and we simply can't fully know yet what all the financial implications of the law will be.

---

b   Please keep in mind that these estimates were released before the Supreme Court decision on the ACA.

Understanding the Affordable Care Act: FAQs

When health care reform was being debated as a bill, much was made of its length. It's long, true. Twice the length of a Harry Potter book, in fact.[1] This section will explain the provisions of the ACA in an intuitive manner. Rather than droning on about details, we focus on answering questions about what those details *mean*. We do our best to cut through the legalese and explain everything in plain English.

How Will Things Change for Individuals?

NEW PROVISIONS: SUBSIDIES AND PENALTIES

The obvious big change due to health care reform is that everyone will have to buy insurance (the "individual mandate"). Beginning in 2014, all American citizens must be insured (except the populations listed in the later question, "Who Will Be Exempt?"), and those who aren't will have to pay a tax. The tax gets phased in, starting at $95 or 1% of income, whichever is greater, in the first year and tops out at $695 or 2.5% of income in 2016. Thereafter, it will increase with cost of living adjustments. Technically, this is not a true "mandate"—it's not a requirement to buy insurance but instead a tax if you don't. If this seems like splitting hairs to you, you're not alone, but it played a role in some of the legal challenges the ACA faced (see "Criticisms and Challenges" at the end of this chapter for more info).

To help those who have trouble affording insurance, the ACA mandates federal subsidies for individuals to buy insurance through the Exchanges (page 202). Subsidies are largest for those under 250% of the federal poverty level, though lesser assistance exists for incomes up to 400% of the federal poverty level.

On one hand, the ACA offers subsidies to purchase insurance for those with low incomes, and, on the other hand, it increases taxes on those with high incomes. It increases taxes in two ways. First, by increasing taxes on the wealthy to fund Medicare Part A; beginning in 2013, the Medicare payroll tax rate increases by 0.9% (to 2.35% total) for all earnings over $200,000 for individual taxpayers and $250,000 for married couples.

(There also will be a 3.8% assessment on unearned income for these taxpayers.) Second, and also beginning in 2013, individuals only will be able to deduct unreimbursed medical expenses from their taxes if these expenses are higher than 10% of income. The prior level was 7.5% of income. Individuals age 65 and older are allowed to keep this original level until 2016.

Things also will change drastically in terms of consumer protections and of regulations on what insurance will cover, how much it will cover, etc. See the "What Will Happen with Insurance in General?" section later in the chapter.

HOW WILL PEOPLE RECEIVE COVERAGE?

The Kaiser Family Foundation offers a handy flowchart explaining where people will receive their insurance coverage under the reforms, which you can check out on the next page.

WHO WILL NOT HAVE TO PURCHASE INSURANCE?

- People with financial hardship (e.g., no plan costs less than 8% of income)
- People with religious objections (e.g., Christian Scientists)
- American Indians (who receive care through the newly reauthorized federal Indian Health Service)
- Those who are uninsured for three months or less
- Those who are incarcerated (who receive care from the federal or state government)

WHO WILL STILL BE UNINSURED?

- Undocumented immigrants
- Those who choose to pay the tax rather than buy insurance
- Those who are eligible for Medicaid but choose not to enroll
- Some individuals for whom insurance will cost more than 8% of their income (they may choose not to purchase it, and their tax is waived)

Employers

Employer requirements for offering insurance depend on the size of the business and number of full-time employees:

▸ **If ≤50 full-time employees:** Not required to provide Employer Sponsored Insurance (ESI). However, these employers are encouraged (with tax credits) to provide ESI, either by purchasing it on the private market or through the Exchanges (see next section).

▸ **If 51-200 full-time employees:** Must offer ESI, and are penalized if (a) they don't offer ESI or (b) do offer ESI, but one or more employees are eligible to receive tax credits in the Exchange (i.e., the ESI is unaffordable or the employees have very low incomes). The tax is $2,000 per full-time employee, minus the first 30 employees. Further, employers that offer coverage but have at least one full-time employee receiving a premium tax credit will pay the lesser of $3,000 per credit or $2,000 per full-time employee, again excluding the first 30.

▸ **If 200+ full-time employees:** Automatic (opt-out) enrollment of all employees into ESI.

The ACA also offers incentives for employers not only to offer insurance but also to develop efforts to increase wellness among their employees. Among these incentives are tax credits to small businesses for 35% to 50% of insurance costs for those that offer insurance to their employees. Also, five-year grants are available to small employers who establish wellness programs, and employers also are encouraged to offer rewards of 30% to 50% of the cost of coverage to employees for participating in and meeting certain health standards. (A few states may receive grants to try the same with private insurance, as with Exchanges.)

In addition, employers who have been receiving tax deductions on Medicare Part D drug subsidy payments for their retirees will no longer receive such deductions, perhaps because the federal government will be providing its own subsidies for the Part D coverage gap.

How People Get Health Coverage
Under the Affordable Care Act Beginning in 2014

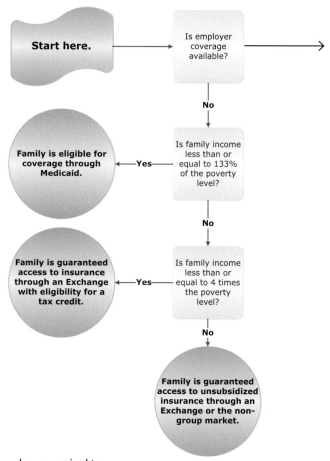

Notes:

1. In general, people are required to obtain coverage or pay a penalty, but those whose health insurance premiums exceed 8% of family income (after tax credits or employer contributions are taken into account) will not be penalized if they choose not to purchase coverage.
2. Employees are eligible for "free choice vouchers" if they must pay 8-9.8% of income for employer coverage, so employees facing premiums of 9.5-9.8% of income under an employer plan are eligible to buy coverage in an Exchange using a free choice voucher or receive a tax credit.

3. Regulations specifying how dependents of workers with employer coverage available are treated have not yet been issued.
4. A "free choice voucher" allows an eligible employee to take the amount contributed by an employer towards health insurance and use it towards the premium of a plan in an Exchange.
5. Certain parts of this flowsheet may not apply in states that choose not to expand Medicaid.

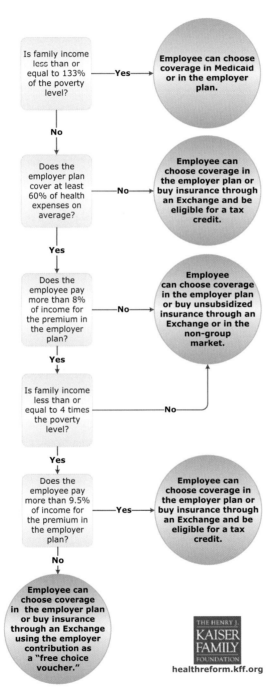

Is family income less than or equal to 133% of the poverty level?

—Yes→ Employee can choose coverage in Medicaid or in the employer plan.

No

Does the employer plan cover at least 60% of health expenses on average?

—No→ Employee can choose coverage in the employer plan or buy insurance through an Exchange and be eligible for a tax credit.

Yes

Does the employee pay more than 8% of income for the premium in the employer plan?

—No→ Employee can choose coverage in the employer plan or buy unsubsidized insurance through an Exchange or in the non-group market.

Yes

Is family income less than or equal to 4 times the poverty level?

—No→ (to non-group market box)

Yes

Does the employee pay more than 9.5% of income for the premium in the employer plan?

—Yes→ Employee can choose coverage in the employer plan or buy insurance through an Exchange and be eligible for a tax credit.

No

Employee can choose coverage in the employer plan or buy insurance through an Exchange using the employer contribution as a "free choice voucher."

THE HENRY J.
KAISER
FAMILY
FOUNDATION
healthreform.kff.org

The Henry J. Kaiser Family Foundation, "How People Get Coverage Under the Affordable Care Act–Flowchart," 2012.
Used by permission.

What Exactly Is an Exchange?

By 2014, every state must have a Health Insurance Exchange. The goal is for states to create and administer these Exchanges themselves, but it's not technically a requirement: if the state doesn't develop an Exchange, the federal government will step in and administer one within that state.

Think of Exchanges as state-run marketplaces for buying insurance—just like you might go to the mall to buy clothes. The mall management decides which stores get in, and it regulates some of their practices in order to be there. The Exchanges are similar but with health insurance plans instead of stores. Each state will create its own, so each exchange will be different.

If this concept still seems abstract, visit the Massachusetts Health Connector website at <www.mahealthconnector.org>. It may make more sense once you see an exchange in action.

WHAT THE EXCHANGES DO

▸ Certify qualified health insurance plans to offer.
▸ Require plans to disclose the following in plain language: claims payment; policies and practices; financial status; data on enrollment, denied claims, and rating practices; information on cost sharing and payments for out-of-network coverage; and enrollee and participant rights.
▸ Require plans to explain what services have co-pays and deductibles.
▸ Assign a rating to each health plan based on relative quality and price.
▸ Use a uniform enrollment form and a standardized format for presenting benefit options for health plans.
▸ Create a calculator to determine the actual cost of a plan for each person, including tax credits, co-pays and deductibles.
▸ Provide a website where enrollees can compare information about each plan.
▸ Inform enrollees about their eligibility for Medicaid, CHIP, or other public programs and coordinate enrollment procedures with them.
▸ Determine which individuals may be exempt from penalties if no

affordable insurance plans are available through those individuals' employers or through the Exchanges.

▸ Award grants to outside entities to educate the public about the Exchanges.

WHAT PLANS THE EXCHANGES OFFER

There are five levels of plans, with premiums scaled down accordingly:

1. **Platinum:** premium accounts for 90% of the full actuarial value of the plan
2. **Gold:** 80%
3. **Silver:** 70%
4. **Bronze:** 60%
5. **Catastrophic:** This is a restricted level, as enrollees must be under the age of 30, and all other plans must exceed 8% of their income.

That "full actuarial value of the plan" can be confusing. The Kaiser Family Foundation explains a Silver plan: "for a standard population, the plan will pay 70% of their health care expenses, while the enrollees themselves will pay 30% through some combination of deductibles, co-pays, and co-insurance. The higher the actuarial value, the less patient cost-sharing the plan will have, on average."[19]

Thus, platinum plans cost more in monthly premiums but cost less in co-pays and deductibles for services, and bronze plans are the opposite.

INDIVIDUALS (ABHP)
- Unincarcerated U.S. citizens and legal immigrants
- No available ESI, ESI premiums cost more than 9.5% of income, or ESI actuarial value is <60%

EXCHANGE

SMALL BUSINESSES (SHOP)
- If <100 employees
- States can restrict to <50 before 2016 or expand to >100 after 2017

INSURERS
- Must offer at least one Silver & one Gold plan
- Meet marketing requirements: not discourage high-risk individuals
- Ensure sufficient choice of providers
- Include providers that serve low-income communities
- Be accredited by the state on clinical quality measures
- Use standard format for presenting benefit plans

WHAT PLANS IN THE EXCHANGE COVER

▸ All plans must cover the following services: ambulatory, emergency, hospitalization, maternity and newborn, mental health and substance abuse, prescription drugs, laboratory, prevention and wellness, chronic disease management, rehabilitation and devices, and pediatric services, including oral and vision care.

▸ All plans must abide by general insurance guidelines concerning premium ratings (meaning insurers can't rate premiums on anything other than age, geographic location, family composition, and tobacco use).

SUBSIDIES FOR THE EXCHANGES

Consumers of plans in Exchanges are eligible for subsidies if their income levels are at or below 400% FPL and they enroll in the least expensive silver plan available. The subsidies are provided as income tax credits, and they reduce premiums as indicated in the table below.

Income % of FPL	Premium Cost as % of Income	Max Out-of-Pocket Expenses
<133%	2%	$1983/person
133-150%	3-4%	$1983
150-200%	4-6.3%	$1983
200-250%	6.3-8.05%	$2975
250-300%	8.05-9.5%	$2975
300-400%	9.5%	$3987

Note: Tax credits also will be available for legal immigrants who aren't yet eligible for Medicaid because they have been citizens for fewer than five years.

What Will Happen to Insurance?

CONSUMER PROTECTIONS

For many Americans, the new regulations on insurance aimed at protecting consumers will be the most noticeable changes of health care reform. The consumer protections on insurance include:

▸ Insurers can't deny coverage based on pre-existing conditions.

▸ The waiting period for new insurance to take effect is capped at 90 days.

▸ Insurers may not cancel policies once policyholders get sick. (This practice, which is based on evidence that a condition existed prior to the beginning of a policy, whether a patient knew it or not, is termed "rescission.")

▸ Insurers may not require co-pays or deductibles for preventive services (largely immunizations and screening for major diseases; must be rated Level A or B by the U.S. Preventive Services Task Force).

▸ Deductibles may be no higher than $2,000 per individual and $4,000 per family.

▸ Insurers may not restrict how much they will reimburse claims either in a year or in a policyholder's entire life. In other words, insurers may not institute annual or lifetime limits.

▸ Insurers must maintain coverage for policyholders' adult, dependent children up to age 26.

In addition, insurance companies will be required to maintain a medical loss ratio of 85% for large group plans or 80% for small group and individual plans (or else provide rebates to policyholders), and insurance companies will be required to develop an appeals process and external review of health plan decisions. Thus, as of 2010, policyholders may now appeal to their insurers when they think their plans are not up to snuff, and states must develop a board to review such plans. State review of insurers is extended through ombudsman programs to advocate for patients in the individual and small group markets. Individuals can get information and assistance from ombudsman offices.

DE-PRIORITIZING CONSUMER-DRIVEN PLANS

Consumer-driven insurance includes such plans as flexible spending accounts (FSAs) and health saving accounts (HSAs). (See Chapter 3 for more information about these plans.) However, tax-free contributions to FSAs are capped at $2,500 each year, to be adjusted annually for inflation, and use of funds in FSAs is restricted to certain circumstances. The funds can no longer be used for over-the-counter, non-prescription drugs (except insulin), and the tax penalty for using account funds for non-medical expenses increases to 20% (from 10%).

HOW MUCH WILL BE NEW, AND HOW MUCH WILL BE GRANDFATHERED IN?

If an individual is already insured and happy with her plan, chances are that very little will change. This is because the health care reform law has a "grandfather" provision, allowing plans in effect as of March 23, 2010, to remain in effect, with the following conditions:

1. Insurers must have made the following changes by 2010: End lifetime limits, end recission, and allow dependents to remain on their parents' policies until age 26; they also must end annual limits on coverage as of 2014.
2. Insurers must *not* make the following changes (or else they become a "new" plan and lose grandfathered status): cut benefits; raise co-insurance, co-pay, or deductible charges; lower the employer contribution to insurance; or introduce or lower an annual limit on coverage.

Individuals will be notified whether their current plans are grandfathered or are changing, and they have the option of sticking with their current plans or choosing new ones.[20]

NEW FEES AND TAXES ON INSURERS

You may consider these Robin Hood measures, or you may consider them unfair taxation. Either way, they will help fund reform.

▸ Yearly fees on insurers. The fees total $8 billion in 2014 and increase to $14.3 billion by 2018.

▸ A temporary reinsurance program (lasting from 2014-16), which accepts premiums from insurers in the individual market, as well as employers, and then provides payments to insurers who cover high-risk policyholders.

▸ An excise tax on insurers of employer-sponsored health plans with expenses that exceed $10,200/$27,500. This is a way to garner revenue for reform while penalizing high-cost insurance.

What Will Happen with Medicare?

In terms of current Medicare beneficiaries, perhaps one of the biggest changes is that preventive services stopped requiring co-pays and deductibles as of January 2011. What exactly a "preventive service" is hasn't been completely defined yet (the U.S. Preventive Service Task Force is working on that; see more information in the glossary), but you can expect it to include things such as colorectal cancer screenings for older adults, annual check-ups, and flu shots. The rationale (and this extends through health care reform in general, not just with Medicare) is to incentivize preventive care in the hopes that this will make people healthier and reduce Medicare spending down the line by nipping costly chronic conditions in the bud.

Along the same lines (increasing short-term spending with the goal of improving the health of the population and thus decreasing long-term spending), Medicare has established or will establish several new programs. They are:

▸ **Accountable Care Organizations (ACOs):** Medicare will allow ACOs to share in any savings they impart. See the next section for an explanation of what ACOs are.

- **Bundled Payments for Episodes of Care:** This is a pilot program to give one lump sum for a course of treatment rather than the traditional fee-for-service payments. An episode of care will begin three days prior to a hospital admission and last 30 days past discharge. This will begin in 2013.

- **Independence at Home Demonstration Project:** This is an experimental program to pay physician and nurse practitioner teams to provide primary care services to some underserved beneficiaries in their homes.[21]

- **Federal Coordinated Health Care Office:** This office (created in 2010) will identify "dual eligibles;" that is, beneficiaries who are eligible for both Medicare and Medicaid. The office coordinates their care between the two programs. (Currently, everything is managed separately.)

- **CMS (Center for Medicare & Medicaid Services) Innovation:** This office, established in 2010, designs, models, and tests new delivery and payment systems for federal insurance programs with the goal of decreasing cost and increasing quality. Interestingly, it accepts suggestions from the public, which you can submit online.

CMS also will expand Medicare eligibility, though only in a very limited category. Medicare now will cover adults under age 65 who have developed health conditions following environmental hazard exposure in an emergency declaration area, though only for certain health conditions, and only for emergency declarations after June 17, 2009 (i.e., no Katrina victims, etc.).

Further, in an effort to reduce fraud and abuse in Medicare (as well as in Medicaid and CHIP), CMS developed new levels of oversight in 2012. Providers, hospitals, and suppliers now will pay increased fees to fund these fraud prevention services.

ACCOUNTABLE CARE ORGANIZATIONS (ACOS)

One of the provisions of the ACA states that qualified ACOs will be able to share in any savings their practices lead to for Medicare. In March 2011, the CMS issued for public review a 400-page document describing the rules ACOs must follow to qualify. Intimidating! Let's break that down into more bite-sized pieces.

The first thing to understand is that an ACO is both a system of delivering care to patients and of receiving payment from insurers. This system could be, for instance, a hospital, in which providers are physically housed together, or it could be more like an HMO, an invisible network connecting providers in different locations. The network provides for patients entirely within its own resources (e.g., any physician the patient sees will be part of the network), coordinates their care within an integrated infrastructure (e.g., same electronic health record, same billing system), and emphasizes primary care (e.g., easy access to a PCP who synthesizes all of your care within the network).

Public health policy experts Drs. Mark McClellan and Elliot Fisher described it in more detail. ACOs include the following core-defining principles:

1. These are provider-led organizations with a focus on primary care. The entire organization is accountable for quality and costs for all care that a population of patients receives.
2. Payments are linked to quality, a move intended to reduce costs in the long-term.
3. The organization focuses on using performance measurements which are reliable, reproducible, and use data to improve over time. These performance measurements support improvements in care as well as savings based on those improvements.[22]

The goal of an ACO is to create "shared savings" for both the health care system and for the government. These savings will ideally accrue from improving the health of individuals and the population as a whole, and from decreased health care costs.

The idea of the ACO pre-dates the health care reform of 2010, but the ACA includes it as a function of Medicare and incentivizes it by allowing ACOs to share in any cost-savings they produce. Some of the criteria ACOs must meet to share savings, though, are:

1. Include at least 5,000 Medicare beneficiaries
2. Agree to participate as an ACO for at least three years
3. Maintain an overall management structure
4. Develop processes to ensure the use of evidence-based medicine and quality measures

5. Ensure patient-centeredness, as defined by clinician and patient surveys or by individualized care plans

MEDICARE ADVANTAGE

Medicare Advantage, as is detailed in the "Medicare" section earlier in this chapter, allows beneficiaries to contract their Medicare benefits through a private insurer rather than through the federal government, potentially paying higher premiums but getting expanded benefits. The reform laws place new restrictions on these plans.

Fee-for-service payments through Medicare Advantage will get increasingly smaller. In 2011, payments didn't increase with inflation and remained at 2010 levels. The affected plans are banned from increasing co-pays or deductibles on certain services, so they can't simply shift this new cost to beneficiaries. In addition, all Medicare Advantage plans will be required to maintain a medical loss ratio of at least 85% beginning in 2014, meaning that these plans will be held to the same standards as all large market insurers.

Reform also reduces payments to Medicare Advantage plans, but it makes up for it by providing bonus payments to Advantage plans that meet quality thresholds. This reduction in payments is being implemented in 2012. The rationale is to incentivize quality improvements and deprioritize Advantage plans relative to regular Medicare.

PART D COVERAGE GAP (THE "DONUT HOLE")

The Part D coverage gap is detailed earlier in the chapter—Medicare doesn't cover prescription drugs costing between $2,700 and $6,154 per year, and patients must pay entirely out of pocket. As you can imagine, this has been a problem for many low- and middle-income Medicare beneficiaries, and the ACA aims to close the gap through several provisions:

- **Starting June 2010:** All Medicare beneficiaries who had to pay out of pocket for drugs due to the coverage gap received a $250 rebate from Medicare.
- **Starting January 2011:** Pharmaceutical companies are required to provide a 50% discount on brand-name drugs for those in the cov-

erage gap, and federal subsidies will do the same for generic pre-scriptions. (As of publication, this has reduced prescription costs on average by $545 per person.)[23]

▸ **Between 2010 and 2020:** The federal government will roll out subsidies for brand-name prescriptions, with the goal of reducing patient out-of-pocket expenses on these drugs from 100% in 2010 to 25% in 2020.

MEDICARE COSTS

Medicare costs have risen dramatically in the last two decades; the pro-gram already spends more than it takes in, and it's forecasted to run out of money in 2024.[24] (Though we should note that many such forecasts have come and gone through the years.) All of the above expansions and added benefits listed above will cost money. As such, the ACA mandates some changes to how Medicare makes reimbursements to reduce spend-ing. (Keep in mind that Medicare already reimburses only 90% of hospital costs—see Chapter 3.)

The ACA also establishes the Medicare Independent Payment Advisory Board (IPAB). This board is tasked with recommending ways to reduce per capita Medicare spending if spending continues to grow past current targets. Its first report of recommendations will be due January 2014. The IPAB's recommendations are especially important because they automati-cally become law unless Congress acts to override them.

In the meantime, ACA makes other changes to Medicare spending:

▸ Updating facility payment rules by reducing annual, market-based updates and adjusting rates for productivity. These changes affect inpatient, outpatient, long-term care, rehabilitation, and psychiatric facilities. These started being implemented at various times in 2011 and continue in 2012.

▸ Adjusting payments to hospitals based on performance in certain quality measures. Further, the ACA mandates plans to implement value-based purchasing programs for nursing, home health, and outpatient surgical facilities. Implementation began in 2012.

▸ Reducing payments to hospitals if they have excess readmissions. This is a measure to incentivize quality care both in the hospital as well as during follow-up after discharge. In addition, CMS counts readmissions to other hospitals, not just the original one. Implementation began in 2012.

▸ Increasing Medicare payments for primary care services—and to general surgeons operating in shortage areas—by 10%. This is both an incentive and a reward for primary care services, and the bonus payments last from 2011 to 2015. Granted, this isn't a measure to save on Medicare costs in particular, but it *is* part of the general thrust in the ACA to boost payments for preventive care in an effort to stem costs down the road.

▸ Shifting more premium costs onto higher-income Medicare beneficiaries. The income threshold for higher premiums in Part B will be frozen at 2010 levels until 2019, meaning it won't keep up with inflation, so more people will have higher premiums. The same provision will reduce the Part D subsidy (described earlier) for those with incomes above $85,000 per individual and $170,000 per couple.

What Will Happen with Medicaid and CHIP?

FEDERAL CHANGES

The general direction of the ACA changes for Medicaid and CHIP is to increase the number of people these programs cover as well as to increase their quality and efficacy. Federal aspects of these changes are:

▸ To increase and extend federal matching funds for states (increasing those for CHIP in 2015 by 23%-100% in each state and extending them until 2015).

▸ To encourage the expansion of Medicaid eligibility in states by covering 100% of costs for these new enrollees from 2014 to 2016. The cost coverage will drop to 90% by 2020.

▸ To expand the Medicaid and CHIP Payment and Access Commission (MACPAC) and charge it with including recommendations on adult services in addition to the recommendations on children's services it already provides. The MACPAC will release these reports twice yearly, providing policy recommendations to the Congress, Department of Health & Human Services (HHS), and states for Medicaid and CHIP.[26]

STATE CHANGES

Of course, if the federal government mandates expansion and changes to Medicaid and CHIP, the states—who administer both programs—have to implement most of the changes.

Originally, the ACA mandated an eligibility expansion by offering a carrot or a stick: the federal government would completely pay for any newly eligible enrollees—but, if states did not comply, then they would lose all of their Medicaid funding. However, in June 2012, the Supreme Court deemed this "stick" to be overly coercive to the states. Now, states must comply with the new stipulations only if they accept the additional federal funding; otherwise, they are free to continue administering their Medicaid programs—and receiving the same federal funds—as before. It isn't clear how many states will decide not to expand Medicaid. We might note that while it's easy for Republican governors to publicly oppose Democratic policies, it's a whole lot harder to turn down extra money. On the other hand, states sometimes do just that: for one example, Arizona refused to set up a Medicaid program at all until 1982, 17 years after Medicaid was formed.

The main way the ACA expands access is by increasing eligibility for Medicaid (again, only in those states that voluntarily comply). This option was allowed beginning in 2010 and will be mandated by 2014. New eligibility extends to those who aren't eligible for Medicare and who have incomes up to 133% of the federal poverty level. This means that more low income childless adults, parents, pregnant women, and children will have access to Medicaid coverage. In addition, hospitals will be able to assume "presumptive eligibility" for patients they know to be eligible but are not already enrolled and bill Medicaid retroactively for their care.

Note, however, that increased federal matching funds will only cover these newly eligible enrollees; those who were previously eligible, even if they hadn't been signed up before, will be subject to the existing federal matching payments. In addition, the ACA requires states to maintain their current eligibility levels for children in Medicaid and CHIP until 2019, so states can't restrict eligibility for children's coverage in their efforts to stem spending.

States will need to make several other changes aimed at providing better coverage for Medicaid beneficiaries. These include new programs and payments:

- **Medicaid Drug Rebate:** Beginning in 2010, Medicaid beneficiaries receive a rebate of 23.1% of the cost of their brand-name drugs and 13% of generics. They get this rebate even if they were in managed care plans.

- **Money Follows the Person Demonstration Program:** This program, along with new initiatives for the Aging and Disability Resource Center, offer increased federal funds for Medicaid beneficiaries who move from long-term, live-in care facilities (e.g., nursing homes) to community-based locations (e.g., back home). These programs were already in effect though, so this just an extension of a trial program until 2014.

- **Extension of Medicaid Services to Homes and Community-Based Centers:** As of 2010, Medicaid covers the complete or partial cost of home or community-based services, such as those by a home health aide or in a nursing home. Along the same lines, Medicaid will use the State Balancing Incentive Program and Community First Choice Option to increase funding and services in home- and community-based long-term care, including for persons with disabilities.

- **Three-Year Grants to States:** States can apply for grants in order to develop Medicaid programs to incentivize healthy lifestyle programs and meet certain health behavior goals. In February 2011, $100 million dollars in grants became available.

- **Bundled Payments for Episodes of Care:** Eight states will run this demonstration project. As with the Medicare experiment, an episode of care will begin three days prior to admission and last 30 days past discharge from a hospital. If the programs improve—or maintain—quality and reduce costs, then they will be expanded after 2016.

- **Medicaid Payments Match Medicare:** Medicaid payments to primary care providers increase to equal the Medicare rates for two years.

- **Increased Federal Matching:** As of 2013, federal matching payments will increase to states in which Medicaid covers preventive services without co-pays or deductibles.

- **Medical Home:** This program allows beneficiaries to designate specific primary care providers as "health homes" and offers 90% federal matching payments for two years for health home-related services.

The Medicaid health home is based on the already-existing concept of the Patient-Centered Medical Home (PCMH), which the CMS defines as "a model for care, provided by physician-led practices, that seeks to strengthen the physician-patient relationship by replacing episodic care based on illnesses and individual's complaints with coordinated care for all life stages […]. The physician-led care team is responsible for coordinating all of the individual's health care needs—including preventive, acute, chronic, and end-of-life care—and arranges for appropriate care with other qualified physicians and support services. The individual decides who is on the team, and the primary care physician makes sure team members work together."[27] Think of a health home as a medical point-of-contact, an advocate, and a guardian to the whole medical world.

The above expansions and extensions of coverage will be costly. To help balance those costs, the ACA also mandates several decreases in Medicaid payments. In 2011, a new ban was implemented on federal funds to Medicaid for services related to hospital-acquired infections (HAIs, page 15). In 2014, the ACA also will reduce states' Medicaid allotments for disproportionate share hospitals (those facilities that treat more Medicaid patients than average); these funds will be distributed elsewhere, as determined by the Secretary of HHS.

What Are the New Insurance Types?

Much of the ACA involves changes to current insurance plans; however, it also creates a few new ones, some temporary and some permanent.

Temporary insurance programs aim to cover early retirees and those with pre-existing conditions. These programs last from 2010-2014, until these populations will be able to receive insurance through the Exchanges. First, the temporary Early Retiree Reinsurance Program offers reinsurance to employers who continue to offer health insurance to retired employees over age 55 who aren't yet eligible for Medicare. The program reimburses either employers or insurers 80% of claims between $15,000 and $90,000. Second, the temporary Pre-Existing Condition Insurance Program (PCIP) insures individuals who have pre-existing conditions and have been uninsured for at least six months. The goal of PCIP is to tide these individuals over until 2014, when insurers will no longer be allowed to deny coverage based on pre-existing conditions.

Further, ACA creates or reauthorizes the following:

- **Health Insurance Exchanges:** Establishes a marketplace for both individuals as well as small employers to purchase insurance from qualified plans.
- **Indian Health Care Improvement Act:** This was a program that lapsed in 2001; it covers American Indians and Alaskan Natives and seeks to erase the health disparities in these populations versus the rest of the general population.
- **Consumer Operated and Oriented Plan (CO-OP):** Fosters the creation of not-for-profit, member-run health insurance companies.

WHAT IS A CO-OP?

CO-OP (Consumer Operated and Oriented Plan) is intended to be not-for-profit, member-owned health insurance. Organizations can form their own plans and apply to be CO-OPs, but they must not be government-sponsored or already in existence as an insurer. They also must offer qualified health benefit plans as well as operate according to majority vote of members. Any profits must be funneled back to all members either through lowered costs or increased benefits.

Will Public Funds Be Used for Abortion?

No. This was a big deal politically while the reform bills were being debated. Here's how abortion is cordoned off from public funds:

- Federal premium subsidies (e.g., for those using the Exchanges) may not be used for abortion unless the reason for termination is rape, incest, or saving the life of the woman.
- States may prohibit all plans that cover abortion from being in an Exchange.
- Abortion may not be listed as part of the essential health benefits package.
- If a state does allow plans that cover abortion in its Exchange, it must create an "allocation account" that separates premium payments that cover abortion from premium payments for other coverage such that no federal funds will be used to cover abortion beyond reasons of rape, incest, or saving the life of the woman.
- Exchange plans may not discriminate against providers who will not provide or refer abortion services.

New Efforts in Research, Prevention, and Serving the Underserved

The ACA aims to improve health care quality. Research is a major force not just in advancing care but also in developing efficient and valuable methods of delivering care. Thus, the ACA also establishes several new avenues of research:

National Health Care Workforce Commission and National Health Care Workforce Analysis: These commissions have two goals: first, to collect and analyze health care workforce data at the state and local level; second, to coordinate workforce activities and make recommendations about policy affecting the workforce.

Patient-Centered Outcomes Research Institute (PCORI): Performs comparative effectiveness research (CER) and publishes its findings and attendant recommendations for care. (Note that it is barred from using any cost-benefit analyses in forming its recommendations.)

Research in Emergency and Trauma Medicine: Establishes a program to develop capacity and preparedness for emergencies as well as to develop new ways to deliver effective care in emergency and trauma departments.

Enhanced Collection of Disparity Demographic Data: HHS is now required to collect patient demographic data such as race, ethnicity, sex, primary language, disability status, and rural underserved. It must collect and analyze this data to better inform policies addressing health care disparities.

Supporting New Ideas in the Private Market: The government will provide tax credits and grants for small businesses that are pursuing new medical therapies, ways to reduce long-term spending, and potential cures for cancer.

One goal of the ACA is to improve primary care medicine, especially preventive services and care for underserved populations. The ACA introduced a number of programs on these fronts, including:

▸ **Strategies:** The development of the National Prevention Strategy and the National Quality Strategy, both aimed at developing a cohesive plan for nationwide coordination of care and delivery.

- **Synchronizing Care for the Underserved:** Community-Based Collaborative Care Networks will encourage cooperation of health care providers to provide streamlined care for underserved populations.
- **Shifting Residencies to Primary Care:** Establishment of "Teaching Health Centers" by providing funding for primary care residencies in community-based, ambulatory health centers. The ACA also redistributes unfilled residency slots in specialty fields to outpatient, primary care settings. This doesn't increase the total number of residencies in the U.S., but it does prioritize primary care slots.
- **New Requirements for Not-For-Profit Hospitals:** Not-for-profit hospitals must conduct community needs assessments and develop plans for financial assistance to the needy. For those that don't meet these requirements, there will be a $50,000 annual tax.
- More money for Federally Qualified Health Centers and the National Health Service Corps.
- **Workforce Shortages:** The Prevention and Public Health Fund aims to address primary care workforce shortages through training programs for low-income individuals wishing to enter the primary care workforce, as well as through wellness (focused on tobacco, obesity, etc.) and immunization campaigns.
- **340(b) Drug Discount Program:** This program provides savings of 20% to 50% on the cost of pharmaceuticals. Eligibility has been expanded to include safety net hospitals.

Medical Malpractice

The ACA does not make any substantial changes to the current medical malpractice system (see the "Criticism" section below), but the federal government will provide $50 million in funding for states to design and test alternative systems. Grant funding will become available in 2013.

Funding Through New Taxes, Fees, Etc.

The ACA is funded in a variety of ways, several of which have been discussed above. In addition, there will be several new taxes and fees that don't fit into other categories, including:

- A 10% tax on indoor tanning services.
- Annual fees for pharmaceutical companies. The fees will increase

from providing a total revenue of $2.8 billion in 2012-2013 up to $4.1 billion in 2018 and thereafter.

▸ A 2.3% excise tax on the sale of any taxable medical device.

Transparency

In Chapter 4, we discussed some of the issues involving financial relationships between industry, physicians, and researchers and how these can lead to conflicts of interest. The ACA seeks to shine a light on these financial relationships, without banning them, by requiring disclosure of financial relationships between health entities, including health care providers as well as hospitals, nursing homes, and manufacturers and distributors of medical goods. Any gift, sponsorship, or ongoing financial relationship must be reported to the federal government, which will in turn make the information available to the general public.

The ACA also seeks to bring transparency to food and nutrition. Beginning in 2014, food vendors and restaurants with more than 20 locations must post the caloric content of their food on all menus. They must also make information about saturated fats, sodium, and cholesterol available upon request. However, some businesses that sell food, such as movie theaters and bars, will be exempt.

Impact of Health Care Reform

Criticisms of the Affordable Care Act

QUALITY

Though the law does include both a National Quality Strategy as well as increased quality requirements for ACOs, hospitals, and insurers, it wasn't—and couldn't be—a magic bullet for quality improvement.

The critiques of the law in terms of quality fall into four camps: (1) providers, not legislators, should be making decisions about quality improvement; (2) quality may be defined in different ways, and the law does not do enough to address this; (3) the law doesn't do enough to incentivize quality improvement; (4) the law messes with structures (such as the market) that produce the best quality already.

EVER-INCREASING COSTS

Even proponents of the law agree that it focuses more on access and quality than on cost. While the law manages to largely finance itself, it does little to reduce the rapidly rising costs of health care in general. (Remember those graphs at the beginning of the chapter?) The law does establish the Independent Payment Advisory Board with the goal of decreasing Medicare spending growth, but this may be woefully inadequate if costs remain so inflationary.

ACCESS

While the ACA does a lot to expand access and reduce the ranks of the uninsured, it's important to note that the law will not cause immediate, universal coverage. The New York Times reports that the ACA is expected to reduce the number of uninsured from 60 million to 27 million. In addition, the law relied heavily on Medicaid expansion to cover the uninsured; since the Supreme Court ruled that states can opt out of Medicaid expansion, this means that the federal government may have a more difficult time expanding coverage to all—or, at least, in making that expansion affordable. The Exchanges may be able to take up the slack in states that won't expand Medicaid, but it's still unclear what this might actually mean in the long term.

IMPLEMENTATION

As wordy as the ACA is, the law is still pretty vague. This is normal for legislation, and it's not unusual for regulations created *after* the law is passed to be more concrete and important than the law itself. But it also leaves a lot of room for interpretation. There will be a lot of costs, resources, and additional controversies that we can't yet know; these will arise from the development of regulations and through the final implementation.

One example of a new controversy comes from the Institute of Medicine (IOM), which published recommendations in July 2011 that the ACA consider birth control to be a "preventive service"—meaning that birth control could soon require no out-of-pocket costs to consumers. The IOM similarly recommends including sexually transmitted infection testing as a preventive service. This became a public controversy in February 2012 when the U.S. Conference of Catholic Bishops spoke out against a requirement that employers provide insurance that pays for contraception.

You can see that what seems benign in the text of the law may give rise to unforeseen controversy when implemented.

CONCERN ABOUT INCREASING GOVERNMENTAL POWER

The ACA expands eligibility for federal programs, expands governmental bureaucracy, increases taxes on corporations, and increases taxes on the wealthy. For someone who takes a dim view of public rather than private administration, and doesn't believe that the wealthy should be taxed to benefit the poor, this law poses some serious ideological concerns.

MANDATES AS THREATS TO LIBERTY

It's true that the federal government doesn't require people to purchase anything, though state governments do for those with cars: all drivers must buy liability auto insurance. (While many people feel they can't choose not to have a car, it is an option, so liability insurance isn't truly a universal mandate.) The individual mandate for health insurance is the first time the federal government has required citizens to purchase something (or face a tax penalty). This fact forms the basis of the claims of unconstitutionality against the ACA.

FRAGMENTATION

Although provisions such as ACOs and streamlined paperwork in the Exchanges do seek to integrate disparate parts of the health care system, the system will remain fragmented. Critics claim that reform didn't do enough to coordinate health care services and that this lack of coordination will continue to affect quality, cost, and both public and provider opinions.

Politics of Reform

COURT CHALLENGES TO THE AFFORDABLE CARE ACT

Scores of lawsuits have challenged health care reform—the first was filed just seven minutes after the ACA was signed into law—and the issue made its way to the Supreme Court. In March 2012, the Supreme Court heard arguments on four issues, and, in June 2012, the Court released opinions. Here is a list of the four issues and how they were decided:

1. Whether the expansion of Medicaid violates state's rights

Issue: The plaintiffs argued that the ACA is overly coercive to states. Medicaid is a joint Federal-State program—the states run Medicaid programs in part with federal money. The ACA mandates that states must expand Medicaid eligibility (the federal government will pay 100% of the cost of new enrollees, but they will only pay at historical rates for all previously eligible enrollees), and, if they don't, then the federal government will retract all funding for Medicaid. States claimed that this was too big of a threat.

Decision: 5-4 opinion that the ACA was coercive to states.

Outcome: Now, states can choose whether or not to expand Medicaid eligibility. If they choose to and accept additional federal money, they must comply with the ACA rules about it. If they choose not to, they will still receive the same historical federal funding for the same Medicaid programs as before.

2. Whether the individual mandate is allowed by the Constitution

Issue: The plaintiffs argued that the individual mandate is unconstitutional because it, in essence, forces individuals to purchase a private product. That requirement on citizens would be beyond the scope of Congress's powers. On the other hand, the federal government characterizes the individual mandate as an acceptable action within Congress's regulation of interstate commerce. Further, the federal government argues that the penalty for not purchasing insurance is levied as a tax, which is also fully within Congress's constitutional powers.

Decision: 5-4 opinion that the individual mandate is constitutional if defined as a tax penalty. Four justices thought that the mandate should be upheld under the Commerce Clause; however, the opinion written by John Roberts was very clear that it is upheld only as a tax, not under the Commerce Clause. This raises complicated legal issues that are beyond the scope of this book.

Outcome: The individual mandate stands as is; it is now defined as a tax penalty on those who can afford insurance but choose not to buy it.

3. Whether the rest of the law can still stand if the individual mandate gets struck down

Issue: The plaintiffs argued that without the individual mandate, the ACA is unworkable and should be scrapped entirely, while the federal government argued that the rest of the ACA should stay in place regardless of what happened with the mandate.

Decision: This point was moot since the individual mandate was upheld

4. Whether the court can even rule on these cases before the individual mandate has come into effect

Issue: A legal point involving the Anti-Injunction Act, an 1867 law concerning jurisdiction of tax lawsuits. In this instance, the Court had to decide if these cases could be decided now, or if they had to wait until the mandate and its associated financial penalties would be implemented in 2014-2015.

Decision: Obviously the court did not decide to wait until 2014.

WHY ARE SO MANY STATES UPSET ABOUT NATIONAL REFORM?

As health policy experts Drs. Benjamin Sommers and Arnold Epstein state in *The New England Journal of Medicine*, "The ACA requires the federal government to pay nearly the full cost of the Medicaid expansion (100% initially and 90% after 2019), and without this expansion millions of uninsured Americans would receive care from public clinics and hospitals that are subsidized by state dollars. So isn't the Medicaid expansion a winning proposition for states?"

Sommers and Epstein outline the following reasons:

- During a recession, Medicaid's ranks swell at the same time that tax revenues shrink, and we've been in the middle of a rather serious recession. Thus, budgets get a double hit right now, making states more upset.
- States had been receiving increased funding from the federal government as part of the economic stimulus package, but that expired in June 2011.
- The ACA mandates increased Medicaid eligibility—and funding—in 2014 but also doesn't allow states to limit eligibility rules until then. Thus, states aren't able to save money in the meantime by rescinding coverage to currently insured individuals.
- The ACA also only offers (near) total funding for *newly* eligible Medicaid beneficiaries; those who were eligible under the old rules will receive the standard matching funds (50-75%). But there are estimated to be millions of uninsured individuals who are currently eligible for Medicaid under the pre-ACA criteria. All of the brouhaha around health reform will likely get these individuals to enroll without actually increasing federal funding for them.
- Politics. It's an easy target for conservative state politicians who may find it politically expedient to counter a Democratic president.[37]

PUBLIC OPINION OF THE AFFORDABLE CARE ACT

Public opinion on reform runs the gamut from people who think it fails because it doesn't establish single-payer nationalized health insurance to people who think it fails because it exists at all. As you can see, levels of support and opposition to the ACA have been neck-and-neck since the law was passed.

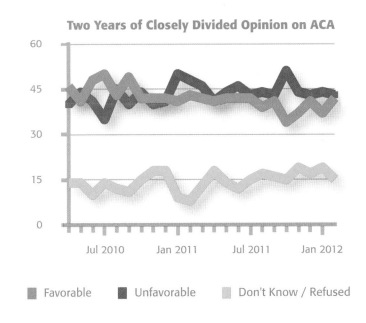

Two Years of Closely Divided Opinion on ACA

■ Favorable   ■ Unfavorable   ■ Don't Know / Refused

"As you may know, a new health reform bill was signed into law earlier this year. Given what you know about the new health reform law, do you have a generally favorable or generally unfavorable opinion of it?"

The Henry J. Kaiser Family Foundation, "Two Years Of Closely Divided Opinion On ACA," March 2012. *Used by permission.*

On the other hand, if you break down the law to its elements, these are remarkably popular across party lines.

Percent who say they feel favorable about each of the following elements of the health law:				
	Total	Dem	Ind	Rep
Require easy-to-understand plan summaries	84%	88%	87%	76%
Tax credits to small businesses	80%	88%	77%	73%
Subsidy assistance to individuals	75%	88%	76%	51%
Gradually close Medicare "dough-nut hole"	74%	86%	73%	63%
Health plan decision appeals	74%	82%	70%	70%
Medicaid expansion	69%	86%	70%	47%
Guaranteed issue	67%	81%	63%	57%
Rate review	66%	78%	66%	51%
No cost sharing for preventative services	64%	68%	65%	53%
Employer mandate/penalty for large employers	63%	79%	59%	39%
Medical loss ratio	60%	72%	62%	48%
Increase Medicare payroll tax on upper income	59%	81%	61%	28%
Increase Medicare premiums for higher income	57%	71%	54%	36%
Basic benefits package, defined by government	53%	73%	49%	31%
Individual mandate/penalty	35%	53%	29%	17%

The Henry J. Kaiser Family Foundation, "Kaiser Health Tracking Poll– November 2011" (8259-C), November 2011. Used by permission.

Note: Items asked of separate half samples. Response wording abbreviated. See Topline: http://www.kff.org/kaiserpolls/8259.cfm for complete wording.

This split of opinion between the law as a whole and the individual components of the law seems odd. But it certainly makes the following graph unsurprising:[41]

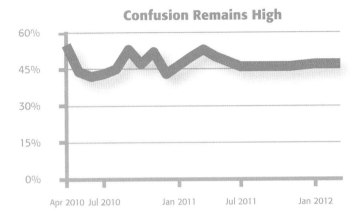

Confusion Remains High

"Percent Who Say That "Confused" Describes Their Feelings About the Health Reform Law" The Henry J. Kaiser Family Foundation, "Kaiser Health Tracking Poll—March 2012" (8285-C). Used by permission.

Those who are dissatisfied with the ACA believe the government should have (and still should) pursue a different type of reform for the health care system. There are as many ideas for health care reform as there are aspects of the system that can be changed. We've mentioned some alternate reform options elsewhere in the book (i.e., malpractice reform), but let's briefly break down a few of the other major ideas in health care reform:

Decrease Insurance Regulation: Eliminate state-specific health insurance regulations, allowing insurers to offer plans nationwide. This would increase choices for consumers, and competition between insurers.

Reduce ESI: Eliminate tax breaks for ESI and transition to a system where insurance is purchased on the individual market. This would increase each patient's "skin in the game" and reduce job lock (page 88).

Single Payer: Cut out private insurers altogether and make health coverage payment a function of government, funded by taxes. Think of the Department of Defense and VA health care systems as models.

Public Option: The government offers a health insurance plan in the market along with private insurance plans. One way to accomplish this would be to allow Americans of any age to enroll in Medicare.

Each of these ideas for reform could—and do— have whole books written about them, and we won't go into details here. Many good ideas are out there, and it's difficult to know what's best; having an opinion about health reform really means going with your best hypothesis. Rest assured that many smart, knowledgeable, well-intentioned people disagree wildly about their hypotheses.

Conclusion

Health care reform is deeply complex and equally controversial. No matter what your political leanings, clearly the state of the American health care system is in need of more than a few bandages. After reading this chapter, you hopefully better understand what health care reform is and what it isn't. We also hope you see how, to some extent, none of us know what the ACA will and won't do. Ultimately, this ignorance about the specifics of the ACA is fitting, because it symbolizes how, in general, our nation stands at a precipice for health care reform. None of us knows what the state of the system will look like in 10 years. Yet, regardless of what is to come, being informed is essential for anyone who provides or receives medical care in the U.S.

Glossary

Beneficiary: A person enrolled in a health insurance plan.

Catastrophic Insurance: An insurance plan that has a minimum of insulation. Low premium, high co-pay/deductible plans that cover costly, unexpected medical services but not routine care.

Co-payment: The dollar amount of an expense incurred by the beneficiary that has to be paid by the individual out of pocket. For example, you might have to pay $15 for each name-brand prescription that's filled, while the rest is covered by the insurance company.

Deductible: An annual minimum amount of costs that the beneficiary must pay entirely out of pocket before the insurance company begins to pay. For example, the first $500 in medical costs incurred per year is paid by the beneficiary; beyond that the insurance company may pay completely or require a co-pay.

Indian Health Service: A branch of the HHS that funds and administers a comprehensive health care system for American Indians. Similar to the VA, it directly employs health care professionals and operates hospitals and outpatient services.

Network Coverage: Certain insurance plans have discount agreements with a number of health care providers; these providers compose the network of options for a beneficiary of that plan. Generally, a beneficiary can visit any health care provider he likes but will have to pay less out of pocket for a provider in the network.

Payout Limit: The total amount of medical care an insurance company will pay for on behalf of a beneficiary. Insurance plans often have annual and lifetime limits. For example, a plan may pay up to $100,000 in costs in any given year and $5 million over the course of a patient's life. After the limit has been reached, any additional medical costs must be paid by the beneficiary out of pocket.

Pre-Existing Condition: A medical condition that was present before enrolling in an insurance plan. Today, regulations about pre-existing conditions vary by state, but many insurance plans can charge higher premiums for customers with pre-existing conditions. Also patients already enrolled in insurance plans may have cost reimbursement denied if the company determines the care was necessary for a pre-existing condition.

Premium: Periodic payment from a beneficiary to the insurance company. Cost varies with type of coverage, risk rating of the beneficiary, amount of co-pay, deductible and payout limits. Most health insurance requires a monthly premium.

Reinsurance: Reinsurance isn't something you can buy—it's the insurance that *insurance companies* buy. This limits their chances of going belly-up if many of their policyholders need a pay-out at the same time, as in an epidemic or natural disaster.

U.S. Preventive Services Task Force (USPSTF): An independent panel of medical experts funded by the Agency for Healthcare Research and Quality (AHRQ) that uses evidence-based medicine processes to formulate recommendations about a broad variety of preventative screening, medication and counseling options, from colonoscopies to vitamin D supplements. Each recommendation receives a grade, from A / Recommend (high certainty of substantial benefit) to D / Recommend Against (moderate or high certainty of no benefit or net harm).

Suggested Reading

Affordable Care Act (full text of the law), http://docs.house.gov/energycommerce/ppacacon.pdf. This lengthy document, obviously, is only for the very interested. If you have a high threshold for legalese, have a lot of time on your hands, and really don't trust summaries, then, by all means, go for it!

"Sick Around the World" (an episode of PBS's Frontline), http://www.pbs.org/wgbh/pages/frontline/sickaroundtheworld/. *This isn't necessarily connected to the ACA, but it does compare and contrast the health care systems of several first-world nations. The differences may give some context for why some of these—and further—reforms get suggested. Plus, the video is only 30 minutes.*

Health Care Will Not Reform Itself: A User's Guide to Refocusing and Reforming American Health Care, by George Halvorson. *This is a book written by the head of Kaiser Permanente, an HMO referenced several times in this book. It's designed to give an opinionated view, which, regardless of your opinion, should give a clue to how a major player in deciding health administration thinks things should be run.*

Kaiser Family Foundation Health Reform Source, http://healthreform.kff.org/. *If we could just force you to go to this website, we would. This is an incredible resource, chock-full of information, well-explained, and free.*

The Urban Institute Health Policy Center: Massachusetts and Health Reform. http://www.urban.org/health_policy/Massachusetts-and-Health-Reform.cfm. *The best compendium of research, analysis, and facts about Massachusetts' 2006 health care reform act and its consequences. The site is updated frequently with new reports so check back often.*

SCOTUSblog—Health Care, http://www.scotusblog.com/category/special-features/health-care/. *If you want to learn more about the Supreme Court cases concerning the ACA but haven't gone to law school, this is the site to check out.*

References

1. Katz A. Length of Health Care Reform Bills Silliness. http://alankatz.wordpress.com/2009/11/27/length-of-health-care-reform-bills-silliness/. Accessed Aug. 5, 2011.

2. National Health Expenditure Data https://www.cms.gov/NationalHealthExpendData/. Centers for Medicare & Medicaid Services. Accessed April 7, 2012.

3. Iglehart JK. Finding money for health care reform—rooting out waste, fraud, and abuse. New England Journal of Medicine. 2009;361(3):229-231.

4. Carrier E, Yee T, Garfield R. The Uninsured and Their Health Care Needs: How Have They Changed Since the Recession? http://www.kff.org/uninsured/upload/8246.pdf. Kaiser Family Foundation. Accessed March 7, 2012.

5. Hoffman C, Damico A, Garfield R. Insurance Coverage and Access to Care in Primary Care Shortage Areas. http://www.kff.org/insurance/upload/8161.pdf. Kaiser Family Foundation. Accessed March 7, 2012.

6. Davis MM, Taubert K, Benin AL, et al. Influenza vaccination as secondary prevention for cardiovascular disease. Circulation. 2006;114(14):1549-1553.

7. Phrommintikul A, Kuanprasert S, Wongcharoen W, Kanjanavanit R, Chaiwarith R, Sukonthasarn A. Influenza vaccination reduces cardiovascular events in patients with acute coronary syndrome. European Heart Journal. 2011.

8. Gonzales R, Steiner JF, Sande MA. Antibiotic prescribing for adults with colds, upper respiratory tract infections, and bronchitis by ambulatory care physicians. JAMA: the journal of the American Medical Association. 1997;278(11):901.

9. Landrigan CP, Parry GJ, Bones CB, Hackbarth AD, Goldmann DA, Sharek PJ. Temporal Trends in Rates of Patient Harm Resulting from Medical Care. New England Journal of Medicine. 2010;363(22):2124-2134.

10. Friedly J, Chan L, Deyo R. Geographic variation in epidural steroid injection use in Medicare patients. The Journal of Bone and Joint Surgery. 2008;90(8):1730.

11. Fiegl C. Medicare private plan enrollment hits 12.8 million. http://www.ama-assn.org/amednews/2012/02/13/gvsb0213.htm. Accessed Feb. 25, 2012.

12. Medicare at a Glance. http://www.kff.org/medicare/upload/1066-13.pdf. Kaiser Family Foundation. Accessed Aug. 5, 2011.

13. Fiegl C. Medicare Doctor Pay Patch Sets Up 32% Cut for 2013. http://www.ama-assn.org/amednews/2012/02/27/gvl10227.htm. American Medical News. Accessed April 12, 2012.

14. Medicaid and the Uninsured. http://www.kff.org/medicaid/upload/7235-04.pdf. Kaiser Family Foundation. Accessed Aug. 5, 2011.

15. Income Eligibility Limits for Working Adults at Applicationas a Percent of the Federal Poverty Level (FPL) by Scope of Benefit Package, January 2012. http://www.statehealthfacts.org/comparereport.jsp?rep=54&cat=4. Kaiser Family Foundation. Accessed April 13, 2012.

16. Health Coverage and Children: The Role of Medicaid and CHIP. http://www.kff.org/uninsured/upload/7698-05.pdf. Kaiser Family Foundation. Accessed Feb. 25, 2012.

17. Health Costs and History. Government programs always exceed their spending estimates. Wall Street Journal. Oct 20 2009 2009 Accessed Apr 7 2009.

18. Holtz-Eakin D, Ramlet MJ. Health Care Reform Is Likely To Widen Federal Budget Deficits, Not Reduce Them. Health Affairs. 2010;29(6):1136-1141.

19. What the Actuarial Values in the Affordable Care Act Mean. http://www.kff.org/healthreform/upload/8177.pdf. Kaiser Family Foundation. Accessed Aug. 5, 2011.

20. Questions and Answers: Keeping the Health Plan You Have: The Affordable Care Act and "Grandfathered" Health Plans. http://www.healthreform.gov/about/grandfathering.html. Department of Health & Human Services. Accessed Aug. 5, 2011.

21. Independence at Home Demonstration Fact Sheet. https://www.cms.gov/DemoProjectsEvalRpts/downloads/IAH_FactSheet.pdf. Center for Medicare & Medicaid Services. Accessed Au.g 5, 2011.

22. McClellan M, McKethan AN, Lewis JL, Roski J, Fisher ES. A national strategy to put accountable care into practice. Health Affairs. 2010;29(5):982.

23. Affordable Care Act Delivers Cheaper Prescription Drugs to Nearly 500,000 People. http://www.medicalnewstoday.com/releases/229881.php. Accessed Feb. 25, 2012.

24. Hensley S. Bad Economy Means Medicare Will Run Out of Cash Sooner. http://www.npr.org/blogs/health/2011/05/14/136278263/bad-economy-means-medicare-will-run-out-of-cash-sooner. National Public Radio. Accessed Aug. 5, 2011.

25. Glossary of Statistical Terms - Productivity adjustment. http://stats.oecd.org/glossary/detail.asp?ID=7163. Organisation for Economic Co-operation and Development. Accessed Aug. 5, 2011.

26. Report to the Congress on Medicaid and CHIP. http://healthreform.kff.org/~/media/Files/KHS/docfinder/MACPAC_March2011_web.pdf. Medicaid and CHIP Payment and Access Commission. Accessed Aug. 5, 2011.

27. Mann C. Re: Health Homes for Enrollees with Chronic Conditions. https://www.cms.gov/smdl/downloads/SMD10024.pdf. Accessed Feb. 25, 2012.

28. An Act Providing Access to Affordable, Quality, Accountable Health Care. http://www.malegislature.gov/Laws/SessionLaws/Acts/2006/Chapter58. Accessed April 7, 2012.

29. Long SK, Stockley K, Dahlen H. National Reform: What Can We Learn from Evaluations of Massachusetts? http://www.shadac.org/files/shadac/publications/MassachusettsNationalLessonsBrief.pdf. State Health Access Reform Evaluation. Accessed April 8, 2012.

30. Long SK, Stockley K, Dahlen H. Massachusetts Health Reforms: Uninsurance Remains Low, Self-Reported Health Status Improves As State Prepares To Tackle Costs. Health Affairs. 2012;31(2):444-451.

31. Ku L, Jones E, Finnegan B, Shin P, Rosenbaum S. How Is the Primary Care Safety Net Faring in Massachusetts? Community Health Centers in the Midst of Reform. http://www.kff.org/healthreform/upload/7878.pdf. Accessed April 7, 2012.

32. Walker E. Primary Care Still Hard to Get in Massachusetts. http://www. medpagetoday.com/Washington-Watch/Reform/26400. Accessed April 7, 2012.

33. Himmelstein DU, Thorne D, Woolhandler S. Medical bankruptcy in Massachusetts: has health reform made a difference? The American Journal of Medicine. 2011;124(3):224-228.

34. Weissman JS, Bigby J. Massachusetts Health Care Reform — Near-Universal Coverage at What Cost? New England Journal of Medicine. 2009;361(21):2012-2015. http://dx.doi.org/10.1056/NEJMp0909295.

35. Courtemanche CJ, Zapata D. Does Universal Coverage Improve Health? The Massachusetts Experience. National Bureau of Economics Research, March 2012.

36. About the Lawsuit. http://www.healthcarelawsuit.us/hc.nsf/pages/About. Office of the Attorney General of Florida. Accessed Aug. 5, 2011.

37. Sommers BD, Epstein AM. Why States Are So Miffed about Medicaid — Economics, Politics, and the "Woodwork Effect." New England Journal of Medicine. 2011;365(2):100-102.

38. Kaiser Health Tracking Poll. http://www.kff.org/kaiserpolls/upload/8082-F.pdf. Kaiser Family Foundation. Accessed Aug. 5, 2011.

39. Public Remains Largely Split on ACA. http://facts.kff.org/chart.aspx?ch=1456. Kaiser Family Foundation. Accessed March 07, 2012.

40. Kaiser Health Tracking Poll: November 2011. http://www.kff.org/kaiserpolls/upload/8259-C.pdf. Kaiser Family Foundation. Accessed March 07, 2012.

41. Kaiser Health Tracking Poll. http://www.kff.org/kaiserpolls/upload/8166-F.pdf. Kaiser Family Foundation. Accessed Aug. 5, 2011.

42. Chen C, Scheffler G, Chandra A. Massachusetts' Health Care Reform and Emergency Department Utilization. New England Journal of Medicine. 2011;365(12):e25.

43. Long SK, Masi PB. Access And Affordability: An Update On Health Reform In Massachusetts, Fall 2008. Health Affairs. July/August 2009;28(4):w578-w587.

44. Miller S. The effect of insurance on outpatient emergency room visits: An analysis of the 2006 Massachusetts health reform. Social Science Research Network.

Index

A

abortion funding, 214
ACA. *see* Affordable Care Act (ACA)
academic medical centers, 5–6, 136
access to health care. *see also* Cost-
	Access-Quality triad
	and ACA, 215, 218
	and health care reform in Mass., 188
	international comparisons, 183
	primary care, 27
	statistics on, 180–1
	uninsured people, 116
Accountable Care Organizations (ACOs),
	190, 205, 206–8
Accreditation Council for Graduate
	Medical Education (ACGME), 31
acute rehabilitation hospitals, 7
administrative services, 7, 10–1, 49, 105
Advanced Practice Nurses (APRNs), 57–8
adverse events, 13–4, 149. *see also*
	infections; medical errors
adverse selection, 98
Affordable Care Act (ACA), 188–226
	changes summarized, 189–93
	court challenges, 101, 211, 218, 220–1
	criticisms of, 217–9
	defined, 31
	effects
		on businesses, 193, 215, 217
		on employers, 191–2, 197, 198, 199,
			202, 205
		financial, 193–5, 207, 209–10, 218,
			222
		on individuals, 192, 195–6, 202,
			203–4
		on insurers, 191, 202, 203–4, 205
		on quality of health care, 209–10,
			215–6, 217–8
		on state governments, 190–1
	fragmentation, 219
	full text online, 228
	"grandfather" provision, 204–5
	and hospitals, 4, 192, 209–10, 213, 216
	implementation, 218–9
	and insurance, 101, 115, 192, 203 (*see
		also* Health Insurance Exchanges)
	insurance plans available, 198–9, 200–
		3, 213–4

	and Medicaid, 4, 190–1, 198, 199,
		210–3, 218, 222
	and Medicare, 4, 189–90, 197, 205–10
	and patient safety, 15
	and politics, 222, 223–4
	and prevention, 203, 205, 215–6
	public opinion on, 222–6
	and research, 215
	and serving the underserved, 215–6
	states' reactions to, 221–2
	and taxes, 191, 192, 193, 195–6, 197,
		202–3, 205, 216–7
Agency for Healthcare Research and
	Quality (AHRQ), 30, 170, 182
Aging and Disability Resource Center, 212
allied health, 31
allopathic physicians (MDs), 64
alternative medicine, 22
ambulatory care. *see* outpatient care
ambulatory surgery centers (ASCs), 21
American Medical Association (AMA), 30
anchoring fallacy, 100
Anti-Injunction Act of 1867, 221
applied research, 134–5
arbitration, 125
assistants and aides, 41, 51
audiologists, 42

B

bankruptcy, medical, 114–5
basic research, 134
behavioral disorder councilors, 45
behavioral economics, 99–100
beneficiaries, 79, 226
Better (Gawande), 124
"biologics," 141–2, 145, 193
"biosimilars," 145–6
biostatistics, 135
birth control, 219
boards of directors/trustees, 7
boutique/concierge practices, 22
Bundled Payments for Episodes of Care,
	206, 212

C

Caplan, Arthur, 102
care teams, 13
Carroll, Aaron, 126
catastrophic insurance, 127, 201, 226
Centers for Disease Control and
	Prevention (CDC), 29
Centers for Medicare & Medicaid Services
	(CMS), 127, 184
Certificate of Need (CON) laws, 117–8

certification, 39
chaplains, 43
charity care, 5, 6, 20, 31, 117, 118
children's hospitals, 6
CHIP (State Children's Health Insurance
    Program), 90, 187, 210–1
chiropractors, 44
chronic care and chronic disease, 101–2
Clinical Nurse Midwives (CNM), 57–8
Clinical Nurse Specialists (CNS), 58
Clinical Practice Guidelines, 154–6
clinical psychologists, 68
clinical research
    controlled/randomized trials, 143, 152,
        157, 170, 171
    defined/characterized, 135
    on drugs, 135, 142–4, 158–9, 160
    and evidence-based medicine, 155
    regulation and oversight, 140–1
CMS Innovation, 206
co-payments, 80, 226
COBRA (Consolidated Omnibus Budget
    Reconciliation Act), 90
cognitive framing, 100
coinsurance, 80
committees in hospitals, 11–2
community health centers (CHCs), 19
community or population health, 135–6
community rating, 85
comparative effectiveness research, 156
complementary and alternative medicine
    (CAM), 22
CON (Certificate of Need) laws, 117–8
concierge practices, 22
conflict of interest, 106–7, 152, 160, 164–
    6, 167, 217
Congressional Budget Office, 193–4
consults, 31
consumer-driven health plans, 84, 191,
    204
Consumer Operated and Oriented Plan
    (CO-OP), 214
controlled trials, 157, 170
corporations. see industry
Cost-Access-Quality triad, 17, 26–7,
    179–83
cost sharing, 79–80
"cost shifting," 119
costs of health care, 94–126. see also
        economics
    and ACA, 193–5, 207, 209–10, 218, 222
    Accountable Care Organizations, 206–8
    and administrative services, 10–1, 105
    and bankruptcy, 114–5

and Certificate of Need laws, 117–8
and comparative effectiveness research,
    157–8
consequences of, 113–8
defensive medicine, 123–4, 126
defraying costs, 112–3
drugs, 108, 145, 146–7, 159, 161–8
emergency departments, 119–21
and employer-sponsored insurance, 89
global comparisons, 179–83
high-tech equipment, 10–1
hospice care, 21
and hospital-acquired infections, 15
inpatient care, 16, 17
insurance, 78–80, 82, 118–9
international comparisons, 183
and lifestyle choices, 102, 108–9
and malpractice, 123, 124, 126
in Massachusetts, 189
Medicaid, 186–7, 211, 222
Medicare, 105–6, 185, 205, 207,
    209–10
patients' decision-making, 103–4, 112
and primary care physicians, 26–7
and quality-adjusted life years, 113
reasons for high costs, 95–112
research funding, 137–9
statistics on, 7, 94–5, 117, 179–83
for uninsured people, 116–7, 118–9
and waste, fraud, abuse, 186–7, 206
councilors, 45
credentialing, 12, 39–40

D
Dartmouth Atlas of Health Care, 158
Dawkins, Richard, 134
deaths, 15, 21, 102–3, 121
deductibles, 79–80, 84, 226–7
defensive medicine, 123–4, 126
dentists, 46
dependents, 79
diagnosis-related group (DRG), 92–3
diagnostic services, 7
diagnostic tests and procedures, 123, 127
dietary supplements, 159
dietitians, 47
direct-to-consumer advertising, 164
"diversion," 121
doctorate degrees, 40, 53–5, 60, 61, 67
Donabedian, Avedis, 169
Donabedian Triad, 169
"donut hole," 184, 189, 193, 197, 208–9
drugs. see pharmaceuticals; prescriptions
DSM IV, 73

E

Early Retiree Reinsurance Program, 213
economics, 77–132. *see also* costs of
    health care; reimbursement
    bankruptcy, 114–5
    concepts related to health care, 96–101
    defined, 77
    and OECD, 171
education
    accreditation of programs, 31
    of health care professionals, 36–76
    patient health literacy, 110–2
    of physicians, 25, 31, 37–9, 64, 73, 216
    teaching hospitals, 5–6
electronic health records (EHR), 150, 171
electronic medical records (EMR), 150
emergency departments (EDs)
    and clinical practice guidelines, 154–6
    costs of uninsured patients, 119–21
    and health care reform in Mass., 188
    outpatient care in, 20
    overcrowding, 121
    research on care in, 215
    statistics on visits to, 120, 121
emergency medical technicians (EMTs),
    48
Emergency Medical Treatment and Active
    Labor Act (EMTALA), 119–20
employer-sponsored insurance (ESI)
    and Affordable Care Act, 191–2, 197,
        198, 199, 202, 205
    Early Retiree Reinsurance Program, 213
    employee contributions to, 199
    history and overview of, 86–90
    reform ideas, 225
end-of-life care, 102–3
epidemiology, 135
episodes of care, 206, 212
Epstein, Arnold, 221–2
ethics committees, 12
ethics in research, 140–1
evidence-based medicine, 153–4, 155–6
Exchanges. *see* Health Insurance
    Exchanges

F

FDA (Food and Drug Administration),
    142–4, 145, 148–9, 158–9, 160
Federal Coordinated Health Care Office,
    206
federal hospitals, 3
Federal Medical Assistance Percentage,
    186
federal poverty level (FPL), 109, 186

Federally Qualified Health Centers, 19
fellowships, 73
Fisher, Elliot, 207
flexible spending accounts (FSAs), 84, 204
food and nutrition, 217
for-profit hospitals, 2, 4, 5
formularies, 146, 147
free/charitable clinics, 20
"free choice vouchers," 198, 199

G

gatekeeping, 82
Gawande, Atul, 105, 124
general hospitals, 5–6
general practitioners. *see* primary care
geographic variation in treatment, 158
gold standard, 171
government
    and abortion funding, 214
    and ACA, 189–91, 219, 221–2
    community health centers, 19
    and costs of uninsured people, 117
    drug regulation, 142–4, 158–9, 160,
        166–8
    health care costs regulation, 106–7
    health departments, 20
    laws on building new facilities, 117–8
    lobbying, 166–8
    medical device regulation, 148–9,
        158–9, 160
    national health care organizations,
        29–30, 29–31
    public insurance programs, overview, 90,
        183–7 (*see also specific programs*)
    research institutions, 137, 138
government-owned hospitals, 2, 3, 4
group practice, 18, 19, 22–3
Group Purchasing Organizations, 28

H

Haldane, Richard, 139
Health & Human Services (HHS), 29
health care administrators, 10–1, 49
health care delivery system, 28
Health Care Education and Reconciliation
    Act (HERA), 188
health care networks, 19, 22–3, 28
health care organizations, national, 29–31,
    167
health care providers/professionals,
    36–76. *see also specific professions*
health courts, 125
health disparities, 110–1, 215
health home, 213

health information technology (IT), 149–50

Health Insurance Exchanges
  and abortion funding, 214
  description of plans available, 200–3
  and employers, 191, 197, 202
  how to get coverage, 198, 199
  and income levels, 202–3
  purpose of, 214
  services covered, 202
  and state governments, 190

Health Insurance Portability and Accountability Act (HIPAA), 141

health literacy, 110–2

health savings accounts (HSAs), 84, 204

health services research, 136

herbal therapies, 159

HHS (Health & Human Services), 29

HMOs (health maintenance organizations), 20, 81–2, 83, 84

home health aides, 50

home health care, 21, 206, 212

horizontal networks, 28

hospice, 21

hospital(s)
  and ACA, 4, 192, 209–10, 213, 216
  accreditation, 30
  business aspects/policies, 7, 10–1
  committees in, 11–2
  costs of uncompensated care, 118–9
  costs of uninsured people, 117
  drugs, 146–7
  issues, 13–7
  laws on building new facilities, 117–8
  lobbying by the industry, 167
  organization of, 7–8
  outpatient care in, 2, 16, 19
  payment-to-cost ratios, 119
  and peer review system, 139–40
  physician-owned, 4, 5
  physicians employed by, 9–10, 19, 22–3
  structure of, 8
  types of, 2, 3–6

hospital-acquired infections, 15, 17, 213

hospitalists, 10

Howard, Philip, 125

I

ICD codes, 93

idiopathic diseases, 156

indemnity insurance plans, 81

Independence at Home Demonstration Project, 206

Independent Payment Advisory Boards, 209

Indian Health Care Improvement Act, 214

Indian Health Service, 227

industry. see also insurance; pharmaceutical industry
  conducting medical research, 137, 138
  conflict of interest, 152, 217
  insurers, 167, 191, 202, 203–4, 205
  medical devices, 148, 158–9, 160, 164–8
  politics and lobbying, 166–8

infections, 15, 17, 213

information asymmetry, 96–7

information technology (IT), 149–50

informational services, 7–8

inpatient care, 2–17, 146–7

inpatient rehab facilities (IRFs), 7

Institute of Medicine (IOM), 30, 168, 218–9

Institutional Review Boards (IRBs), 140–1

insurance. see also Health Insurance Exchanges; uninsured and underinsured people
  and Affordable Care Act
    employers, 190–1, 197, 198, 199, 202, 205
    individuals, 192, 195–205
    mandates to purchase, 195, 219, 220–1
    plans available, 200–3, 213–4
    restrictions on insurers, 191, 202, 203–4, 205
  catastrophic, 127, 201, 226
  concepts and terminology, 79–80
  and "cost shifting," 119
  and costs of health care, 79, 80, 82
  defined/characterized, 78–9
  drugs, 146–7
  employer-sponsored, 86–90, 190–1, 199, 213, 225
  enrollment statistics, 84, 86
  government programs, overview, 90
  and health care reform in Mass., 188–9
  lobbying by the industry, 167
  malpractice, 121, 122, 123
  medical loss ratios, 85–6, 105, 191, 204, 208, 224
  Medigap, 184
  not-for-profit, member-owned, 214
  payout limits, 80, 97, 115, 191, 203, 227
  premiums, 79, 85–6, 87, 122, 201, 227
  reimbursement systems (see reimbursement systems)
  types of, 81–91

intellectual property, 144–5

internships, 37
Investigational New Drug (IND), 143, 144

J
The Joint Commission (TJC), 30

L
length-of-stay, 10, 15–7
licensing, 39, 40. *see also specific professions*
lifestyle choices, 97–8, 102, 108–9
lobbying, 166–8
local hospitals, 3
long-term acute care hospitals, 6
long-term care, 212

M
malpractice, 121–6, 140, 216
managed care organizations, 81, 83, 84
marriage and family therapists, 45
Massachusetts health care reform, 188–9
Massachusetts Health Connector, 200
McArdle, Megan, 115
McClellan, Mark, 207
MDUFMA (legislation), 160
Medicaid
    and ACA, 4, 190–1, 198, 199, 210–3, 218, 222
    costs of/funding, 186–7, 211, 222
    coverage, 186
    defined, 31, 90
    eligibility, 185–6, 210, 211, 222
    and emergency department visits, 120
    and primary care, 27
    state changes in, 211–2
    and undercompensated care, 119
    waste, fraud, and abuse, 186–7, 206
Medicaid and CHIP Payment and Access Commission (MACPAC), 210
Medicaid Drug Rebate, 212
Medicaid Money Follows the Person Rebalancing Demonstration Program, 212
medical assistants, 51
medical billing, 104–5, 150
medical coders, 52
medical devices
    benefits of, 147–8
    conflict of interest, 160, 164–6
    costs of, 10–1
    excise tax on, 217
    largest companies, 148
    lobbying by the industry, 166–8
    regulations, 148–9, 158–9, 160, 166

medical errors. *see also* adverse events
    causes of, 14, 38, 39
    death rates, 13, 121
    defined, 13–4
    and malpractice lawsuits, 121–6
    reducing/preventing, 15, 39
    types of, 14
medical home, 22, 212–3
Medical Injury Compensation Reform Act, 125
medical loss ratios (MLRs), 85–6, 105, 191, 204, 208, 224
medical malpractice, 121–6, 140, 216
medical records, 149–50
medical scientists, 53–4
medical students, 25, 27
medical transcriptionists, 54
medical underwriting, 85
Medicare
    and ACA, 4, 189–90, 195, 197, 205–10
    costs of, 102, 105–6, 205, 207, 209–10
    coverage, 184
    defined, 31, 90
    and diagnosis-related groups, 93
    eligibility, 183–4, 210
    and end-of-life care, 102
    funding, 185
    income and premiums, 210
    and length-of-stay, 16
    Part D drug subsidy, 184, 189, 193, 197, 208–9
    and physician-owned hospitals, 4
    and primary care, 27, 210
    regional differences, 105–6
    reimbursement, 4, 16, 93, 103, 185, 209–10
    supplemental insurance, 184
    and undercompensated care, 119
    waste, fraud, and abuse, 186–7, 206
Medicare Advantage, 184, 187, 190, 208
Medicare Independent Payment Advisory Board (IPAB), 209
Medigap insurance, 184
members (beneficiaries), 79
mental health councilors, 45
meta-analyses, 155–6, 171
midwives, 57–8
misinformation, 111–2
moral hazard, 79, 97–8

N
National Health Care Workforce Analysis, 215
National Health Care Workforce Commission, 215

National Institute for Health and Clinical Excellence (NICE), 157–8, 160, 171
network coverage, 227
networks, health care, 19, 22–3, 28
New Drug Application (NDA), 143, 144
NIH (National Institutes of Health), 29
not-for-profit hospitals, 2, 3–4, 5, 216
Nurse Anesthetists (NAs / CRNAs), 58
Nurse Practitioners (NPs), 40, 57
nurses, 55–9
nursing homes, 6, 167

O

occupational therapists, 60
Office of Research Integrity (ORI), 140
optometrists, 61
Organization for Economic Co-operation and Development (OECD), 171
"orphan drugs," 144, 163
OSHA (Occupational Safety and Health Administration), 29
osteopathic physicians (DOs), 64–5
Ottawa Ankle Rules, 154–5
out-of-pocket max, 80, 203
outpatient care, 2, 15–28, 147
overtreatment, 105–7

P

palliative care (hospice), 21
paramedics, 48
patient care teams, 13
patient-centered medical home, 22, 213
Patient-Centered Outcomes Research Institute (PCORI), 113, 157, 215
patient dumping, 31
patient privacy, 141
Patient Protection and Affordable Care Act (ACA). see Affordable Care Act (ACA)
patient safety. see also medical errors
    adverse events, 13–4, 149
    in clinical research, 140–1
    drug regulations, 142–5
    hospital-acquired infections, 15, 17, 213
patient variation, 158
pay-for-performance (P4P), 92
payout limits, 80, 97, 115, 191, 203, 227
PDUFA (legislation), 160
peer review system, 139–40
personal health aides, 50
personal health records (PHR), 150
pharmaceutical industry
    and ACA, 193, 216–7
    annual fees for, 216–7

conflict of interest, 160, 164–6
legislation regulating, 160
lobbying, 167
marketing and advertising, 162–4
pharmaceuticals. see also prescriptions
    and ACA, 193
    costs of, 108, 145, 146–7, 159, 161–8
    defined/types of, 141–2
    340(b) Drug Discount Program, 216
    efficacy: clinical vs. statistical significance, 160
    FDA approval, 142–4, 145, 159, 160
    and flexible spending accounts, 204
    generic, 145–6
    and health care costs, 108
    Medicaid Drug Rebate, 212
    Medicare coverage, 184, 189, 193, 197, 208–9
    placebos, 151
    regulation of, 142–4, 158–9, 160, 166–8
    research on, 108, 135, 142, 143–4, 151–3, 158–9, 161–2
pharmacists, 62
pharmacy benefits manager, 146–7
physical therapists, 63
physician(s)
    admitting or attending, defined, 12
    and Clinical Practice Guidelines, 154–6
    conflict of interest, 106–7, 165–6, 217
    education, 24–5, 31, 37–9, 64, 73, 216
    employment/practice, 9–10, 19, 22–3
    geographic variation in treatment, 158
    hospitalists, 10
    income of, 37, 65, 107–8
    industry connections, 165–6
    job description, 64–5
    limiting numbers of, 25, 107–8
    and malpractice, 121–6, 140, 216
    MDs and DOs, defined, 64
    payments to under Medicare, 185
    primary care vs. specialists, 26–7, 65
    shortage of, 24–8, 127
    statistics on, 18–9, 64–5
physician assistants (PAs), 66
physician-hospital relationship, 4, 5, 9–11, 19, 22–3
Physician Payments Sunshine Act, 166
physician shortage area, 127
placebo effect, 151
podiatrists, 67
politics, 166–8, 222, 223–4
population or community health, 135–6
POS (point-of-service) plans, 83

poverty and/or low income
   and ACA, 195, 198, 199, 202–3
   and children's health care, 187
   and emergency department visits, 120
   federal poverty level, 109, 186
   and health/heath care costs, 109–10
   lack of insurance (*see* uninsured)
   and Medicaid, 185–6
PPO (preferred provider organization),
   82–3, 84
practical nurses (LPNs), 59
Pre-Existing Condition Insurance Program
   (PCIP), 213
pre-existing conditions, 127, 227
premarket approval (PMA), 149
premiums, insurance. *see also* insurance
   under ACA, 198–9, 201, 205
   defined, 79, 227
   in employer-sponsored plans, 87
   and malpractice, 122
   setting rates, 85–6
prescriptions. *see also* pharmaceuticals
   electronic, 150
   by non-MDs, 40, 44, 62, 66, 68
   "off-label," 159
prevention, 102. *see also* lifestyle choices
preventive services, 203, 205, 215–6, 219
primary care
   and ACA, 206, 210, 215–6
   and health outcomes, 26–7
   in HMO, PPO, POS, 83
   and physician-hospital relationship, 23
   physician shortage, 26–8, 127
prison hospitals, 2, 3
privacy, 140
private hospitals, 3–4, 5
private practice, 18–9, 22–3
privileges, defined, 12
psychiatric hospitals, 2, 6
psychologists, 45, 68
public health research, 135–6
public (government) hospitals, 2, 3, 4
publication bias, 152

Q
quality-adjusted life years (QALY), 113
quality of health care. *see also* Cost-
      Access-Quality triad
   and ACA, 209–10, 215–6, 217–8
   categories of failures in, 182
   and defensive medicine, 123
   defined, 168
   and health care reform in Mass., 189
   international comparisons, 183

   measuring, 169–70
   and primary care physicians, 27

R
"rack rate," 108
randomized trials, 143, 152, 157, 171
rationing health care, 113–4
reform. *see also* Affordable Care Act (ACA)
   Massachusetts health care, 188–9
   torts/malpractice, 123, 124, 125–6
rehabilitation councilors, 45
rehabilitation facilities, 7
reimbursement, iterative, 108
reimbursement systems
   and ACA, 203, 206, 209–10
   length-of-stay/outpatient care, 10, 16
   Medicaid, 119, 213
   Medicare, 4, 16, 93, 103, 119, 185, 206,
      209–10
   and transparency, 103–4
   types of, 91–4
reinsurance, 227
relative value unit (RVU), 93–4
religious hospitals, 4, 5
rescission, 203
research, 134–41
   and ACA, 215
   clinical, 135, 140–1, 142, 155, 158–9
   comparative effectiveness, 156–8
   conflict of interest, 152, 164–6
   controlled trials, 157, 170
   drugs, 108, 142, 151–3, 158–9, 161–2
   ethics in, 140–1
   evidence-based medicine, 153–4,
      155–6
   funding, 136, 137–9
   institutions for, 136–7
   issues and problems, 150–60
   medical scientists, 53–4
   meta-analyses, 155–6, 171
   online registry for, 152
   and patient health literacy, 110
   peer review system, 139–40
   process of, 139
   publication bias, 152
   randomized trials, 143, 152, 157, 171
   regulation and oversight, 140–1
   types of, 134–6
   validity concerns, 151–3
residents and residency programs, 24–5,
      37, 38–9, 216
retail clinics, 20–1
rural health, 110
RVU (relative value unit), 93–4

S

S-CHIP. *see* CHIP
safety. *see* patient safety
Scalia, Antonin, 101
scope of practice, 40
secular hospitals, 4, 5
sensitivity and specificity, 127
significance, statistical, 160, 171–2
single payer, 225
skilled nursing facilities, 6, 167
social workers, 69–70
solo practice, 18, 19, 22–3
Sommers, Benjamin, 221–2
specialty hospitals, 6
speech-language pathologists, 71
speech therapists, 71
state hospitals, 3
statistical significance, 160, 171–2
subscriber, defined, 79
substance abuse and behavioral disorder
    councilors, 45
substantial equivalence, 148–9
supply-induced demand, 98–9
support services, 8
Supreme Court, 101, 211, 218, 220–1
Surgeon General, 30
Sustainable Growth Rate formula, 185
systematic reviews, 171–2

T

taxes
    and ACA, 191, 192, 193, 195–6, 197,
        202–3, 205, 216–7
    and flexible spending accounts, 204
    on insurers, 205
    on medical devices, 217
teaching hospitals, 5–6
technicians and technologists, 72
therapeutic services, 7
time inconsistency, 100
To Err is Human (IOM), 13, 15, 121–2
tort system/reform, 123, 124, 125–6
translational research, 134
transparency, 103–4, 217

U

UCCs (urgent care centers), 20
uncompensated and undercompensated
    care, 118–9
uninsured and underinsured people
    under ACA, 196, 218
    access to health care, 116, 180–1
    costs of defensive medicine, 124
    defined/characterized, 91, 115–6

    and emergency departments, 119–21
    and health care reform in Mass., 188
    statistics on, 91, 116–7, 180–1
The Uninsured: A Primer, 115–6
urgent care, 20, 127
US Preventive Services Task Force, 228

V

validity, in research, 151–3
vertical networks, 28
Veterans Affairs (VA) hospitals, 3
Veteran's Health Administration, 90
vocational nurses (LVNs), 59

W

Wachter, Bob, 169

Y

Yglesias, Matthew, 112

About the Authors

Elisabeth Askin and Nathan Moore are students in the M.D. program at the Washington University School of Medicine in St. Louis, Missouri. They both graduated from the University of Texas at Austin and took time off after graduating. They met in medical school and bonded over how much they miss breakfast tacos.